Harriett's Walk

How to make wiser choices for a better life

Harriett's Walk

*How to make wiser choices
for a better life*

Lucia Matthews (signature)

LUCIA MATTHEWS, PhD

Two Harbors Press

Two Harbors Press
212 3rd Avenue North, Suite 290
Minneapolis, MN 55401
612.455.2293
www.TwoHarborsPress.com

The advice and strategies contained in this book are not intended for use as a substitute for adequate and professional mental health treatment. Please consult a qualified practitioner if you are dealing with serious mental health concerns or issues. The characters and scenarios portrayed in the book are contrived and do not represent any actual person or event.

ISBN: 978-1-937293-67-3
LCCN: 2011941076

Distributed by Itasca Books

Cover Design by Jill Kennedy
Edited by Marly Cornell
Printed in the United States of America

TO MY CLIENTS:

Your willingness to persevere is my inspiration.

CONTENTS

FOREWORD

Lucia Matthews' brilliantly written book is a valuable asset for anyone interested in making better choices, whether that's people looking for ways to improve their quality of life or professionals working with clients. *Harriett's Walk* reads like a novel and anyone (man/woman, young/old) can easily identify with the main character whose issues are shared by so many. There is a piece of Harriett in each one of us and that's what makes her story relevant and applicable to so many different walks of life.

Dr. Aye, the psychologist who counsels Harriett, shows her that all behavior is a choice. She teaches Harriett the "9 skills" and walks her through strategies that enable Harriett to practice and apply the skills. A valuable aspect of this approach is that each skill stands alone as usable and independent of the others. Even after learning and practicing just one of the skills in this book, it's possible to begin moving toward a better life.

Readers can follow along and practice each skill in their own lives, which provides an immediate substantiation of the practical and useful guidance provided. Walking with Harriett along her journey reminds us that we are not alone in the very human issues we all face. The story offers hope that we *can* make changes to attain more of what we want—the best possible life.

I have taught Choice Theory for almost twenty years and often use different case studies to help demonstrate how to apply the concepts when working with clients. What is different about this book from other teaching tools is that it illustrates the work with just one client over time, showing how her world of unsatisfying behaviors is transformed by choices that lead her to a better life—albeit with some unexpected revelations.

I became acquainted with Lucia Matthews about fifteen years ago when she was a doctoral candidate in Counseling Psychology. The topic of her dissertation was Choice Theory (CT) and Reality Therapy (RT), and I was on her committee. A quality friendship evolved out of our common interest in applying CT/RT concepts to help people make better choices in their lives. Each year, for the past six years, I have asked her to spend a day with the graduate students in my Reality Therapy course, sharing how her strategies move clients forward. The feedback is always positive, and my respect for Dr. Matthews as a psychologist and helping professional continues to grow. I plan to require *Harriett's Walk* as supplemental reading for my course and I encourage everyone teaching a skills building class for helping professionals to do likewise.

Readers are invited to walk along with Harriett as she learns how to make better choices.

~Mary E. Watson, MSCP, EdD, Northeastern University
Bouvé College of Health Sciences

INTRODUCTION

Who is Harriett?

Harriett is a fictional character I created to exemplify how to cope when life begins to feel overwhelming. Harriett is a daughter, sister, wife, mother, and friend. She is a strong, resilient, and committed woman who, until recently, managed everyday stress in ways that felt effortless and fulfilling. Now, these same stressors feel burdensome and Harriett cannot understand what has changed. She senses her quality of life slipping away, but is unable to pinpoint why. She is confused and apprehensive. She feels vulnerable and her vulnerability causes her to behave unwisely. Harriett's voice embodies how the contrariness of life can leave anyone feeling helpless and uncertain.

Harriett personifies ways to discover personal strengths and use them to enhance the quality of our lives. Through her, we can learn ways to cope when feeling burdened by life's challenges. Her story teaches skills that help us control our emotions long enough to make wiser choices. I invite you to adapt Harriett's story to your own storyline, and use it to attain a happier, more fulfilling life.

1

Acting Emotionally

I wish people would stop asking me what happened. I don't know what happened! One minute I was chopping cabbage, and the next I lunged at my husband with the knife. How could a day that started like most, end so badly? I just don't understand...

I woke up at 6:30 to take a walk before the day got too hectic. I like to keep myself trim and I'm partial to jogging. However, I just can't seem to find the oomph to enjoy a good run. Walking is far less satisfying, but I guess it's better than nothing. If I have to be honest, oomph seems to be missing from most aspects of my life.

The morning was bright and sunny, a treat for early March in New England, and the forecast looked great. I was relieved because that meant favorable conditions for my seventeen-year-old son's soccer game. Matt's a goalkeeper on his high school team and the boys were playing a night game under the lights of the outdoor stadium. College coaches were supposed to scout the game and Matt wanted to impress them with one of his signature saves.

I imagined my tall, lanky son, body fully extended, using his fingertips to flick the soccer ball over the upper right-hand corner of the net. The roars of delighted spectators filled my ears as I double-checked my mental checklist. I'd already forgotten to do one thing and I wanted to make sure there wasn't anything else I needed to do to insure my son's success.

Did I remember to wash Matt's lucky shirt? I'm glad I got him those wool liners to wear under his soccer socks. They'll keep his feet nice and warm while he's standing in the goal. I'm so annoyed at myself for forgetting to order his new soccer cleats. The field will probably be muddy from all the melting snow and I'm worried that his old cleats might cause him to slip. Maybe the new ones will arrive today. Rob at the Soccer Locker said there was a good chance. I can't believe I forgot to order them. I'm usually on top of important things like that!

A worrisome thought slowed my pace. *What if Matt has a bad game?*

The roars of delight changed to groans of frustration, and my heart broke for my son because I knew he'd be so disappointed. Matt's entire being is focused on earning a college soccer scholarship; and, as a devoted soccer mom, I will do anything to make my son's dream a reality.

Except that I forgot to order his soccer cleats.

I felt my chest tighten as I dredged up other mistakes I'd made in recent weeks. Mistakes like forgetting to make phone calls soliciting donations for the local food bank or neglecting to stop by the town's assisted living home to visit a resident whose family lived out of state. I felt so sad, knowing that my failures had disappointed my son...and other people.

I picked up my speed and tried to stay focused on my walk.

Bayview is a small, beachy community whose streets contain renovated, single-story cottages with lawns that end at the Narragansett Bay. The sound of waves breaking gently on the coastline usually cures my woes, but for some reason all I could think about was how disturbed I was over a recent article in the *Providence Journal* that portrayed the people living in Bayview as arrogant and entitled.

I wonder what made that reporter describe us that way, when I know the people here are caring and hardworking.

I'm a staunch supporter of my adopted hometown and glad I live in a place that's safe and the people dependable. I try to be an involved member of the community, always ready to lend a hand to my friends and neighbors, and I join any campaign devoted to preserving the natural beauty of Bayview's waterfront. Just last week, I walked the beach with a group of volunteers for the town's annual spring clean-up. I felt good clearing away the litter and debris left over from the winter. I only wish there was a way I could do the same thing with my thoughts...

I've always been happy with who I am and what I do, and thought that people liked me. But maybe I'm wrong. I don't think I'm arrogant, but I am usually able to get people to agree with how I see the situation. Not that I'm a bully, but... Oh, I don't know... I used to feel so satisfied with my life, but lately things just don't feel the same. Why is it that what used to be satisfying now seems so stressful?

The question made me think about an ongoing argument with my husband. Jake's begun to doubt the choice we made to move the family from Boston to Bayview in order to take advantage of the town's excellent school system. He thinks the change may not have been worth the stress of living so far from where he works—not to mention the financial strain incurred by the high property taxes associated with a Rhode Island suburb. It's not anything serious, but we do struggle, and sometimes things feel a bit daunting. However, I'm determined to provide my children with every advantage we can afford, even if I have to pinch pennies.

So why do I worry that I should be doing more? Maybe it's because of the constant challenge to make ends meet. I've been thinking about going back to work, but who would hire someone who's been out of the workforce for more than seventeen years? Lately, I'm plagued by the notion that I don't measure up to other people's standards and, if I'm being really honest, I'm not sure I'm living up to my own standards...

"Hello there, Harriett!"

The sound of my neighbor's voice made me wince. As the self-anointed mayor of the neighborhood, Phil finds it necessary to broadcast a weekly report regarding the neighborhood's compliance with the "rules" of trash day. Ordinarily, I manage to escape scrutiny by conforming to his harmless covenants, but for some reason, on this trash day, I sensed danger.

"Hi, Phil, what has you out so early?"

"That wind last night really did a number on the trees, and did you notice the garbage all over the street? I keep telling everyone not to put the trash out the night before pick-up day."

Phil's pointed stare seemed filled with annoyance, and I was sure the source of his displeasure was Jake.

I've repeatedly told Jake to wait until Friday morning before dragging the garbage cans to the end of the driveway, but he thinks I'm silly for worrying about what Phil thinks. If he'd only listen to me, I could avoid these types of unpleasant encounters.

Realizing I'd lost track of the conversation, I looked up in time to see an impatient frown flash across Phil's face. Obviously, I'd missed hearing something that Phil thought was important.

"I'm sorry, Phil, what did you say?"

"The meeting with the zoning board is Wednesday night! I'm counting on you to tell people why the Ferros shouldn't get permission to add a second level to their house. You know that will make the water view even more obstructed from the other side of the street. I'm sure one of your impassioned speeches about protecting our natural resources will do the trick."

Even though I knew Phil was asking for my help, he has a way of making me feel like I owe him something. I'm sure his comment about the Ferros was intended to make me feel guilty. Thirty-three years ago, an out-of-state couple bought a piece of waterfront property and built the house we now call home. The moment Jake and I saw the three-bedroom cape style house, with its beautiful view; we knew we'd found the perfect place to raise our family. Unfortunately, our house blocks the water for people living on the other side of the street and, on multiple occasions, I've had to listen to war stories about the neighborhood's unsuccessful fight with the zoning board. On top of that, my devotion to conservationism conflicts with the fact that I live right on the water's edge.

Wanting to avoid further upset, I searched for an excuse to end the conversation. "I won't forget, and I promise we'll talk again before Wednesday. But right now, I've got to go. I need to finish my walk in time to see Jake before he leaves for the office. Say hi to Mildred for me. Tell her I haven't forgotten Monday night's book club."

I kept my secret to myself. You see, book club was in three days and I'd barely read the first chapter, even though I love to read and typically finish a book weeks before the discussion. Jake laughs at how I'll read anything, even the public notices posted in the local newspaper. However, I haven't been able to enjoy this month's book because my wandering mind makes staying focused impossible. If it weren't for the responsibility I feel to attend the meeting and make the discussion interesting, I doubt I'd push myself to finish.

I could almost hear my mother's admonishment, "Harriett, if you are going to join the group, you must be a reliable member."

I can always count on one of Mother's "constructive admonishments" to make me do the right thing.

Besides, book club is usually a highlight of my month. I look forward to the change of pace and enjoy the lively banter provoked by the discussions. Only lately, I feel more like a disinterested bystander, with nothing worthwhile to contribute.

"Is that man of yours still commuting to Boston on the train?"

Phil's question startled me and once again, I realized I was lost in my own thoughts. I struggled to pretend I'd been listening, and covered my uneasiness with a nervous laugh. "The train's the only part of commuting that Jake likes! He says a long train ride is what keeps him sane because it's his only chance to get some me-time."

The phrase echoed inside me as I proffered a final wave. *I wonder what it would feel like to have a little "me-time." No matter what I do or how hard I work, there's always something or someone needing more of me.*

I headed home feeling tired and drained. Rather than being energized by my walk, all I wanted was a nap.

A nap? Really, Harriett, a nap? Women considering going back to work don't think about napping. They think about the stress involved in keeping their lives organized enough to manage both their career and family. If I don't even have the energy for a power walk, where would I find the energy to juggle work and family?

According to Jake, I spend too much time worrying over things being perfect. He says I should adopt his motto—success comes to those who can multitask. However, I don't think success has anything to do with multitasking. I'm a champion multitasker! It's just that I can't enjoy anything I've done unless I think I've done it the right way.

I wondered if a vacation would perk me up and hoped Jake might be able to take some time off from work during the kids' spring break. Knowing how much energy was involved in turning my hopes into a reality made me shake. I was certain that Matt and Katie would complain and lobby to stay home without any supervision. They balk every time I even hint at a weekend trip to Cape Cod.

What happened to the days when they were young, and Jake and I could bundle them into the car and steal away to Granddad's bungalow at the cape? They used to love when I showed them where I spent my summers, and we'd spend hours collecting seashells and making sand castles. Those weekends were such fun. My biggest worry was remembering to cover the kids in sunblock!

I stood in the middle of the street, contemplating my quandary and feeling caught between the desire to recapture the joy of the past and my responsibility to my family. I didn't know what to do...

I thought about asking my mother to baby-sit, but wasn't sure she'd be up to the challenge. Raising teenagers requires constant attention and I didn't think my mother could manage my children's hectic schedules. Besides, I figured Jake would argue that planning a trip at the last minute wasn't cost-efficient and that his work schedule wouldn't allow for a vacation. Deciding that the whole thing wasn't worth the effort, I sighed and abandoned my hope of any type of respite.

Seeing our trashcans neatly stacked at the end of the driveway made me feel a bit better. Then I spied several items that I knew would require both my husband's and my "me-time." The buds forming on our thirty-year-old ornamental maple tree always means it's time to schedule a family-day spring cleanup, and fertilizing the lawn is not how Jake prefers to spend the weekend.

Most New Englanders wait until May to prepare their outside for the summer season. However, I insist that mine be ready by Easter. I don't care if that means lugging the front-door planters into the garage each night to protect the annuals from an unexpected frost. The effort is worth it when I compare the vibrant colors of my home to the neighboring houses still cloaked in the drabness of winter. The contrast fills me with delight because it offers proof that I what I do matters.

So, if I've always been willing to work hard for what I want, when did life become such a burden?

Ignoring a question that had no answer, I continued my inventory. The mulch in the garden beds looks drab and we need to buy chemicals for our pool. I'm a bit worried about the pool because last year the heater gave us problems and I'm not sure we can afford a new one. Katie loves having her friends over to swim and I hate when she's disappointed by things that are within my power to fix, including finding the money to heat our pool.

Oh, I know that, in the scheme of life, worrying about things like cold pool water sounds trivial and makes me appear exactly how that reporter described the people living in Bayview—arrogant and entitled—especially when there are so many people in this world coping with unbearable stress and heartache. I don't mean to belittle anyone's problems. In fact, I don't usually share my worries because they sound so trite—even to me!

I just wish I could go back to a time when I felt happy. A time when I didn't feel so weighed down by trivial details. A time like when I was my daughter's age and the only worry I *did* have was an unheated pool!

Every summer, my grandfather relocated the family from our brownstone in the heart of downtown Boston to a cozy bungalow nestled amongst the reedy coastline of Cape Cod. As teenagers, my sister and I spent our vacations lying on the sandy beach, our bodies bronzed by the sun's warmth and filled with the newfound discovery of feminine wiles that made flirting fun and exciting.

Even though Granddad is one of Boston's most esteemed lawyers, he's never forgotten the lessons learned from his parents—Irish immigrants who taught him the value of a dollar. I suspect the only reason Granddad agreed to buy the bungalow was because my grandmother convinced him it would be perfect for his "girls." Granddad will do anything to make his family happy, even if it means spending money on things that clash with his Puritan New England mentality. The purchase of a second home most likely made his stomach ache; and, the fact that the purchase included a heated pool probably made him cringe!

I remember how he and I would quarrel over turning on the pool's heater because I thought it made no sense to swim in cold water when we owned a perfectly good heater. While my reasoning did little to sway Granddad, a quiet intercession from my grandmother curtailed the quarrels and got the pool heated. Granny always knew what was best for her family and accepted nothing less. Her life epitomized what it means to behave with grace and elegance.

Yet, even with Granny as a role model, I'm still confused. Why do I find it so difficult to handle my life as easily as she handled hers? Why do I always feel I've done too little, too late? Why does life seem so bleak these days? What's happened to my zest for living? I've always been pleased with my life and proud of my accomplishments. When did my pleasure turn into indifference? Worse, when did pleasure turn to dread?

My confusion swirled within me as I walked to the front door. In retrospect, I knew something was amiss, but I resisted acknowledging how bad I felt because admitting something was wrong would be akin to denouncing everything that's important to me. I was also afraid that complaining would make people think I'm spoiled and ungrateful for my wonderful life.

Defeated, I walked into the kitchen to find my daughter wearing my new sweater. "Katie! I just bought that! I never said you could wear it!"

"But, Mom! Today's my presentation at school and my favorite sweater's still in the laundry. You're always telling me it's so important to pay attention to how I look. I didn't think you'd want me to go to school in a dirty sweater."

"You're right. I want you to pay attention to how you look. But what I really wanted was for you to think about your outfit last night when I asked what you were wearing. This way I could have washed *your* favorite sweater rather than have you wearing *my* newest one."

Despite my annoyance, I secretly approved. The sweater was perfect for my daughter's presentation. The color green brought out a hint of amber in her eyes that made her look lovely and astonishingly grown-up. She looked exactly like I want to look. These days I stare into the mirror and see only crow's feet and sagging skin. Why shouldn't I let Katie enjoy wearing something that can never hide the fact that I've become a middle-aged hag?

Reluctantly, I conceded. "Please be careful. I bought that sweater for tomorrow night's client dinner that your father's hosting."

"Don't worry, Mom, I promise. I'll return it to you good as new." Her eyes sparkled as she added, "And you'll look almost as hot as I do!"

Too tired to take offense, I smiled a weary smile, opened the refrigerator door, pulled out the lunch I'd prepared, and handed it to my daughter.

I'm lucky to have Katie in my life since difficulties with Matt's birth almost ruined our chances for a bigger family. Now I truly feel that what I have is perfect—a great husband, one amazingly athletic son, and an equally exquisite daughter.

The thought of Matt made me uneasy, and Katie's response to my question about his whereabouts confirmed my fear.

"Where else? In bed." Unconcerned, she tossed the words over her shoulder and went outside to wait for the school bus.

"Not again!" My words were followed by a second sigh as I realized that another tardy was about to blemish my son's less-than-stellar attendance record. Matt seems unfazed by his nasty habit of sleeping through first period. Despite my escalating concern, his response is always the same, "What's the big deal? It's only study hall. I'm never late for second period."

Of course he's never late! I'm so worried about him getting into trouble that I nag him until he gets up and then I drive him to school. I'm beginning to think he's using me as a way to avoid what he considers "the indignity" of riding on a bus. Although..., maybe I'm blowing things out of proportion. After all, isn't the common wisdom these days not to sweat the small stuff?

As I climbed the stairs to coax my wayward son out of bed for the third time in a week, I wondered how I could make him understand the importance of being responsible and doing the right thing.

"After all, rules are rules," intoned my mother's voice.

Yes, Mother, I hear you.

I woke Matt and headed towards the master bedroom. I felt my face light up when Jake greeted me with one of his endearing smiles. The sight of my husband always makes me feel better. He was, and still is, a great catch. He's good-looking, and his graying temples, combined with tight abs and a few laugh lines, make him even more distinguished. His rock-steady character is a reassuring constant in my life. I often tell people how Jake's last name, Sterling, symbolizes everything about my husband, and I feel lucky to be married to him.

I met Jake the summer after graduating from college. I was interning at Granddad's law firm and on track to enter law school. Jake was a rising young associate and, after one date, I knew he was perfect for me. Marrying Jake derailed my aspirations and changed my life forever.

I sometimes question what life would be like had I pursued a law degree, but Granddad was certain that marrying Jake guaranteed a secure and economically sound future. My grandfather's opinion is important to me and knowing that he approved of my choice made me feel safe. I also suspect that Granddad's words were a reminder not to make the same mistakes as my mother.

Mother...hmmm...how do I explain my mother? She grew up in a world that valued all things prim and proper, but by every account, she was a hellion who rejected everything that Granddad and Granny believed was important. She dismissed social conventions and barely stayed on the right side of the law. Mother even rejected the idea of a traditional education by defying Granddad's insistence that she finish college.

In sophomore year, she fell in love with an adjunct professor who swept her off to Italy, raving how they'd spend the summer touring the

Amalfi coast, teaching transfer students about *Dante's Inferno*. According to Granddad, Mother couldn't understand why she should sit in class reading about the world when she had the chance to experience it up close and personal.

The couple returned home, tanned and engaged. Despite his reservations, Granddad consented to the marriage. However, my father absconded the moment Mother learned she was pregnant with Faye and me. Maybe he could have handled one baby, but never twins! He told Mother he couldn't stand having his wings clipped, and simply walked away.

"Hey!" Jake's voice shook me out of my daydream. "I said I'd be home a little early tonight. There's a luncheon and seminar in downtown Providence. I'll head home after it's over and should be here around five."

The change to our routine was welcome news because it meant we'd finally have a chance to sit down to dinner as a family. Jake's been so busy with work that we're never all together in the same place at the same time. I decided to fix a delightfully perfect meal, complete with Jake's favorite dessert and fresh flowers to celebrate both the event and the beginning of spring. Then I remembered the soccer game and worried if I'd have enough time and energy to get everything done. *Yes, because I'm determined to make this work!*

"Great," I replied, forcing myself to sound more cheerful than I felt. "I'll make a special dinner. This way we'll have a chance to reconnect and log some quality family time."

"Reconnect?" asked Jake. "Over what? School? Work? Committee meetings? Sometimes I feel like our lives are as scripted as the movie, *Ground Hog Day*—same old stuff, just a different day. Please, Harriett, you don't have to plan everything down to the smallest detail. Let's just have a simple potluck dinner so we can relax and not rush to make everything perfect before Matt's game."

Panic rose in my chest the way it always does when Jake's unhappy because I think I'm to blame, and lately his comments contain a subtle sarcasm that has me really worried. Doesn't he understand that making things perfect is what I do? How can he not see that I want to create something wonderful to make our family time special? If he'd only take the time to listen to what I'm saying, he'd understand that what I'm doing is trying to keeps things organized so that everyone's happy and things work the way they should.

I knew from experience that telling Jake how I felt or complaining about our lack of communication was useless. He doesn't really listen to me anymore. Over the last three months, he's become ornery and talking to him is difficult. Yet, when I ask him about what's going on, his answer is always the same. He just sighs and says the new case he's working on is stressful.

I gave Jake's request serious consideration and mentally pared down my plans for the night's dinner. While I wasn't happy, I figured I could strike a workable compromise. Instead of telling him I was disappointed that he didn't share my enthusiasm, I hid what I was feeling behind a hollow laugh. "Don't worry, honey, I'll keep it simple and promise I won't use any silver or crystal! But seriously, Jake, we haven't had any family time lately and I want to make tonight special. Are you telling me not to bother?"

I watched my husband's shoulders slump, as he shook his head. "No, I just wish..."

"What do you wish?" I interrupted, fearful that his answer would tarnish my illusion of a perfect meal.

"...that life was a little less predictable."

I painted a phony grin on my face and asked, "How can life be predictable with two adolescents?" Then I held my breath, waiting to hear Jake's response.

Regret washed over my husband's handsome features but before he could say another word, Matt barged into the room.

"Mom! We have to leave now if you don't want me to be late!" As he turned to go down the stairs, I heard him add, "I don't know why I can't drive myself. I'm only weeks away from turning eighteen!"

Matt's protests about driving usually set my teeth on edge, but this time I sighed with relief. The timing of his interruption meant I could avoid hearing whatever Jake was about to say.

I gave my husband a quick kiss on the cheek and promised I'd make sure to plan a fun and relaxing night. I returned to the kitchen where I caught Matt snatching the car keys off the counter.

He looked me straight in the eye and said, "Since you insist that I wait till I'm eighteen to drive myself to school, you have to ride shotgun! I'll meet you in the car."

Once again, I was too tired to argue.

While looking for my purse, I also searched for the words I thought might make Matt understand why it's important to obey things like driving laws and all the other responsibilities that are part of growing up. I hope we did the right thing by having him repeat fifth grade prior to entering middle school. The choice seemed wise at the time, but lately I worry that being the oldest junior in his school puts too much pressure on him.

Why can't I get him to understand that just because his friends are eager for him to become their personal chauffeur, doesn't mean he's ready for all the responsibility that comes with driving? I wish I knew a way to make him see how one mistake could ruin his entire life!

Knowing that any kind of lecture would fall on deaf ears, I climbed into the passenger seat and resorted to persuasion. "Listen, Matt. I know you think it's silly for Dad and me to make you wait until you're eighteen to drive the car alone, but those are the rules. Have patience, my love. Good things come to those who wait, and in a few weeks you might find that red Saab you saw in the used car lot sitting on our driveway."

As I said earlier, the day began like most—an odd mishmash of disturbing thoughts and emotions, but nothing earth shattering, and certainly no indicator of things to come. Jumbled thoughts and jangled nerves prevented me from returning serve after serve at tennis. At the end of the game, I watched my partner throw her racquet in disgust.

"Harriett! Where's your mind today? I would have been better off playing doubles with a mannequin!"

I apologized profusely, knowing she was right. Too ashamed to risk the scrutiny of the other players, I avoided the locker room and retreated to my car, intending to hide behind the Jeep's tinted windows. I couldn't believe that I'd played so badly and knew that what I'd done wasn't fair to my partner. Tennis has always been a fun activity, but maybe I should hang up my racquet!

I was tired and out of sorts, and briefly considered backing out of the promise I'd made to meet friends for lunch. I also wanted to make sure I saved enough energy to make Jake his special dinner. But then I thought, *For heaven's sake, how much energy does it take to have a sandwich with friends? I'm acting as if I'm so overworked, when all I've accomplished is a mediocre walk and an atrocious tennis game. Stop acting like a rich, overindulged princess. I made a commitment, now do what I'm expected to do—keep it!*

Worried about Matt's soccer cleats, I used my cell phone to make a quick call to the Soccer Locker before I put the Jeep in gear and headed for the local deli. Relieved that the shoes had arrived, I made a mental note to pick them up in between my shift at the food bank and shopping for dinner.

The sight of my good friend, Sharon, seated in one of the deli's over-sized booths made me glad I'd kept my promise to have lunch. We haven't spent much time together since her husband took a job that means traveling between Bayview and Albany. Seeing Sharon reminded me of Jake's complaint about life being too scripted. I wondered if he'd trade our life for one that demanded the upkeep of two homes and a three-hour commute each way over snow-packed roads in the winter.

A short time ago, I would have jumped at the challenge, but now it seems too overwhelming. These days all I want is for things to be simple, or at least not so complicated. I don't like how I seem to panic every time something unexpected happens, like the morning's conversation with Jake. Little did I know that my morning's panic was a harbinger of how the day would end...

I gave Sharon a quick hug and plopped myself next to my friend Lissa, whose life exemplifies the stress-free lifestyle I crave. A transplant from Alabama, Lissa retired from teaching and followed her husband to Rhode Island, searching for lucrative work that never materialized. Despite their limited means, Lissa always manages to make their lives comfortable. Both are only children with no living parents and no children of their own. They minimize expenses by restricting their travel, and Lissa fills her time gardening, taking long walks, and staying connected to long-distance friends via the Internet. To me, Lissa oozes contentment and I wish my life were as simple as hers. Maybe then I could lose some of this stress that seems to follow me wherever I go.

Not having much to say, I listened to the idle conversation of my friends and, just for a moment, allowed myself the pleasure of their company. I wonder why I've become so unsociable when being with my friends feels so good? Now that's a silly question, because the answer's obvious—I've got too much to worry about to waste time eating lunch and chitchatting with friends!

I looked over at Brenda, an equally close friend, who'd decided to give herself a fortieth birthday present by becoming pregnant with her third child. Her unabashed joy makes me wonder if I should add a third child to my family.

Ha! Like I have the energy to even think about sex, let alone getting pregnant! Besides, I should be happy with what I have. Most women think mine is a fairytale existence and, most of the time, I think they're right. *So what makes me so miserable?*

"Hey!" Lissa snapped her fingers in my face. "Where'd you zone out to?"

"Pardon? Oh, sorry, I was thinking about what to make for dinner. Jake's been putting in long hours and traveling all over the East Coast, so it's been a while since we've sat down as a family and I want to make him something special."

"Why not Stroganoff?" Sharon suggested. "Yours is great and you're always telling me it's one of Jake's favorites."

"Stroganoff! Great! Easy, fast, and Matt can eat the leftovers if he's still hungry after the game."

Dismissing the pleasurable company of my friends, I rummaged through my purse, found a pen, pulled a napkin from the dispenser sitting at the end of the table, and composed a shopping list. Shoving both the pen and napkin into my bag, I gathered my things.

"I've gotta run. I'm late for my shift at the food bank. I hate when the other volunteers get there first. I feel like a slacker."

Both Sharon and Lissa protested, arguing that I had plenty of time before my shift started and complaining that they missed my company. But I was adamant, even though what I really wanted was to stay right where I was.

"Hold on a sec," said Brenda. "I'll walk out with you."

She scrambled from the booth, and we headed for the door. There was something about the look on my friend's face that made me suspect she wanted to talk. How I wish I'd kept walking...

"Harriett, can I speak with you a moment?"

"Of course," I replied, still unaware of the looming disaster. "Do you need a favor?"

"No, I just wanted to ask if things are okay between you and Jake."

"Why?"

"Well, I heard you say Jake's been away a lot, and that made me remember that I saw him and some woman going into the Crowne Plaza Hotel last Thursday. I thought it odd because it was in the middle of the day, but I figured it was for one of those lawyer seminars he's so fond of attending. It's just that, when I waved at him, he seemed to purposely ignore me."

I shrugged. "He didn't mention anything to me."

"Just be careful," Brenda warned. "You know I love you and I don't want to see you hurt."

"Oh, for heaven's sake, Brenda! Everyone knows about your penchant for seeing conspiracy in people's behavior! Even if it was Jake, I'm sure there's a perfectly good reason why he was at the Crowne Plaza. Are you positive he ignored you? It's more likely he just didn't see you."

Brenda remained skeptical.

"Look," I said, more to placate my friend than to validate her suspicions.

16

"I'll ask Jake about it tonight. I'm certain the explanation's a lot more innocent than the one floating around in that suspicious brain of yours!"

I turned away, intending to walk across the road, up the cobblestone stairs and into the stone building that housed the food bank. I was halfway across the common when I realized that Jake was spending more and more time in Providence. Then the ominous thoughts began...

*Not only has he been missing a lot of dinners and traveling more than usual, he's also been going into the office on Saturdays, and that's not something he's ever done. And...*my heart raced...*when was the last time he initiated sex? What do the pundits say? Where there's smoke there's often a torrid affair?*

"Oh, knock it off!" I scolded out loud. "Sure Jake's been preoccupied, irritable, and wishing for some spontaneity. But, an affair? My Jake? Who would he even approach?"

My stomach dropped because I know Jake's first love practices law in the same town as the Crowne Plaza. I closed my eyes and pictured Julie, a beautiful girl with big breasts and turquoise eyes.

Jake and Julie were the talk of Granddad's law firm when they were both associates. I'll never forget the surprise I felt when Jake asked me out. I thought I'd won the lottery! Even so, I was relieved when Julie got an offer to practice corporate law at a firm in Rhode Island because it meant I no longer had to worry about competing for Jake's attention. Julie always struck me as the perfect combination of brains and beauty.

The image of Julie made me remember how Jake recently raved about her being an accomplished lawyer with a thriving private practice. We were out to dinner with a group of friends and I heard Sharon's husband ask Jake for a referral regarding issues at his plant near the Crowne Plaza. Even from my vantage point way at the other end of the table, I saw the animated expression on Jake's face when he recommended Julie.

But, Jake, my Jake? Is it possible he regrets marrying me?

Pulling my cell phone from my purse, I used speed-dial to call Jake's office in Boston.

"Smyth and Poole, Mr. Sterling's line," answered Shelley, Jake's long-time secretary.

"Hi, Shelley, it's Harriett Sterling. I was wondering if Jake's left for the seminar yet."

"Seminar?"

"Yes, he mentioned it this morning. Is he there?"

"Nooooo."

The caution in her response made me suspicious. *Might she be covering for her boss?*

"He's not here. He told me he had a luncheon meeting with a client and would leave for home directly from the meeting. He said he'd be available on his cell. Have you tried calling him?"

"Yes, but he's not answering," I lied, my incredulity mounting because I recalled Jake specifically said he was going to a seminar. "I'll give him another try."

I hung up and shook my head, trying to erase the uncertainty within my mind. *Jake and Julie? Impossible!*

I stared at the cell phone's monitor and made a choice. Punching a new set of numbers, I waited...

"Verizon four-one-one Connect. City and State," said the automated voice of operator assistance.

"Warwick, Rhode Island," I replied, my voice strangled by taught nerves pressed against my vocal cords.

"How may I help you in Warwick, Rhode Island?" queried an anonymous voice.

"I need the number for a lawyer, last name..." I urged myself to think. "Butler! Yes. That's it! Julie Butler!"

"Connecting your call to area code 401-555-4411."

"Law office of Julie Butler," stated another disembodied voice.

"Is she in?" My heart felt ready to explode from my chest.

"Ms. Butler's left for the day—a luncheon meeting with a client and then home. Can I take a message?" offered the stranger who had unknowingly rocked my world.

In disbelief, I ended the call, returned the phone to my purse, and sank onto the park bench adjacent to the food bank.

Now, Harriett, get a grip. Coincidences do happen and I can't jump to conclusions based on a coincidence. Besides, what would Jake think of my wild imaginings? Stop making mountains out of molehills.

There had to be another explanation and I was determined to find it. With an unexpected spark of energy, I vowed to confront Jake that evening and insist on a family vacation. I decided that springing the idea on him at the last minute would give him some of the spontaneity he'd been craving.

I walked into the food bank, concealing my worries behind a fake smile.

Most days, the time flies by in a frenzied rush to greet patrons and tend to their needs, but on this day, time seemed interminable as I watched the clock slowly creep towards quitting time.

Come on! Come on! I've got a ton of things to do before I can get home and get dinner on the stove. Besides food shopping, I want to swing by the florist and hand pick an extra special bouquet of flowers to put in the middle of the dinner table. I also want to stop by the bakery for some really fresh sourdough bread. Should I pick up one of their apple cobblers? Jake says theirs tastes almost as good as mine.

Looking at my watch, I decided there was just enough time to make one from scratch. After all, nothing tastes better than homemade, even if it meant I'd be a bit rushed.

My obligations at the food bank satisfied, I cast a final glance at the antiquated timepiece hanging over the exit door. *Phew*, I released the breath I'd been holding. It was only two o'clock. Plenty of time to go shopping, rush home, and get dinner started. Since it was Friday, I didn't have to nag the kids to get their homework done before Matt's game, but I groaned when I remembered that Granddad expected my whole family to attend the client dinner that Jake was hosting. While this was not my children's preferred way to spend a Saturday evening, I was in no mood to tolerate anyone's nonsense, especially Jake's!

After the florist and bakery, I zipped up and down the grocery

19

aisles, pulling items off the shelves and checking them off my list: *On-ions*—check. *Mushrooms*—check. *Sour cream*—check. *Mustn't forget my secret ingredient—fresh dill weed. Do I have everything I need for the cobbler? Yes, I bought a bag of apples the other day.*

Halfway through the list, I experienced the overwhelming fatigue I've come to regard as my constant companion. My exhaustion makes no sense because I just had a checkup, eat well, and exercise regularly. Yet, most mornings I wake up tired, no matter how much sleep I get.

Relieved to escape the market unscathed by acquaintances wishing to engage in useless conversation, I headed home with thoughts of a perfectly delightful family dinner dancing in my head...until the image of Julie inserted itself into the picture.

Jake and Julie. Jake and Julie. The phrase became a mantra inside my brain. My stomach muscles clenched and I felt nauseous.

As soon as I'd unloaded the groceries, I opened the cabinets to take out the ingredients for dinner. I rummaged the fridge, looking for the apples and found the bag nearly empty.

"Matt!" I yelled, furious at my son's voracious appetite. "Did you eat all these apples?"

"I guess," he hollered from his bedroom. "Was I not allowed?"

Now what was I supposed to do about Jake's dessert? How can a dinner be perfect without dessert? All I wanted was to make him a pleasant meal—one that would vanquish any thought of Julie. *If there are even any thoughts to vanquish.*

Shaking my head in weary resignation, I turned away from the fridge and wondered if there was time to pick up more apples. For some reason, I was sure there was something else I was supposed to pick up...

My heart sank. THE SOCCER CLEATS!

In a panic, I grabbed the keys from the counter, intending to make a beeline for the Soccer Locker. That's when I noticed the flashing red light on the answering machine. I pushed the play button and heard the programmed voice announcing a single message. Sadly, that solitary message eclipsed my trip to the soccer store and dispelled any thoughts of a perfect dinner.

ACTING EMOTIONALLY

"Mr. and Mrs. Sterling, this is Vice-Principal Bartlett. I'm calling about Matt. He was absent from the last period of school today and there's no documentation excusing him. This, along with chronic tardiness, is becoming a disturbing pattern. I've scheduled a meeting for eight o'clock on Monday morning. We need to discuss the issue and develop a plan so that Matt's college aspirations aren't jeopardized."

Livid, I shouted up the stairwell. "Matt, you better get yourself down here right now!"

I turned to find Katie standing in front of me and the guilty look on her face made me sigh. "What now?"

"Oh, Mom, I'm really sorry. There must have been gum on one of the chairs at school and I think your sweater's ruined. Please don't be mad. I really didn't mean for it to happen."

That's when things become a bit hazy. I do remember being at the stove stirring that dammed Stroganoff. Matt was pleading his case for why skipping the last period of school was okay and that a command meeting with the vice-principal was, in his favorite phrase, "no big deal"—at least not big enough to warrant grounding for the entire weekend. Katie hovered around me, her remorse genuine; but I continued ruminating over her flippant care of my sweater. The shade of green perfectly matched a pair of slacks I already owned. Katie's negligence meant I'd have to settle on an old outfit for the client dinner and that meant every woman in the room would outshine me.

In retrospect, everything sounds so embarrassingly trite and mundane...

Desperate for space to breath, I replaced the lid on the Dutch boiler and shooed the kids out of the kitchen. I assembled what I needed to make vegan coleslaw and took the heavy chopping knife out of the knife block. Unlike the weather, my thoughts were dark and stormy.

Damn it! Instead of making Jake his favorite dessert, I'm worrying about soccer cleats, unexcused absences, what to wear tomorrow night, and making Katie vegan slaw because she thinks eating vegan clears up acne. I cater to these kids and give them every opportunity to succeed. I'm beginning to think all I've done is raise two pampered, overindulged brats!

21

I yanked open the utensil drawer, pulled out the wooden cutting board, slapped it down onto the counter and began chopping the cabbage. The thump of steel against wood accentuated my anger. That's when Jake—*poor Jake, dependable Jake, responsible Jake*—walked into the house and shouted, "I'm home! What's for dinner?"

His question made me grit my teeth and I felt the burn of angry bile gather in the back of my throat.

Everyone wants a piece of me! I bet Julie doesn't have to worry about cooking the perfect meal or making sure her kids act responsibly. She probably still looks gorgeous, without a single worry line. In fact, I bet she's even more alluring than she was twenty years ago!

Ignoring the fury provoked by Jake's innocent question required all my willpower; but somehow, I managed a calm reply, "I'm in the kitchen. Supper's almost ready."

Just like every other workday, Jake turned left into his study to rid himself of his briefcase and jacket. Then he checked mail and plugged in his laptop. His routine epitomizes the stability and reliability of my husband and usually makes me smile. This night however, his behavior made me incensed.

Why do I always come second? THUMP! *Shouldn't Jake want to greet me first?* THUMP!! *Shouldn't Matt know the importance of behaving responsibly instead of expecting me to keep fixing his mistakes?* THUMP!!! *And, even at fifteen, Katie should know to be more careful with my things.* THUMP!!!!

My thoughts felt like a runaway train, going downhill and gaining speed; and Jake's entry into the kitchen did little to slow them down. I stood at the counter, breathing heavily as Jake reached around me to sneak a piece of cabbage. My anger grew...

"What's cooking?" He bent over, kissed the top of my head, moved to the stove and lifted the lid off the steaming pot of beef.

"One of your favorites," I replied as calmly as possible. "Beef Stroganoff."

"Oh," Jake responded with disappointment. "That's what I had for lunch."

I always pooh-pooh stories about out of body episodes. However, I think that's exactly what I experienced. It's as if I was in the audience of an off-Broadway, badly directed play. I watched myself turn towards Jake in slow motion and heard myself scream. Did I even realize I still had the knife in my hand? I don't think so.

"For lunch? You had Stroganoff for lunch? Who has beef Stroganoff for lunch?"

Then I lunged.

Frankly, I'm not entirely sure what stopped me from thrusting the knife into my husband's well-toned stomach.

2

The Difference Between
Acting Emotionally and Behaving Wisely

Harriett stood in the middle of the small, private waiting room, torn between the desire to run and the knowledge that if she did, her marriage would be over and her children ripped away.

What am I doing here? I'm not crazy. I just lost it one time. How in the world is some psychologist going to fix what's already happened? My life's in shambles and will never be the same again. I'm not crazy, but being here is crazy!

The thought of counseling made her upper lip curl in distain. Therapy was for people who are weak or unable to help themselves. Her mother didn't go to counseling when her father left. She simply put her nose to the grindstone and got on with life. However, Jake was adamant about protecting the children from a potentially dangerous situation. He'd mandated that either Harriett see someone or he'd remove Matt and Katie from the house. Between Jake's threat and the worry over a nasty custody battle, Harriett believed she had no other choice but to comply with her husband's mandate.

How could one lapse lead to such a state of affairs? She pressed her hands against her face, appalled by the consequences of her behavior. *I can't fathom how talking about what happened is going to fix anything and I resent being judged by someone who can't possibly understand why I did what I did!*

She heard the door open. Feigning a polite smile, Harriett turned to meet her fate. The sight of a small, non-descript, middle-aged woman wearing a pair of slacks and a blue sweater set intensified her dismay. *This woman doesn't even look like a professional! She looks like someone I'd see in the stores across the road. How can someone so ordinary understand how out of control my world's become?*

"Hi, Harriett? Welcome, I'm Dr. Aye." Smiling, the woman extended her hand.

Harriett froze. *What do I do? Should I smile back? Offer to shake her hand? Mutter a polite thank you? Whatever I do, I'd better do it quickly because this woman's obviously expecting some kind of response.*

Her innate breeding produced a reflexive nod of acknowledgment.

"Why don't you come into my office where we can talk?"

The distinct New York accent reminded Harriett of the therapist in the HBO television series, *The Sopranos*. Indeed, everything about the situation felt like a parody.

Talk? She screamed inside her head. *Talk? What does she want me to talk about? My father didn't abuse me! My mother loved me! I had a perfect life until I lost it. How is talking going to make anything better?*

"Have a seat."

Harriett cast a nervous glance around the room. There was a choice between a teal-colored loveseat, a matching oversized chair or a brown leather swivel. Her survey reinforced the belief that being there was a mistake. *Where's the desk? Isn't this woman a doctor? Doesn't she at least need a pad to take notes?*

She attempted to portray a cool aloofness that was the exact opposite of what she felt. "Where would you like me to sit?"

"Wherever you'd like, the choice is yours."

Sensing a trap, Harriett asked, "Does that mean you're going to analyze me based on where I sit?"

Dr. Aye chuckled and shook her head. "That's what everyone asks. I don't care where you sit. I care that you make the choice."

"I would rather you tell me where to sit," Harriett responded aloud, while in her mind she plotted. *If I wait until she tells me where to sit, then I won't supply her with ammunition that she can use against me.*

"Sorry, I can't do that. Pick a seat, any seat." Dr Aye waved her arm around the expanse of the office. She waited until Harriett positioned herself on the edge of the loveseat, then sat in the swivel.

"Great, I always worry that a new client will take my chair."

"What would you do if they did?"

"Kick them out, of course."

"Would you really do that?"

Dr. Aye smiled at the look of horror on Harriett's face. "Of course not. I appreciate how coming to counseling can be unsettling, so I use humor to alleviate the tension."

"I find that rather insulting. There is nothing funny about my situation and I resent your attempt to humor me out of my problems. I told you on the phone. I almost stabbed my husband!"

"What stopped you?"

The abruptness of the question was unsettling. "Pardon?"

"I asked, what stopped you?"

Once again, Harriett replayed the fiasco in her mind.

I'm sure the debacle began with that stupid, little word—Oh! Jake sounded so annoyed and bored about the Stroganoff. I felt like he was dismissing all my efforts and...dismissing ME! I know he tried to explain when he saw my reaction, but nothing he said made any difference because that single word was roaring in my head—blocking out all sound, all composure, and all reason. I wanted Jake to appreciate me and to reassure me that everything was okay. I wanted to get his attention. I didn't want to hurt him. The knife just happened to be in my hand.

"What stopped me?" repeated a puzzled Harriett. "I didn't want to hurt my husband."

"Yes, but what did you want?"

"What do you mean what did I want? I certainly didn't want to wind up *here*." Her hands flew to her mouth, horrified at the derogatory tone in her voice. She always behaved with decorum, yet here she was acting snarly and critical. *What is it about this woman that feels so threatening?*

Dr. Aye persisted. "I understand you'd prefer not to be here, but what were you hoping to achieve when you lunged at your husband?"

The question seemed to contain a mixture of interest, patience, concern, and something Harriett couldn't quite identify. Looking up, she met Dr. Aye's gaze for the first time and experienced a brief glimmer of hope. *Is it possible this woman really understands?*

"I just wanted...I wanted...not to be dismissed." The tremulous timbre of her voice and unbidden tears belied the depth of Harriett's despair.

"Well, I guess you succeeded, because no one's dismissing you now."

Despite her distress, Harriett wiped her eyes with the back of her hand and returned a wry smile. "That's for sure."

"So, Harriett, how can I help?"

The question unleashed a fresh set of tears. In a practiced move, Dr. Aye handed Harriett several tissues from the wooden box sitting atop her credenza and waited.

Drying her tears, Harriett replied, "Oh, Dr. Aye, I wish I knew, and I'm afraid you can't. I feel like my world's in chaos. I'm the talk of the town. My children say I've embarrassed them and Jake doesn't know what to do. He's become overprotective of the kids and tiptoes around me, acting as if his slightest comment will have me running for the knife."

"Do you blame him?"

"Pardon?" Harriett wished the woman would stop asking such unexpected questions—questions that felt brusque and flippant. *This isn't what I expected. I feel like a four-year-old running to keep up with a faster, older sibling. Where's the soothing tone that's supposed to placate my raw emotions?*

"Do you blame him?" repeated Dr. Aye. "If asking 'What's for dinner?' made you lunge, imagine the commotion a more demanding question like 'Where are my keys?' might provoke."

"That's ridiculous! I only lost it once! I don't intend to lose it again." Harriett's smoldering resistance reignited. *This so-called counselor is toying with my emotions. I'm not some plaything. I'm a real person with a really, big problem!*

She sat in stony silence, waiting and watching.

Dr. Aye returned her stare. "Did you intend to lose it the first time?"

"No! Of course not!"

"Then how does Jake know what might cause you to lose it again?"

Harriett sank into the loveseat, stunned by the implication. *If I can't be certain of my own behavior, how can I expect Jake to trust me? No wonder he's so skittish around me and adamant about protecting the kids.*

The realization produced a wail. "What can I do?" she asked, fearful that any answer would be woefully inadequate.

Unfazed by her wail, Dr. Aye replied, "That's a great question and perhaps I can help you find an answer."

Harriett was adrift in a sea of confusion. *This woman's supposed to tell me the answers! What's the point of coming here if she expects me to answer my own questions? If I knew the answers, I could fix my problems myself. I don't need her to ask me questions. I need her to give me answers!*

She struggled to maintain her composure, searching for a neutral response. "I don't understand."

"That's okay. Let me explain what I do and how I work and maybe that will help you understand." Before proceeding, Dr. Aye took Harriett's history, explained the details behind confidentiality and HIPAA privacy laws and established that Harriett was currently not a danger to herself or anyone else.

At least she's acting more like a professional.

"My goal is to help people figure out what they want and teach them ways to achieve what they want. Think of wants as pictures inside your head. My approach explains how to develop those pictures and bring them into sharper focus. I also teach a set of skills that help you identify ways to satisfy your wants and choose the option that has the highest likelihood of success. All nine skills have the same purpose—to help you stop acting emotionally and start behaving wisely. The question, 'What can I do?' is excellent because changing your behavior is the only way to improve your situation."

Harriett resented the implication. *I'm not the only one whose behavior needs changing! I know going after Jake with a knife was wrong, but the thought of him having an affair makes my blood boil!*

Working hard to hide her resentment, she asked, "Doesn't it take two to have a fight? Isn't Jake at fault for making me feel so out of control?"

"The only behavior you can change is your own," replied Dr. Aye. "Changing your behavior is also how you'll get what you want."

"But that's the problem! I have everything I want and I'm afraid of losing it!"

"What would it mean if you lost it?"

The question challenged Harriett to look inward. She stared down at her hands folded limply in her lap and reflected on the mess she'd made of her life. "That I'd be left with nothing," she replied, her despair obvious.

"Oh, you'd be left with something, just not what you want."

Harriett shook her head. "That doesn't make sense."

"Then help me understand what you're afraid of losing. Paint me a picture. What do you see when you picture yourself holding everything you want?"

Harriett looked within and saw Jake, Matt, and Katie. It was a glorious summer day and they were all in the pool, laughing and playing water volleyball. Her friends suddenly popped into the scene followed by her mother and grandfather. Tentatively, Harriett described the picture.

"Thank you," said Dr Aye. "You've helped me understand some of the things that satisfy your need for love and belonging—the need to feel connected to people. Each of us has the need to feel connected to others, but the way we satisfy the need varies from person to person. You seem to have several options that help you feel connected. You have your husband, your children, other members of your family and your friends. Those pictures inside your head are the wants that satisfy your need. Wants come from the combination of your unique personality coupled with the unique set of experiences you've encountered throughout your lifetime. Both of us need to feel connected, but our uniqueness makes your wants different from my wants."

"But if I have what I want, why do I feel so miserable?"

"Perhaps other needs aren't being satisfied. In addition to love and belonging, there's power, freedom, and fun. The description of yourself laughing as you played volleyball in the pool is an example of satisfying your fun need. What pictures might represent your need for power and freedom?"

"How can you picture power?"

"The power need is the need to achieve something we believe is important. A tennis player's picture of power might be of herself returning a ferocious serve. For a plumber, turning on the tap and watching water flow from newly installed pipes might be an image of power. Most every high school senior who dreams of opening that first college acceptance letter is picturing power. There are countless ways to satisfy the need for power, but each of us has a different picture of how to feel powerful."

Harriett began painting a picture that depicted the perfect meal. She saw her grandfather's face crinkle in delight when she presented her renowned lemon meringue pie derived from an old family recipe and modernized by using phyllo dough cut into triangles to form individual packets filled with airy yellow sweetness. The blowtorch she used to brown the peaks of the meringue, combined with a few fresh raspberries placed next to the sumptuous treat, added just enough color to create a perfect balance of look, taste, and texture. Her efforts achieved notoriety in last year's Best of Rhode Island Bake-Off competition.

The vividness of her description made Dr. Aye plead, "Stop! You're making my mouth water."

Painting a picture of freedom was more troublesome, even after Dr. Aye encouraged her to describe pictures of other people upholding their freedom.

"I still don't think I understand." Admitting she was confused intensified Harriett's discomfort.

"The freedom need is the need to assert free will. We all need to view ourselves as independent beings, capable of choosing how to live our lives. While I cannot presume to know for sure, I often speculate that the satisfaction of his freedom need played a part in Senator John McCain's ability to survive his ordeal as a prisoner of war. Even under the most restrictive of circumstances, Senator McCain asserted his free will and chose to remain a prisoner rather than participate in the Viet Cong's propaganda campaign to portray itself as humane."

Harriett leaned into the loveseat and absorbed the meaning of freedom.

Dr. Aye continued. "Your difficulty painting a picture of freedom is likely due to your husband's mandate that you come to counseling—the choice wasn't yours. I suspect your lack of pictures means you're overwhelmed and feeling helpless, powerless, and out of control."

Harriett sat upright, pressured to dispute an allegation that conflicted with her staunch desire to be in control of every situation. *I don't allow myself to become overwhelmed. I just work harder to make the situation perfect!*

Determined to refute Dr. Aye's assessment, she argued, "I'm not sure I understand why having a picture of freedom is important. Maybe I don't have a need to assert my free will."

"The needs are basic and exist in each of us. The unique combination of personality and experience creates a need profile that is uniquely different for each individual. A need profile evolves over the course of a lifetime and changes based on the attainment of our wants. When our wants are satisfied, the need is less. When we're not getting what we want, the need feels more urgent and motivates us to find ways to satiate the urgency."

"But," Harriett protested. "You just said the reason I feel so awful is because I don't have any pictures of freedom. If the need is so urgent, why don't I know what I want?"

"Sometimes situations conspire to undermine the attainment of our needs and we become besieged by negative feelings. These feelings are so overwhelming that they inhibit our capacity to create pictures of what we want. That's when we act emotionally instead of behaving wisely." Dr. Aye emphasized her point with a question. "Didn't you tell me you lunged at your husband because you wanted his attention?"

Harriett shuddered. "Yes, but look where it got me."

"Your behavior got you here, and your behavior will get you where you want to go," observed Dr. Aye.

"Pardon?"

"While you may still want your husband's attention, I presume you'll avoid lunging at him with a knife in your hands?"

The question was so obviously rhetorical, Harriett merely nodded. "Why?"

The horridness of the memory elicited a whispered response, "Because I never want to feel like that again."

"The consequences associated with what you did are what will stop you from lunging. The outcome didn't satisfy your need."

Dr. Aye offered a gentle smile. "Oh, your behavior got you Jake's attention, just not the attention you wanted. That's why being specific about your wants is important. Specificity optimizes the odds of getting what you want and improves the chances of choosing the most suitable behavior. For instance, if I want ice cream and ask my husband to get me what I want, he might bring me vanilla when what I really wanted was chocolate."

Harriett was having difficulty absorbing how needs provoked wants that translated into behaviors. "I think I need you to elaborate."

Hearing her words made Harriett wonder, *Is that a need or a want?* Thoroughly confused, she remained silent.

Dr. Aye provided an example. "The need for freedom is usually dominant in a teenager's life because adolescence is about developing an identity that's autonomous from the rest of society. I'm sure you can cite many times when your children have exerted their free will."

Harriett grimaced as she pictured Matt lounging in bed despite knowing he'd be late for school. Her scowl deepened at the image of Katie wearing the new sweater without permission.

"Your children's need profiles contain a high need for freedom and that makes them want to assert their independence. As a result, they often behave in ways that disregard you and Jake. The consequences of their behavior shape the pictures inside their heads. Positive consequences enhance their picture of freedom and motivate them to embellish their behavior. Negative consequences are discordant with their picture and motivate them to adjust their behaviors to ones that assert their free will, but with a higher regard for what you and Jake believe."

Harriett felt compelled to object. "I think the topic of consequences sounds more like a discussion about the need for power."

"Do you know what you just did?" asked Dr. Aye.

"Pardon?"

"You epitomized the concept of self-evaluation. You paid attention to what I said, evaluated your reaction, and chose a behavior that was consistent with what you wanted. You wanted to voice your objection, so you told me what you thought. We are always self-evaluating our reaction to a situation. However, many of us are unaware of how we use self-evaluation to achieve what we want."

Harriett's eyes filled with tears of frustration. "You know what, Dr. Aye? I really don't care. All I want is to fix what I broke so I can move on with my life."

"And how do you propose to get what you want?" The tone of Dr. Aye's voice made the question sound like a challenge.

Harriett was too upset to recognize the self-evaluation question. "I don't know!" She began to cry.

"That's why you've come to me. I'll teach you how to achieve what you want."

Harriett reached for another tissue and wiped at her face. "And you're saying self-evaluation is what I'll use to get what I want?"

Dr. Aye nodded. "Asking self-evaluation questions helps you identify behaviors that will get you what you want. Self-evaluation also helps you choose the behavior that has the highest likelihood of success and motivates you to initiate the behavior."

Upset but intrigued, Harriett asked, "What is a self-evaluation question?"

"I've asked you several since we've met."

Harriett's blank look prompted Dr. Aye's next query. "What happened when I asked about Jake not knowing what might cause you to lose it again?"

Harriett recalled her reaction. "The question made me realize I can't expect Jake to trust me if I can't trust myself."

"My question challenged you to evaluate how your behavior impacts the situation. Self-evaluation is the hallmark of a psychological perspective called Choice Theory/Reality Therapy, developed by William Glasser in the 1970s. As a Reality Therapy certified practitioner, the questions I pose demonstrate how you can use self-evaluation to attain a quality life."

"A quality life?" Harriett repeated.

"Everyone wants to live a quality life—a life that's satisfying, rewarding, and gratifying. Achievement of a quality life occurs by identifying your wants and evaluating if what you're doing is getting you what you want."

Until recently, I thought I was living a quality life. I wonder what changed.

Dr. Aye explained. "Unfortunately, the external world sometimes thwarts our ability to get what we want to the point where the brain is so overwhelmed with emotion that it shuts down, making a thorough self-evaluation impossible. Most people describe their brain shutting down as feeling out of control. They behave impulsively, without regard for the consequences of their behavior. I call this acting emotionally."

Harriett recounted the out-of-body feeling she experienced prior to lunging at Jake. "Is that what you mean by acting emotionally?"

"What do you think?"

She's forcing me to self-evaluate. That's why I've been feeling odd throughout this session. Her questions challenge me to analyze my thoughts and feelings. I've become so accustomed to others telling me what to think and how to feel that it's uncomfortable to stop and consider what I want and what I feel.

The glimmer of hope she experienced earlier in the session grew brighter. "I think I was acting emotionally the night I lost it with Jake and

I would like to know why." The forcefulness of her delivery was startling. "How does it feel to know what you want?"

Harriett expelled a deep sigh. "Frankly, your questions make me feel like a student in a graduate level psych course that I'll never master."

"No, Harriett," Dr. Aye corrected. "That's what you *think*."

"Pardon?" She silently rebuffed her repeated use of the word. *I sound like a parrot, but this woman has me on an emotional roller coaster!*

"You said you *feel* like you're a student in a graduate level psych course that you'll never master. That's a thought, not a feeling. You've confused the two several times since we've begun talking."

Harriett's shrug was dismissive. "What's the difference? It's just semantics."

"There's a major difference between a thought and a feeling. I want you to become acutely aware of how your thoughts impact your feelings."

"Why?"

"A thorough self-evaluation requires an understanding of the source of your feelings. Thoughts provoke feelings, and feelings motivate behavior."

Dr. Aye leaned over, pulled open a drawer in the credenza, removed a yellow pad and drew a diagram depicting a continuously revolving cycle of behaviors, thoughts, and feelings.

"Think of yourself as a system comprised of three components—behaviors, thoughts, and feelings. The components are interrelated, so changing one component forces change in the other two components. I help you change your behavior and analyze how the change impacts your thoughts and feelings. If you like the consequences, you do more of the behavior. If your self-evaluation causes you to conclude that you don't like the consequences, you choose a different behavior."

"But I don't want to change what I do! I just want to feel better!" Harriett's wail unleashed a fresh set of tears that splashed onto her lap.

"Harriett." The gentleness in Dr. Aye's voice caused Harriett to look up. "I understand how badly you want to feel better. I promise I can help. However, the choice to change must come from you, not me or anyone else, including your husband."

"But what choice do I have?"

"The choice to work hard to find behaviors that help you get what you want."

"But I don't know what I want!"

"That's why you've come to me. I'll teach you how to figure out what you want. I'll show you how to make achieving what you want a reality."

"Can you really do that?"

"With your help."

Harriett's frustration swelled. "But I came to you for help! How am I supposed to help you?"

"By committing to a process that requires experimenting with new behaviors, evaluating your thoughts and feelings, and devising an alternative strategy when you realize that what you're doing isn't having the desired effect on your thoughts and feelings."

Harriett used the damp tissue to wipe her nose. "You make it sound so simple."

"My approach is pragmatic and based on observation combined with practical experience. Behavior is more easily observed than thoughts or feelings because behavior is binary—either it is or it isn't. Either you change your behavior or you don't. Whatever you do or don't do provides information that becomes the topic of our discussions."

"What will we discuss?"

"All behavior produces consequences. Consequences force change in thinking, which in turn provokes a shift in feelings. We examine the consequences and evaluate the subsequent changes. If you like the shift, you do more of the behavior. If you don't like the shift, I'll show you how to plan a different behavior."

Harriett was dubious. *Does this woman really believe that what I broke is so easy to fix?*

"Harriett." The warning in Dr. Aye's voice demanded attention. "Do not underestimate the effort required to change your behavior. You must be diligent and committed to doing the homework I assign."

"I have to do homework? I'm too tired to do homework! I was almost too tired to keep today's appointment. Now you're telling me I have to work hard and do homework?"

"I guarantee the homework requires less energy than you currently expend dwelling over past mistakes and worrying about the ones you might make in the future."

"Then why call it hard work?"

"We're emotional beings and all our behavior is provoked by emotion. Earlier you said you lunged after Jake because you lost it. What did you lose?"

Harriett cocked her head to one side, focused on a picture of two swans in a bookcase across the room and pondered the question. *What did I lose? I was so angry that I couldn't reason nor could I stop myself from screaming and running towards Jake. I was out of control.*

She turned her head towards Dr. Aye. "I lost control." Harriett's response was soft.

"Control of what?"

"Control of my anger."

"Anger is an emotion and emotions are hard to control. When we lose control over our emotions, we behave unwisely. Keeping emotions under control requires hard work—that's the bad news. The good news is

38

that I can show you how to keep your emotions under control long enough to behave more wisely."

"What's the homework assignment?" The question popped out of Harriett's mouth. *I can't believe I'm working with this woman!*

"Does that mean you'd like to return for another session?"

Harriett felt conflicted. While less resistant, she was still angry over Jake's mandate and doubtful that Dr. Aye's approach could really help her regain the life she lost.

"I don't know," she replied.

"I appreciate your honesty. And, with your permission, I'd like to make an observation."

A nod indicated Harriett's consent.

"I believe your uncertainty is a resistance to the concept of counseling in general." Harriett opened her mouth in protest, but Dr. Aye put up her hand. "Let me finish before you dispute what I say. I appreciate how you've tolerated my questions long enough to allow me a glimpse into your world. Exposing ourselves to strangers is difficult and I imagine it's especially difficult for you. Maintaining a façade of perfection seems important to you and my self-evaluation questions challenge you to examine your flaws."

Harriett struggled to remain silent, but lost the battle when Dr. Aye posed the next question. "What role does perfection play in your life?"

Harriett's eyebrows rose in righteous indignation as extreme rage replaced the blood in her veins. "Perfection plays a vital role! You make it sound like a fault. If I can't be perfect, what's the point of trying? I set my standards very high and try not to make mistakes that might cause me to look foolish or disappoint someone." The frost in her voice chilled the room.

Unconcerned, Dr. Aye asked, "How's that working for you?"

Looking around an office that felt more like a prison, Harriett answered, "Obviously, not well."

"What would you like to do?"

Harriett closed her eyes, wishing she had the energy to leave the office and retreat to the sanctity of her bedroom. Opening her eyes, she muttered, "Do I have a choice?"

"You always have a choice. The choice to change your behavior, gather data on the outcome, evaluate the results, and plan the next behavior."

"Oh, goody." Harriett's voice dripped with sarcasm. "You want me to fix my life by running experiments."

"In a way," agreed Dr. Aye. "Scientific research papers include a discussion section that objectively evaluates the findings of an experiment. There's no judgment on the results, only an analysis of how the results support the hypothesis. If the hypothesis isn't supported, then recommendations are made for future experiments."

The experiment analogy actually relieved some of Harriett's anxiety. *I was certain this woman would judge me harshly for lunging at Jake, but it sounds as if assigning blame is not as important as understanding why.*

She took a tentative step forward and asked, "What's my homework?"

"Does that mean you'd like to give my approach a try?"

"I think so."

"Because?"

Another self-evaluation question.

Harriett considered her answer before responding. "If I understand you correctly, keeping my emotions under control will be hard, but learning to keep them under control will help me change my behavior and that will change how I think and ultimately change how I feel."

Dr. Aye nodded. "Are you ready to make a commitment?"

Reluctant to relinquish her resistance, Harriett countered, "Is that another choice?"

Dr. Aye provided a serious response to the obviously derisive question. "You always have a choice. The goal is to pick the choice that maximizes the pros and minimizes the cons. However, that's a skill I teach in later sessions."

"Skill?"

"Skills help identify other behaviors to choose when your current behavior is not getting you what you want. I will teach you these skills *if* you decide to return. Therefore, I'd like an answer to my question."

"Must I give you my answer today?"

"Take all the time you need; but I warn you, progress will not occur until you make a commitment."

"A commitment to what?"

"To the process we've been discussing. The longer you remain resistant, the longer it takes to reap the rewards."

The reference to resistance stung, but she squelched the urge to argue. "What's so important about making a commitment?"

"Think about dieting. Your goal is to lose ten pounds and to accomplish your goal requires that you eat twelve hundred calories per day and exercise three times a week. However, you're not really committed to your diet. One day you don't exercise and compensate by eating nine-hundred calories, and the next day you exercise but consume seventeen hundred calories. How fast will you shed the weight?"

The example coalesced many of the concepts heard throughout the session. She might want to lose weight, but sticking to a weight loss plan required hard work and acceptance that the results she sought would not be instantaneous. Dieting required a commitment to stay the course and the perseverance to find an alternate plan when the original plan wasn't working.

Harriett made a choice. "I'll commit to doing the homework you give me at this session. Then I'll return at least one more time to let you know what I think. Is that enough of a commitment?"

"As long as you don't make any excuses if you fail to do your homework."

"Excuses?"

"We make excuses whenever we justify our inability to honor our commitments by blaming an external event. An excuse is an attempt to avoid accountability by rationalizing our behavior."

"But sometimes there's a valid reason why something didn't get done!"

"A failure identity emerges when we habitually blame an external event for our inability to honor a commitment. Conversely, a success identity develops whenever we seize control over an external event in a way that lessens its negative impact on our thoughts and feelings. Some liken a success identity to making lemonade out of lemons."

"Even when the lemons are rotten?"

Dr. Aye shrugged. "Perhaps the choice is to drink a different beverage if what you want is to quench your thirst. While rotten lemons might leave you feeling powerless, the choice to drink a different beverage mitigates the feeling."

"All that from rotten lemons?" A scornful smile accompanied the question.

"All that and more," promised Dr. Aye. "Shall I assign your homework and see how committed you are to the process?" She watched the conflicting emotions wash across Harriett's face, and offered a soft, "Thank you."

Confusion added to Harriett's mix of emotions. "For what?"

"Before this meeting, I was a stranger that you would have passed in the street without any acknowledgment. I know it was hard to tolerate my questions long enough to allow me a glimpse into your life and I appreciate your hard work."

Harriett responded with a muted, "Thank you," as her eyes filled with tears. "I needed to hear that."

"I will always believe in your capacity to live a quality life."

Dr. Aye waited as Harriett dried her face. "Shall I assign the homework?"

Despite her weariness, Harriett nodded.

"Earlier we discussed the impact thoughts have on feelings. I want you to gain a fuller appreciation of how your thoughts influence your feelings and how changes in your feelings impact your motivation to behave. This awareness is the foundation for changing your behaviors to ones that have a higher likelihood of getting you what you want."

Harriett held her breath, worried that she'd never be able to grasp the difference between a thought and a feeling.

"Your homework is to focus on how people confuse thoughts and feelings. Notice how they substitute the word *feel* for the word *think*. For instance, count how many times politicians say something like, 'I feel like this country is going to hell in a handbasket.' That's a thought that generates different feelings, depending on the politician's unique personality combined with a unique set of experiences. Candidates running for president might feel excited by the thought the country is going to hell in a handbasket because the chance of election increases. Whereas, the same thought might provoke anxiety in a presiding president whose job is to fix the problem. A lame duck president might feel relieved because the problem will soon be someone else's to fix. The more aware you become of other people's misuse of the words, the more conscious you'll become of how *your* thoughts impact *your* feelings."

The homework assignment changed Harriett's worry. *What if it's not enough to convince Jake that I'm complying with his mandate?*

"What else do you want me to do?" she asked.

"Excuse me?"

"The assignment's too simple. There must be more than differentiating between a thought and a feeling."

Dr. Aye emitted another chuckle. "Your question confirms that I'm working with an overachiever. Oh, wait! A perfectionist!"

The perfectionist comment rankled and Harriett opened her mouth to protest, but then she had a flash of insight. *The inane assignment might actually be a way out of this mess. If I tell Jake, maybe he'll agree that counseling's not the answer.*

Her distain obvious, Harriett replied, "Since you seem to think I'm a perfectionist, doesn't it make sense that I'd try to be a perfect client? That's of course, *if* I decide to be your client."

Ignoring the insolence, Dr. Aye wrote their next appointment on one of her business cards. Rising from her seat, she walked across the room towards her new client.

"Remember, Harriett, a quality life is attained one choice at a time. I'll be your teacher, coach, and mentor; but you have to walk the walk."

Handing Harriett the card, Dr. Aye instructed, "Do the homework.

I don't care if you succeed or …"

"I know," interrupted Harriett, walking towards the door in a daze. "You only care how I behave."

3

Differentiating Thoughts from Feelings

Harriett walked to her car, unlocked the door and slipped into the driver's seat. The sun heated the interior and the leather of the Jeep's bucket seat invited her into its soothing warmth. She rested her head against the headrest, trying to summon the energy to put the car in gear. She was uncertain whether to embrace Dr. Aye's promise to help or simply succumb to her fatigue, fall into a deep sleep, and dream about her problems fading away.

On some level, Harriett knew she had a choice—the choice to do the hard work Dr. Aye believed could change her life or the choice to continue wishing the change would magically occur.

The idea that changes in behavior promote changes in feeling is intriguing and certainly different from how I thought counseling would work.

Harriett suddenly remembered her reason for selecting Dr. Aye's name from the list Jake had compiled. "And forced on me," she added with a grumble. During last month's book club, she'd overheard Amy, one of the women in the group, raving about Dr. Aye's unorthodox style.

I wonder if Amy felt this confused after her first session.

Harriett sat up straight in the seat. *Did I just have a thought or a feeling?*

She puzzled over the question and concluded it was her thought, but Amy's feeling. She experienced an urge to jump out of the car and run back into the office, heralding her deduction to Dr. Aye.

Am I an eight-year-old? Do I really need to run to the teacher to have my homework approved?

A resigned sadness ensued as she acknowledged her need for reassurance, the type a child gains from earning a gold star. She repeated the question Dr. Aye posed earlier, "What role does perfection play in my life?"

A picture developed in her mind. Her third-grade teacher, Mrs. Fletcher, was returning the previous night's homework to the class, announcing how "only the best" would be on display for parent's night. Harriett recalled the thrill she felt when Mrs. Fletcher selected her homework to adorn the classroom wall.

I was so excited and couldn't wait to tell Mother. I raced home, pushed opened the door and yelled for her to come quick. Even Mother's admonishment to, "Stop that racket," didn't diminish my excitement. I announced my news and watched her beam with pride.

The words, "I expected nothing less from a Smyth," still echoed in Harriett's brain.

Little girl Harriett waited in eager anticipation the morning after parents' night, anxious to see her mother's reaction to the homework. The assignment was to write an essay using descriptive words to convey a favorite memory and she'd worked hard to capture the memory of a day at the beach with her family. Her mother's silence at the dining room table made Harriett worry that Mrs. Fletcher had said something bad.

"Did you see my homework?" she asked.

"Yes, Harriett, I did."

Mother's quiet response confirmed that something was amiss and a pit began growing in Harriett's stomach.

"What did you think?" Little girl Harriett wasn't sure she wanted to know.

"I think your penmanship requires more effort," Mother replied. "In comparison to the others, yours was quite sloppy."

"Did you like what I wrote about the day at the Cape?" persisted little girl Harriett.

Mother smiled. "Yes, sweetheart, you described the day very nicely. I could almost feel the sand between my toes."

The words abated some of Harriett's worry, but her distress escalated when Mother scolded, "Harriett, I am very serious. You must work harder on your handwriting. Proper penmanship reflects good manners."

Little girl Harriett vowed to her mother and to herself that she'd do better next time.

Forty-two-year-old Harriett shook her head and sighed. *It's odd that something as trite as a third grader's penmanship could elicit such a stern warning. I've often wondered if Mother's preoccupation with the opinions of others stems from her failed marriage to my father.*

As a rebellious twenty-year-old, her mother rejected her own parents' warning that the man she wanted to marry would not be a good provider. Mother refused to listen and was devastated when the marriage ended, leaving her alone, pregnant, and penniless. Her welfare and the welfare of her twin daughters became the responsibility of Harriett's grandparents.

Mother transformed herself in a matron of old Bostonian society when she saw how rebellion contributed to her demise and she was determined that I avoid repeating her mistakes.

A glance at the dashboard's clock interrupted Harriett's musings. It was late and the kids were waiting. She started the Jeep's engine and backed out of the parking spot, still mulling the memory. *What on earth made me remember Mrs. Fletcher? I had a perfect childhood and I refuse to waste time dissecting my memories.*

Harriett drove out of the parking lot, resolving to remain reticent if Dr. Aye attempted to explore her past.

Hold on, am I really considering a second visit? All I'd have to do is leave a short message on Dr. Aye's answering machine, canceling the appointment. Then I won't have to worry about dissecting my past.

"So why," she asked, "am I reluctant to choose that option?"

While the empty car offered no answer, another glance at the clock distracted her thoughts. *I have to pick up Katie and then get Matt to his soccer match. I hope Katie doesn't give me a hard time about staying to watch the game. She keeps moaning how I've embarrassed her SOOOOO much. Maintaining my composure in public is hard enough. I don't need the added worry of Katie and her friends.*

News of the lunge had spread with stunning swiftness...

I suppose it makes for a good gossip. I was in such a state, screeching and flailing the knife at Jake. I was deaf to his pleas to stop and I never heard the kids running down the stairs. I can't imagine what the scene was like from their perspective!

She trembled at the memory of her children rushing into the kitchen to find their father cornered against the hot stove, waving his arms in a frantic attempt to avoid the sharp blade of the knife. Katie had grabbed the phone, dialed 9-1-1 and screamed for help, while Matt wrapped his arms around his mother in a stranglehold similar to ones she'd seen in an action movie.

At least I regained my composure before the Bayview police started banging on the door. I suppose it mitigated some of the calamity that followed.

Two officers entered the house, silently surveyed the scene, assessed it was a domestic dispute and escorted her into Jake's study where she sat alone, breathless and mute.

Thank goodness they accepted Jake's assurances that everything was under control.

She re-experienced the relief she felt when they agreed to let Jake handle the situation. However, they took a report and warned that a second incident would result in a more serious outcome. Foolishly, Harriett expected the incident to die a quiet death, but the nightmare continued...

The flashing lights of emergency vehicles parked in the driveway alerted the neighbors and provoked curious inquiries. Then a notice appeared in the police log of the local newspaper publicizing that officers had responded to a domestic disturbance at her address. Details of the event began to leak out like water into a sinking boat. The analogy made Harriett cringe and she decided to skip Matt's game. *He can hitch a ride with one of his teammates and then call me when the game's over.*

She rationalized how her decision was better than sitting in the bleachers, surrounded by prying eyes. *Besides, my outburst rattled Matt and made him play terribly the other night. The last thing I need is for the other parents to make me feel guilty for causing the team to lose the game. I already feel guilty enough!*

Harriett's choice proved regrettable in that it produced more turmoil, which intensified her guilt. Katie whined because Harriett had "destroyed" her plans to sit with friends and Matt moaned how she'd reneged on her promise to videotape the match. A coach wanted to critique his game, but her failure to keep her promise meant he had nothing to show the coach.

Matt accentuated his anger with an additional grievance, "I waited forever for you to pick me up. I don't know why I can't just drive myself to and from the games."

Harriett sighed in defeat when she attached a third consequence to her choice. Her retreat from scrutiny created more time to be alone with her thoughts and she spent the time in her bedroom, reliving the nightmare over and over. The dwelling left her sad, listless, and too exhausted to interact with anyone, including those who cared about her.

"Please, Harriett," Jake coaxed from the other side of the locked door. "Just come downstairs. I sent the kids out for pizza with their friends. Can't we at least talk about what's going on?"

NOOOOOO! The word screamed inside her head as fear supplanted her guilt and sadness. *What if he starts talking about Julie? Then what?*

Hiding in her room was safer, even if it meant she had more time to dwell.

"I told you, I'm fine. Just leave me alone!"

The sound of retreating footsteps made her ambivalent. Part of her was relieved and part of her yearned for Jake to break down the door, hold her in his arms, and promise that everything would be all right.

Harriett plodded through the week, too tired to paint pictures of what she wanted and certainly too worn out to consider how she might change her behavior. However, she occasionally remembered snippets of the conversation with Dr. Aye. *She'd probably challenge me to self-evaluate and probably say I'm using my fatigue as an excuse to avoid dealing with all my woes...but I don't care. I'm exhausted!*

Harriett also noticed how people on television and talk radio confused thoughts and feelings. She became a bit over-zealous while watching a televised debate between school committee members who repeatedly told the audience they felt like the school budget was out of control.

"That's what you think," she yelled to the television. "And when you think the school budget's out of control, how do you feel?"

Several feelings came to mind—anger, concern, disgust...

Unfortunately, her newfound awareness became problematic while out to dinner with Sharon and her husband. Tim and Jake were talking about golf when Harriett heard Tim complain, "I feel like I'm not connecting with the ball as well as I did last year."

Harriett suppressed an urge to observe, "No, Tim, that's what you think; and when you think that, how do you feel?" Instead, she picked up her wineglass and took a long swallow. Over the rim of the glass, she saw Jake scowling in disapproval. A knot formed in her stomach—*Now what?*

"I'll tell you what!" Jake fumed during the car ride home. "You had three glasses of wine and listening to you slur your words was embarrassing! Haven't you caused enough commotion without the whole town gossiping that you're a drunk?"

Harriett didn't have the energy to argue. "I'm sorry."

"Damn it! Stop telling me you're sorry. I know you're sorry, but you don't seem motivated to fix it. All you do is mope around the house, avoiding people, and refusing to answer the phone. I had to pry you out of the bedroom just to eat dinner. For God sakes, Sharon and Tim are loyal friends! If they don't understand, who will?"

"Do you?"

"Do I what?" Jake cast a nervous glance in her direction.

"Do you understand why I did what I did?"

"I don't think I will ever understand," admitted Jake. "That's why I insisted you see someone. You haven't been yourself for weeks. I've been concerned, but thought you'd eventually snap back to your old self. The other night was the final straw." He reached for Harriett's hand and gave it a gentle squeeze. "I'm hoping Dr. Aye can help us both understand."

Encouraged by Jake's unexpected show of tenderness, Harriett took a deep breath and confessed her uncertainty.

"...and I'm not sure I want to see her again," she finished.

To her surprise, Jake didn't respond with a rant nor did he repeat his threat to take away the children. He simply wondered, "Why?"

"I'm not sure she's right for me. I found an article online that discussed the ten top reasons to run from a therapist and I'm beginning to think some of those reasons apply to her."

"Such as?"

"Well, she tried to make me laugh and one of the reasons to leave a therapist is if you feel you're being treated with contempt or disdain."

"And do you?"

Harriett evaluated her answer. While she might expect a little more commiseration from a counselor, she couldn't honestly say that Dr. Aye treated her with disdain.

"No, not really, but Dr Aye thinks looking at the bright side of life makes things a little less overwhelming. She calls it a success identity and wants me to make lemonade out of lemons."

"That sounds more like common sense than contempt."

"The article also said you should see someone else if you feel worse after your session."

"And do you?" Jake repeated.

"Not worse, but what she wants me to do is hard."

"What does she want you to do?"

"Change my behavior whenever I'm upset."

"Well, what's wrong with that? You certainly can't keep coming after me with a knife!"

Harriett bristled at the edginess in Jake's voice and she briefly considered confronting him about Julie. *No. I don't have the stamina to tolerate his excuses.*

Instead, she used her last vestige of energy to plead her case. "Oh, Jake, I know what I did was wrong, but please don't overreact."

"Don't overreact! How should I react? What is proper etiquette for when your wife attacks you with a weapon?"

She lost the fragile grip on her emotions and began crying softly. Jake's question mocked her devotion to acting correctly and truncated further conversation. The couple retreated to their respective corner of the car and completed the ride home in silence. Harriett stared out the window, her thoughts remorseful and foreboding.

She dragged herself up the stairs in wounded defeat, intending to crawl into bed and pull the covers over her head. As she rubbed cream into a face etched with dejection, she remembered what the article said to do if a therapist promises a quick and easy cure—RUN!

Dr. Aye certainly didn't promise any magic cures. But, she did offer to help me make better choices and I certainly need to start making some.

Harriett stared into the bathroom mirror and saw a woman desperate to salvage her marriage and her family. "What choice do I have?" She sighed and resolved to keep the appointment.

The day of the session was rainy, raw, and cold, adding to Harriett's already gloomy outlook. She backed the Jeep out of the garage and made her way across town, reflecting on the days since her last meeting with Dr. Aye.

"Miserable," she concluded. "I was naïve to think counseling would be the solution to my problems."

Her resolve weakened.

Dr. Aye's assertion that all behavior is a choice is absurd! What choice do I have if Jake's having an affair? My only choices are to ignore it or divorce him and neither choice works for me! I'm stuck in a situation that I did not choose—and don't want!

Harriett yanked the steering wheel left towards Dr. Aye's office. From somewhere within the recesses of her mind, a niggling little voice asked the question she'd shunned throughout the week, "What do you want?"

Staring through the misty windshield, Harriett replied, "I wish I knew."

Exhausted, she ruminated on Dr. Aye's repeated reference to hard work. *How can that woman expect me to work hard when I can barely get through the day?*

Harriett knew she was being obstinate, but didn't care.

Imagine accusing me of making excuses for what happened with Jake! Besides, I don't think it's ethical to deride a person's desire to be perfect!

Her resistance rose as the distance between client and counselor shortened.

That woman wants a commitment from me?

Resistance morphed into rebellion.

I think...no, wait! I FEEL LIKE she needs to be committed to me!

The Jeep came to a halt outside the large white colonial that housed Dr. Aye's office. Instinctively, Harriett sensed she had a choice. She could act emotionally, put the car in reverse, and run away—or—she could behave wisely and keep the appointment.

Both choices seemed fraught with consequences.

4

Skill #1
Tolerate

Harriett fidgeted on the couch, impatient for Dr. Aye to call her into the office. *Last week I wondered why I needed a counselor...this week I'm wondering why I need this counselor!*

Her angry thoughts propelled her out of her seat the moment the waiting room door squeaked open. She rushed ahead of Dr. Aye, positioned herself on the teal loveseat and waited...

"So, Harriett, how was your week?"

"Do you really care?" Her prepared response concluded with a silent, *Ta-da!*

"Not really."

Harriett gasped, astonished at the careless dismissal of her question. *That's not what I wanted! What I wanted was to put this woman on notice. If she wants me to work hard, then I intend to make her work just as hard!*

"Pardon?" Harriett cringed as the word fell from her mouth. *Please stop repeating that inane word,* she begged herself.

"How did you expect me to answer?" replied Dr. Aye.

Harriett's shoulders rose in helpless surrender.

"Harriett." Dr. Aye's tone demanded attention. "I'm willing to work as hard as you require. I want to help make your situation better. However, I will not work harder than you're willing to work for yourself.

Spending your day devising snappy responses to my questions is a waste of your energy and my time."

Dr. Aye's tone softened as she suggested they start over. "How was your week?" she repeated.

"Not much different from last week," Harriett admitted. "I thought coming to you would make a difference, but I think maybe I'm even more confused, more tired, and more afraid that things will never be the same as before."

"I wish I could wave a magic wand and make your world shiny and bright," replied Dr. Aye. "Unfortunately, a magic wand isn't the secret to a quality life. A quality life unfolds through a combination of faith and hope. Faith in your ability to make the changes necessary to get what you want and hope that you'll find behaviors that make you feel less confused, less tired, and less afraid. I'll be your keeper of hope until you're confident in your ability to add quality to your life."

Holding Harriett in a steady gaze, Dr. Aye asked, "What would you like to do?"

Please don't ask me to self-evaluate.

Tempted to curl up into a ball and tuck herself in a corner of the loveseat, Harriett remembered the desperate face of the woman in the bathroom mirror.

"I understand how the four needs create wants that are represented by pictures inside my head, but how do I change my behavior to get what I want if I don't know what I want?"

"First, we ascertain the need represented by the picture, then look for alternative behaviors that might conceivably satisfy the same need. For instance, a picture of me at the movies with my husband might represent the need for fun. I might change my behavior and take my husband bowling if there's no suitable movie playing at the cinema. However, if the need for love and belonging is the reason my husband's in the picture and he suddenly has to work, I might satisfy the need by calling a friend who likes to bowl."

Dr. Aye smiled at her client's repugnant look. "You don't like bowling? Perhaps you prefer rock climbing?"

Harriett shook her head. "Why can't it just be a quiet dinner?"

"As long as the behavior isn't dangerous to yourself or someone else, I don't care what you do. I only care that the behavior you choose has the highest likelihood of satisfying your needs."

"But that's the problem! I don't have the energy to think about my needs, let alone change my behavior!"

"I understand," assured her counselor. "Today I'll explain how we become energized enough to identify our needs and also how to develop a hypothesis about behaviors that might satisfy them. Then you'll run the experiment and assess the results. If the results support the hypothesis, you continue the behavior. If they don't, I suggest you conduct a different experiment."

Harriett's mind focused on her hypothesis about Jake and Julie. *Careful, don't go jumping to conclusions—even if I know I'm right!*

Cautioning herself to remain silent about the affair, Harriett asked, "What if the choices aren't worth running the experiment?"

"Sometimes the choices are less than ideal," conceded Dr. Aye. "However, the realization that we have control over our response to a situation helps us avoid feeling stuck and powerless."

That's exactly how I feel about Jake.

Harriett was tempted to share her thoughts with Dr. Aye, but fear made her reticent. *I don't trust anyone's ability to help me.*

Dr. Aye continued. "Last week I mentioned nine skills that help control your emotional response to a situation long enough to consider other ways to behave. The skills give you the energy required to make difficult choices."

Tears of frustration welled in Harriett's eyes. "I still don't understand! How will all this help me fix what I broke with Jake? You ask me what I want when all I know is that I want my life back! I'm tired of hiding from people...tired of feeling ashamed...tired of being overwhelmed. I'm just tired! I'm so tired that I'm not sure I have the energy to do the hard work you want me to do."

Bending over, she sobbed into her lap. Eventually, she lifted her head and cast a sideways glance at Dr. Aye, worried about her counselor's response. *I might not know what I want, but I do know I'd be devastated if I failed at being the client she expects me to be.*

"I understand," replied Dr. Aye, her voice quiet.

The gentle response was surprising. Relieved, Harriett repositioned herself on the loveseat. "I'm sorry for being so obstinate."

"Harriett, you're not being obstinate. Your reaction is valid given your circumstances. I think it's time I explained the purpose of skills training and how the skills provide the energy to work hard. Are you ready to listen?"

Dr. Aye waited as Harriett evaluated her options.

Sighing deeply, Harriett nodded.

"I use a synthesis of different perspectives to explain my point of view on how people can fill their lives with quality. While I predominantly subscribe to the Choice Theory model, I also draw upon concepts from Dialectical Behavior Therapy and my experiences in engineering. As a result, the set of skills I teach are uniquely mine and sprang from the KISS principle—Keep It Simple and Straightforward. My colleagues consider my approach quirky because I use daily life experiences to exemplify complicated psychological paradigms."

"Like lemonade?"

"Like lemonade," agreed Dr. Aye. "My job is to walk you through the process while making the journey as comprehensible as possible. And...," her eyes twinkled. "...there's no harm in having a little fun along the way."

"But what if I can't keep up?"

Dr. Aye held up her hand, curbing Harriett's trepidation. "It's your journey and I'll walk alongside you. Think of me as your guide, shining a light in the direction you want to travel."

"You sound more like a cheerleader."

Dr. Aye chuckled. "I wanted to be a cheerleader in high school, but was too short to make the squad. See, I found a different behavior to get what I want!"

Harriett rolled her eyes. "What do you mean when you say the skills give me energy?"

"Think of a battery. The power inside a battery provides energy to make something work. The energy dissipates every time the battery's used, making the battery less effective. Now visualize yourself as a battery. Your energy is psychic energy and dissipates each time you engage in a behavior. Unproductive behaviors waste energy and cause you to feel sluggish, tired, and listless. Behaviors that achieve what you want are productive and energizing. Productive behaviors recharge the battery and provide the motivation to continue working hard."

I'm not sure I like the analogy of myself as a battery. It seems a rather simplistic way to explain why I feel so fatigued.

However, the more she evaluated how unproductive behaviors were a waste of energy, the more Harriett embraced the concept. "Last week you told me to make lemonade out of lemons. What you meant was to stop wasting my energy moaning about the lemons and start behaving productively by making something good to drink."

"Give that girl a gold star."

Mrs. Fletcher flashed before Harriett's eyes and she experienced the same satisfaction she felt as a child.

"Were you able to complete your homework?" asked Dr. Aye.

"I was surprised," she admitted. "Once you made me aware of the difference, I noticed how often people mistake their thoughts for feelings."

"What did you notice about yourself?"

"Sometimes my thoughts and feelings are so interconnected that distinguishing between the two is difficult."

"There's a concept in Dialectical Behavior Therapy that helps differentiate the difference. Marsha Linehan, the therapy's creator, maintains that human beings have three minds—reasonable mind, emotional mind, and wise mind. All three are important, but for different reasons. Reasonable mind is where data reside. Every fact we've ever learned is stored in reasonable mind and stays in storage until a situation arises that requires accessibility to the pertinent facts."

"Like a computer?"

"Exactly like a computer. Let's use the radiator in my office as an example. If we were sitting here and I saw smoke coming from the radiator, reasonable mind would think, *Smoke. Smoke's turned to flames. Wall's on fire. Room's smoky. Client's coughing. I'm suffocating. I'm dying.*"

Dr. Aye waited before asking, "What's wrong with this scenario?"

"You're not doing anything."

"We literally cannot live in reasonable mind because there's no motivation to behave. Emotional mind motivates behavior. Emotional mind contains every emotion we've ever experienced—love, hate, fear, anger, passion, fury, disillusionment, sadness... All emotions, regardless of subtlety or intensity, exist in emotional mind. Like reasonable mind, living exclusively in emotional mind is fraught with consequences."

Responding to Harriett's puzzled look, Dr. Aye explained. "An emotional mind response to smoke would be to jump up and scream, 'Danger! Run! Get out!' I might drag you out of the office and scramble to pull the fire alarm."

Studying her client's reaction, she asked, "What's wrong with my behavior?"

"It seems a little excessive."

"Just a little?" Dr. Aye's eyebrows raised in exaggerated surprise. "Emotional mind contains no censure on behavior. We feel therefore, we behave. Which mind do you think you were in when you lunged at your husband?"

"Since I wasn't acting reasonably, I'd have to guess emotional mind."

"And that's what I mean by acting emotionally! Now let's teach you how to behave wisely!"

"You mean the skills?"

Dr. Aye nodded. "The best options for less impulsive behavior reside in wise mind. Wise mind is the part of our brain that balances the facts pertinent to the situation with the amount of emotion appropriate to the situation. The behavioral options contained in wise mind are always more controlled. I call them—*wise*."

Pausing for effect, she continued, "A wise mind response to smoke might be concern which would motivate me to get up from my chair and examine the radiator. The absence of flames might allay my concern, but I know that smoke is often an indication of fire. Still motivated to act, I'd contact maintenance and report the problem. Then, I'd resume our session, but watch the radiator closely."

"Are you saying wise mind controls emotional mind?"

"A filter between emotional mind and wise mind prevents over-saturation by allowing only the correct amount of emotion to enter into wise mind. When the proportion between reason and emotion is balanced, the brain's creative energy produces productive behavioral options. Think of wise mind as an engine that requires gas."

"Oh, great," Harriett moaned. "Earlier I was a battery and now I'm an engine. Soon I'll be a whole car!"

Amused, Dr. Aye described her picture of new clients. "I see them as trucks stuck in the mud with their wheels spinning, but going nowhere."

"That's exactly how I feel," replied Harriett.

"I have an image of myself cheering as I watch my clients use their creative energy to rock themselves out of the mud. What color truck would you like to be?"

Harriett pictured a bright-yellow Hummer.

"Can you attach your picture to a need?"

She recalled the four needs and mentally evaluated how they related to her picture. *Perhaps power, because rocking myself out of the bog would feel amazing! On the other hand, maybe freedom, because becoming unstuck would feel liberating and I'd be free to travel wherever I wanted. Then again, a Hummer would be a fun way to explore undeveloped trails.*

Harriett relayed her thoughts to her counselor.

"You self-evaluated nicely," affirmed Dr. Aye. "By evaluating the information contained in reasonable mind, and assessing the impact on your feelings, you've created several pictures and given yourself multiple options. Now choose the behavior that's most likely to achieve what you want."

The choice was surprisingly easy. "I want to hear why you think wise mind is like an engine that requires gas."

"Gas engines cannot operate without the proper amount of gasoline. They might be precise and highly efficient, but won't work if the gas tank's empty or the engine's flooded with too much gas. Think of emotions as gasoline. If there's no emotion in wise mind, there's no ability to initiate behavior and too much emotion floods wise mind. Do you know what to do when an engine's flooded?"

"Wait for the gas to dissipate?"

"And when the proportion of gas is correct, the engine operates properly," finished Dr. Aye. "Combining the proper level of emotion with the facts pertinent to the situation allows wise mind to operate properly."

Harriett leaned against the back of the loveseat. "I think I understand, but how does the concept apply to my situation with Jake?"

"How do you think the concept applies?"

The constant challenge to self-evaluate was annoying and felt similar to being on a roller coaster. One minute she was on top of the conversation and the next, her emotions plummeted. Tired, testy, and irritable, she asked, "Why can't you just tell me?"

"I can, but conducting your own evaluation is more productive."

Harriett expelled another weary sigh. "I think I was in emotional mind when I lunged because I felt Jake wasn't appreciating me. I've been feeling like that for a while and I snapped."

"Snapped?"

"I guess wise mind got flooded and I went crazy." Looking at her counselor, Harriett asked the question that had plagued her mind for the past two weeks. "Does that mean I'm crazy?"

"Let's examine your question within the context of your homework. You *thought* Jake didn't appreciate you and that made you *feel* crazed. As a result, you behaved crazily—you snapped."

Harriett's patience waned. "I still don't understand! What good does it do me to understand why I snapped? My life's still in shambles!" Rekindled frustration provoked fresh tears.

"My skills transition you from emotional mind into wise mind whenever you're involved in an emotionally laden situation. In wise mind, you're able to resist acting impulsively, evaluate the problem, and craft wiser options. Wiser options are more productive and expend less energy. Using the skills makes you feel less fatigued and more invigorated to initiate a different behavior. Would that be helpful?"

"It might help Jake be less afraid of me," she admitted.

"Is that something you want?"

Very much. If Jake were less afraid of me, I might be able to put this ugly mess behind me and get back to normal.

The thought made her ambivalent. *What does normal mean? Do I really want to return to a life that feels dominated by everyone else's demands? What if Jake is having an affair? Doesn't that change everything? Can life ever be normal after an affair?*

Her ambivalence grew with each question and ultimately brought her to the same conclusion. *I have no idea what I want.*

The sound of Dr. Aye calling her name refocused her attention.

"I'll show you how to establish what you want by teaching you a skill every time we meet," said Dr. Aye. "Your homework is to practice the skill and collect the data. Together, we'll analyze your findings and plan new behaviors. My process facilitates answers and each answer adds quality to your life."

The words diminished Harriett's distress. She nodded when Dr. Aye asked if she was ready to learn about the skills.

"The transition from emotional mind into wise mind occurs throughout the day, often without conscious effort. I developed skills and gave them pithy names to help people access wise mind when they feel overwhelmed. There are nine skills because different situations require different interventions. Some situations necessitate controlling the feelings provoked by the circumstances, while other situations demand managing your thoughts. Differentiating between thoughts and feelings enables you to select the skill most appropriate to the situation."

Harriett's interest deepened as Dr. Aye introduced the first skill.

"Last week I thanked you for tolerating your resistance long enough to allow me a glimpse into your life. Tolerate is the name of the first skill and its purpose is to help you endure your feelings long enough to behave less impulsively."

Harriett shrugged. "I try to ignore my feelings all the time."

"There's a significant difference between ignoring your feelings and tolerating your feelings. I don't want you to invalidate your feelings by ignoring or denying them. I want you to validate your feelings and make a conscious choice to tolerate them. When emotions threaten to flood wise mind, I want you to acknowledge the feeling, grit your teeth, and endure the feeling long enough to consider wiser behaviors—ones that are less emotional and less impulsive."

Dr. Aye held out her hands and pushed downward. "Think of the Tolerate skill as a way to dampen down your emotions in the same way gas dissipates from a flooded engine."

"Can you give me an example of how ignoring and tolerating are different?"

"Let's use the emotion of lust. When couples behave too amorously in public, spectators yell, 'Get a room!' They're not telling the couple to deny or ignore their feelings—only to put a damper on their emotions and tolerate their feelings long enough to behave with more decorum. If everyone experiencing lust acted emotionally on the feeling, the streets of Bayview would be filled with rampant sex."

The absurdity of the example made Harriett rise off the loveseat, eager to avoid hearing another ridiculous analogy or metaphor.

Dr. Aye requested one last self-evaluation. "Before you scurry out of my office, humor me with an example of how you intend to practice the Tolerate skill. I don't care if you only practice one time, but remember to collect the data required to analyze the outcome."

"I'm sure I'll have many opportunities to practice," Harriett remarked with rueful awareness.

A sudden thought entered her mind. *Experimenting with the Tolerate skill might be useful the next time I have to pry Matt out of bed.*

She explained her plan while Dr. Aye wrote their next appointment on her business card.

Dr. Aye placed the card in Harriett's outstretched hand. "Good luck and remember…"

"I know," interrupted Harriett. "You don't care if I succeed or fail. You only care how I behave." She walked towards the door, mindful that the anger she'd felt entering the session had been replaced by a modicum of energy.

"…remain aware of the difference between a thought and a feeling *and* practice the skill. Your use of energy will be more productive than devising snappy rejoinders to my very important questions."

Chastised, Harriett beat a hasty retreat to her car.

5

Changing Behavior as a Way to Change Thoughts and Feelings

The small amount of energy she experienced inside Dr. Aye's office ebbed as Harriett stepped over the threshold and walked across the parking lot. *I wish I understood why I feel hopeful inside Dr. Aye's office when, out here in the real world, life feels so daunting.*

Her shoulders slumped as she trudged towards the car, tempted to retreat to the safety of her bedroom, but obliged to drive across town and pick up her children. She drove through the streets, using the car's quiet solitude to sort through the day's session.

Dr. Aye gives me reason to believe there's a way out of this mess.

"So, Harriett," she asked, adopting her counselor's New York accent. "When you think there's a way out of this mess, how do you feel?"

Posing the question produced a startling response. "I feel slightly less apprehensive."

That makes no sense. How can words make me feel better? Just because there might be a light at the end of the tunnel, how do I know it's not the headlights of an oncoming train?

A shiver of fear ran down her spine and yet, the light beckoned...

I wonder if alleviating some of the emotion from my wise mind can really make things better.

Dr. Aye's suggestion to dampen her emotions made Harriett recall the previous summer's conversation with the chimneysweep after finding the damper opened in her fireplace. *He said the room's cool air was escaping up the chimney and wasting energy.*

Harriett imagined a wide-open damper between her emotional mind and wise mind.

According to Dr. Aye, the Tolerate skill is the equivalent of closing the damper.

Suddenly curious, Harriett wondered, *Can I possibly tolerate my emotions long enough to change my behavior?*

She resolved to conduct the experiment and find out, but her next thoughts sapped her resolve. *What if I use the Tolerate skill and the behavior I choose makes the situation worse? What if Dr. Aye's skills are inadequate and I can't cope?*

Her despair returned, along with its cohorts of hopelessness, helplessness, panic, and exhaustion.

The next morning Harriett was too tired to argue over Matt's boycott of first period. She sat in the passenger seat, agitated by the way her son's head bobbed in contented rhythm to the music playing on his favorite radio station.

Great, on top of all my other woes, I feel guilty for not doing my homework!

Harriett excused her behavior by rationalizing. *Dr. Aye said I only have to do my homework one time. I'll think about it tomorrow.*

Feeling a bit like Scarlett O'Hara, she wondered, *Is feeling like a person, a thought or a feeling?*

The tomorrows came and went. Matt's rebelliousness continued, as did Harriett's choice to ignore him. She also turned a blind eye to Jake's increasingly odd behavior. He seemed disengaged, when his usual behavior was to take control in a crisis—just as he'd done in the aftermath of the now famous lunge...

Huddled alone in the study, she'd listened to him reassure Matt and Katie. "Mom's fine. She just needs a bit of space."

She'd felt an onslaught of guilt when she heard Jake consoling Katie. "I promise, honey. Getting gum on your mother's sweater isn't what made her upset."

Unable to bear her family's distress, she'd begged Jake to take Matt to his soccer game and then escaped to the bedroom. Jake even went to the Monday meeting with the vice-principal and developed a plan to keep Matt focused on his goals.

However, over the past two weeks, her husband had become increasingly remote—disinterested in Matt's noncompliance with the plan and distracted when Katie tried to engage him in a daddy-daughter chat. While Harriett could accept his aloofness towards her, Jake's withdrawal from the children was baffling and fueled her worry about Julie...*the trollop.* Merely thinking about Julie made Harriett's skin crawl.

Remembering Dr. Aye's reference to specificity, Harriett challenged herself to dig deeper. *When I think of Julie, I feel...what? Annoyed? Scared? No! When I think of Julie, I feel frantic!*

Harriett flashed a bitter smile as she imagined Dr. Aye's nod of approval.

I bet Dr. Aye would have a field day with that piece of information! I wonder if I should tell her about my suspicions. She'd probably ask, "Whose behavior can you change?" How do I change the fact that my husband is having an affair?

"*If* he is having an affair," she amended, even though she knew she was right.

The following morning, Harriett dragged herself up the steps to wake Matt.

I'm nothing more than an alarm clock.

Stopping midway up the stairs, she realized she didn't like the feeling provoked by her thought. She felt annoyed, and mentally emphasized the feeling with a capital "A" accompanied by a bold underline.

"How's that for being specific?" she asked aloud.

Thrusting her chin forward, Harriett made a choice. "This is as good a time as any to try my homework. If I fail, I'll use the evidence to refute Dr. Aye's logic!"

She continued up the stairs, pleased to rediscover her resolve.

"Matt, are you awake?"

"Yeah," Matt answered from under the chocolate-brown duvet adorning his bed.

"Well, listen up. I'm tired of being your alarm clock. If you want a ride to school, you need to be in the car in fifteen minutes. If you're not, then find your own ride, or don't go. The choice is yours."

Matt lifted his head slightly from his pillow and poked his face out from under the comforter, grinning from ear to ear. "Does that mean I can stay home?"

"I said the choice is yours. If you choose to stay home or go in late, I will report you as unexcused. Remember what Mr. Bartlett said about incurring another unexcused tardy or absence. You will be suspended."

Determined not to wheedle or cajole, Harriett used soccer as her ally. Matt knew a suspension from school also meant suspension from playing soccer and this weekend's match was an important prelude to the state championships. She hoped Matt's passion for soccer would be enough motivation to leave the comfort of his bed. Harriett turned and left the room before her courage flagged.

Regrettably, her feelings didn't transform into wild jubilation. Rather, a sense of conflicted uncertainty invaded every aspect of her being. *What if changing my behavior causes Matt to miss an important soccer game? His dreams of a scholarship might be destroyed!*

Panic rose into her throat, causing her to turn and head back to Matt's room. *Perhaps I can convince him to make the right choice.*

TOLERATE!

The word reverberated throughout her mind, stopping her in mid-stride and urging her to self-evaluate. *Can a single word really assuage my panic? I'm supposed to acknowledge the feeling and tolerate it long enough to change my behavior.*

Harriett stood frozen with ambivalence and heard the seconds tick away. Somehow, someway, she found the wisdom to change direction. *I've come this far, I might as well complete my homework.*

Fifteen minutes later, Harriett sat in the car, stunned.

I'm absolutely stunned, she repeated to herself, as *she* drove Matt to school, listening to *her* music on *her* favorite radio station.

Matt's pace had slowed when he walked into the garage and saw his mother sitting behind the wheel, but he didn't dare complain or even comment.

Was he happy? *No.* Did she care? *No! I only care about his behavior!*

She also cared about her subsequent feelings of power. Thinking her behavior had elicited a change in her son made Harriett feel invigorated and in control. *If this is the definition of a success identity, I want more!*

Feeling energized, Harriett decided to apply her energy towards doing the laundry and even tackled a pile of ironing she'd been neglecting for the past two weeks. While minor, she felt victorious because yesterday the pile seemed insurmountable.

Picking her daughter's sweater from the basket, she recalled how angry she'd become over Katie's careless disregard of the new green sweater. Assessing her anger within the context of Dr Aye's belief that the only behavior we can change is our own, Harriett reached a provocative conclusion. "If I wasn't prepared to risk having Katie disregard my sweater, I should have insisted she wear another outfit."

She passed the iron over one of Jake's shirts and contemplated other points from the sessions with Dr. Aye. *I've been making excuses for Matt's behavior when the reality is that I can't make him get to school on time—that's my lemon. However, by changing my behavior, I made a tasty batch of lemonade!*

She pressed the hot iron into the fabric and watched a puff of steam envelope the shirt.

I'm not sure what I'd have done if Matt's behavior hadn't changed.

Smoothing away the wrinkles, she hypothesized, *I guess I'd have to tolerate my negative feelings long enough to let Matt suffer the consequences.*

Hot water spit from the iron.

Would I have the gumption to follow through on that type of consequence?

Harriett thought about how she always bragged that hard work didn't faze her. "I might have to retract that statement."

Reaching into the bottom of the basket, she considered another option. "I could make sure that I only set consequences that I'm prepared to administer."

Marveling at the extent of data gleaned from just one experiment, Harriett plowed through the last of the laundry.

I used the Tolerate skill to keep my emotions in control long enough to change my behavior and doing so changed my thinking, which is why I feel better.

She also acknowledged how running the experiment used less energy than worrying about Matt's tardiness. Behaving productively was more energizing and the empty clothes hamper was her proof!

Perhaps Dr. Aye's reliance on daily life experiences isn't such an odd way of counseling.

Closing the ironing board, Harriett summarized her findings. "Dr. Aye says being in control is a want that represents my need for power. The reason I feel more energized is because my behavior matched a picture of myself exerting control."

"Behaving wisely certainly feels better than acting emotionally," she confessed to the empty basket.

Sadly, Jake's footsteps announcing his arrival home from the office robbed Harriett of her newly minted energy.

Confused, she worked hard to recapture the precious resource, but to no avail. Instead, familiar feelings of dread and shame filled the void. Tense and tired, she lacked the energy to tell Jake about the morning's success and retreated to her bedroom immediately after dinner. She buried her head in her pillow and had a final thought before closing her eyes—*Following Dr. Aye's advice may produce enough energy to empty a clothesbasket, but seems woefully inadequate to rid my life of the really, dirty laundry.*

6

Skill #2
Stop Thinking! Start Doing!

"So, Harriett, how was your week?"

"Okay." Harriett knew the lackluster response wasn't what Dr. Aye wanted, but was all she could muster.

"Just okay?"

She braced for another round of question and answer ping-pong, wondering how to convey her uncertainty regarding Dr. Aye's approach to counseling.

"I don't really know what to say. I managed to get through the week without doing anything horrid and I did the homework, but I still feel awful."

Harriett recounted how the homework made her feel energized and how her feelings plummeted after Jake got home. "What good is using the skills if they only work for a little while? I'm still so worried about Jake and the children." Her eyes filled with tears of discouragement.

Dr. Aye studied her client before asking, "What makes you so discouraged?"

"Because nothing special occurred, except my laundry basket got emptied!" Harriett knew she sounded petulant, but didn't care. *I'm determined to make this woman understand that I don't need help surviving life's daily monotony—I need help repairing the destruction I've caused!*

"I disagree," replied Dr. Aye.

Harriett heard the hiss of deflating determination.

"The monotony of life contains vital data that goes unnoticed unless we make a concerted effort to pay attention and process what we learn. So tell me, what did you learn?"

"I did notice how behaving wisely felt better than acting emotionally. But what made my energy disappear when Jake came home from work? What's the sense of switching from emotional mind into wise mind if the energy's not enough to get me through the day?"

"Let's examine the other things you learned before I answer your question. You also learned that differentiating between a thought and a feeling enabled you to take control of the situation with Matt, and using the Tolerate skill allowed you to find a more productive way to help your son make a responsible choice. Doing the homework also shows how feelings aren't what get us into trouble, but how we behave on our feelings can be troublesome. When you were upset with Matt, you behaved wisely and felt energized. When you're upset with Jake, you act emotionally and feel drained."

"Are you telling me I'm not capable of being in wise mind even when I want to be?" The thought of not being in control was terrifying.

"Quite the contrary. The reason you made it through the week without doing anything horrid is because you spent the majority of your week in wise mind. You weren't conscious of using skills to keep your emotions under control, but I promise, that's exactly what you did."

Harriett shook her head in vehement disagreement. "I don't care if I'm in wise mind at the grocery store! I need to be in wise mind when I'm around my husband!"

"And you are," countered Dr. Aye. "You mentioned your worry about Jake's behavior with the children. What stops you from being overwhelmed with worry and lunging?"

"Pardon?"

How is her question even logical! I might be worried over Jake's behavior, but certainly not worried enough to make the situation worse than it already is!

Dr. Aye explained. "Even though you're worried about Jake, you're tolerating your worry long enough to behave wisely. Oh, I understand you want to behave more wisely. However, isn't escaping to your bedroom wiser than lunging with a knife?"

Harriett barely nodded.

"With Matt, you made a conscious choice to tolerate your feelings. You're choice to tolerate your worry as it relates to Jake is less obvious, but just as wise. Paying attention to your success with Matt made you feel energized. With Jake, you feel defeated because you're focusing on your feelings and ignoring how your behavior keeps you in control."

"Is that why you tell me you don't care how I feel, only how I behave?"

Dr. Aye nodded. "Practicing the skills increases your ability to stay focused on behaving wisely. Over time, your energy will become more stabilized and your feelings more regulated."

Harriett evaluated what she'd just heard. *The quicker I use a skill to control my emotions, the less time I'll spend in emotional mind where all I do is waste energy and, when I acknowledge my wise behavior, my energy increases.*

She looked at Dr. Aye, intending to share what she'd learned. "Instead of wasting energy being annoyed with Matt, I tried the Tolerate skill..."

"No," corrected Dr. Aye. "You did more than try."

"Pardon?"

"In the first *Star Wars* movie, Yoda teaches Luke Skywalker how to become a Jedi warrior." Adopting a grave and solemn tone, Dr. Aye offered her client the wisdom of Yoda. "Do or do not...there is no try."

What in the world? Harriett stared at her counselor in puzzled silence.

"Behavior is binary," explained Dr. Aye. "Either we behave or we don't. You might want to do better, but you're always doing."

Dr. Aye affixed a stare on her client. "Tell me what you *did*."

"Instead of arguing, I gave Matt a choice."

"And what happened?" Breathless, Dr. Aye sat forward on the edge of her seat.

Harriett smiled at the dramatics. "He was in the car and on time for school."

Dr. Aye shook her head in exaggerated wonderment and flopped back in her chair. "How did that make you feel?"

"I'm not sure. At first, I was impressed with my ability to use the skill, but then I got upset. Ultimately, I was pleased and relieved when he made the right choice."

"Emotions are transient. They last for only a short time and change as the situation changes. Living life impacts our emotions with a speed and abruptness that often feels like riding on a roller coaster. I created the skills to make the ride a bit more stable."

Dr. Aye switched topics by asking a self-evaluation question, "How hard was it to tolerate your feelings long enough to change your behavior?"

"I found it hard to resist the urge to go back upstairs and try to coax Matt into making the right choice."

Harriett heard herself stumble over the word "try" and saw a slight smile flash across her counselor's face.

"What stopped you from going back upstairs?" asked Dr. Aye.

"I wanted to make sure Matt knew I'd no longer be responsible for making his choices!"

Saying the words made Harriett feel powerful.

Dr. Aye expelled an exaggerated sigh and patted the left side of her chest. "Be still my heart!"

Harriett emitted a disparaging, *pshaw*. "Enough with the drama—it's not such a big deal."

"I disagree! Celebrating our successes harnesses the energy required to continue working hard."

Secretly, Harriett agreed. *Acknowledging my success does feel energizing, so I guess it is a big deal!*

"Remind me again," requested Dr. Aye. "What happened to your thinking and feeling after you changed your behavior?"

"At first, I didn't like either because I thought changing my behavior would destroy Matt's dream of playing soccer in college. The thought made me panic."

"Help me to understand. What made you panic?"

Despite thinking the question redundant, Harriett replied, "I was worried that Matt would be suspended and become ineligible to play his next match. He'd lose the opportunity to showcase his talents."

The ensuing silence made her fidget. "If Matt was suspended, then I'd be at fault if he didn't get showcased," she explained.

Dr. Aye's quiet scrutiny increased Harriett's discomfort.

"Don't you see?" she asked. "If he made the wrong choice and I refused to excuse him, then I'd be responsible for the suspension. The thought that, as his mother, I wasn't doing everything possible to help my son achieve his dream made me panic!"

"Are you saying you must protect your son from the consequences of making poor choices; and, unless you're there to protect him, your son will fail?"

Harriett's nod was emphatic. "How else can I insure his success and happiness? I feel the same way about Katie. Isn't that what a good mother does?"

"I think that's rather egotistical."

"Pardon?"

"Thinking you're responsible for Matt's success or failure is somewhat egotistical—and minimizes your son's capabilities."

This woman's so busy devising clever analogies, she hasn't listened to a word I said!

"I'm proud of Matt!" Harriett rebutted.

"I never said you weren't proud of your son, but I do think your thoughts around who's responsible for getting him into college are somewhat distorted. This notion of perfection seems to keep rearing its ugly head."

"Only because you keep bringing it up!"

Dr. Aye held up her hands in mock surrender. "Okay. Okay. To quote my very British husband, *Don't get your knickers in a twist*."

She gave Harriett time to regain her composure before suggesting they finish processing the homework.

Harriett struggled to remain civil long enough to describe how she'd felt better once Matt was in the car.

"Define 'better.'"

"Relieved, calmer, and in control of the situation."

"Did your hard work pay off?"

Harriett pictured the empty laundry basket and shrugged. "Only for a short time."

"Success is achieved by improving one situation at a time. Each improvement becomes the foundation for future improvements. In this case, your change in behavior produced the change you wanted in Matt. Well done."

Harriett flushed with pleasure. *I feel so silly. What difference does it make if this woman is proud of me?*

"I see a success identity written all over your face," observed Dr. Aye.

It obviously makes a big difference.

"I have one more question," said Dr. Aye. "Did changing your behavior expend more or less energy than previous choices regarding Matt's wake-up call?"

"Definitely less."

"Even though you went down the stairs worried over what he would do?"

Machiavelli must have been one of this woman's relatives! I'm sure playing devil's advocate satisfies her need for fun!

Despite the irreverent thoughts, Harriett reported her findings. "The energy I expended getting my son out of bed was less than the energy I've expended on past behaviors. Even though I wasted energy worrying if I'd failed Matt, my successful use of the Tolerate skill produced more energy than I wasted."

Harriett heard the triumph in her voice. Again, she flushed with pleasure. Feeling energized, she requested additional information. "I have a question."

Dr. Aye glanced at the clock sitting in her bookcase. "I don't have time for questions. I have skills to teach."

She watched the look on Harriett's face change from pleasure to horror, to confusion, to frustration. "Gotcha," she said with a chuckle. "I'm glad you have a question. That's how I know you're evaluating what you've learned throughout this session."

The vain attempt at humor was infuriating, and Harriett clenched her hands into tight fists. She squelched an angry retort by urging herself to tolerate Dr. Aye's unorthodox and unsettling counseling style. A sudden realization washed over her—*I just used the Tolerate skill to change my behavior!*

Relaxing her hands, Harriett's lips curled into a tiny grin.

"What just happened?" Dr. Aye demanded.

"Pardon?"

"I watched your jaw muscles tighten in response to my joke. In fact, your entire body stiffened. Then your body relaxed and you grinned. You had an affect shift—something in your thinking changed and provoked a shift in your feelings that made your behavior change. What happened?"

Recalling the diagram of a continuous cycle, Harriett ruefully revealed her thoughts.

"Acknowledging the shift in emotions that accompanies the successful use of a skill reinforces your hard work," said Dr. Aye.

"That's what my question's about," replied Harriett. "Talking about changing behavior and using skills is easy when I'm here with you, but seems so hard out in the real world. Why?"

"Learning the skills inside this office is like reading about them in a book. You're in wise mind, so the concepts sound simplistic and easy to apply. Things are harder in the real world because emotions cloud our ability to think clearly. The value of the skills lies in their ability to gain control over the emotions imposed on us by the real world. However, proficiency in any game requires practice, including the game of life."

Matt's coach says that becoming a better goalkeeper requires learning skills and practicing new ways to use them in a game. He also says becoming a better goalkeeper requires risk. Well, if Matt can do it, so can I!

Harriett chose to take a risk. "Your repeated references to perfectionism jogged an odd memory of third grade," she began. "...and I vowed to do better. All my life, I've tried to do things just a little bit better, but lately I feel like no matter how hard I try, my efforts are never good enough."

"Feel?"

"Oh! That's a thought and I definitely don't like the feeling it provokes!" Searching her counselor's face for answers, Harriett asked, "How do I change?"

Dr. Aye cocked her head, but remained silent.

Harriett expelled a deep sigh. "I understand the way to change is through my behavior, but change my behavior to what?"

"You're not going to like my answer..."

Harriett waited, certain she agreed.

"Because the answer is always the same—change your behavior to one that has a higher likelihood of achieving what you want."

"But I've told you repeatedly. I don't know what I want!"

"I beg to differ. You know your control over the situation with Matt made you feel energized and you like the feeling. I think you want to continue behaving in ways that make you to feel more in control."

Bewildered, Harriett fell back into the loveseat. "Can that really happen? Can you really make me feel more in control?"

"No, only you can do that, but I can show you how."

In her mind, Harriett saw herself hike up her britches. "Then let's get started!"

Her response provoked a quiet laugh. "Oh, Harriett, you've already started."

"I have?"

"You took the first step the moment you made a commitment."

Feeling empowered, Harriett demanded, "Teach me the next skill."

"How should I interpret your, uh, request?"

A slow smile spread across Harriett's face, dimming the sadness in her eyes. "I find it difficult to understand how keeping things simple and straightforward works on something as complicated as emotions; so let's just say I'm cautiously optimistic."

"Fine, then I'll teach you the next skill," replied her counselor.

"Stop Thinking, Start Doing is a skill based on distraction. A distraction is any behavior that interferes with your ability to concentrate. Stop Thinking, Start Doing focuses on thoughts and distracts your mind when you're dwelling on thoughts that disturb you. The objective is to find behaviors that are engrossing enough to absorb your interest and keep you focused on what you're doing, not what you're thinking. Stop Thinking, Start Doing diverts your energy away from unproductive dwelling and worrying."

"What are some examples of distracting behaviors?"

"Only you can answer that question. Each of us has different activities that we find engrossing. As for me, I like watching television shows about murder."

Harriett's head snapped up. "Pardon?"

The air filled with a chortle that made Harriett cringe—*The woman's duped me again!*

"Sorry, I couldn't resist a bit of humor," confessed Dr. Aye. "The specific behavior isn't important, as long as it's not dangerous to you or to others."

Harriett worked hard, but couldn't identify any behavior engrossing enough to distract her from obsessing over the lunge, or worrying about the affair. Dejected, her eyes welled with tears.

"Do you know the television show, *Grey's Anatomy*?" asked Dr. Aye. Harriett nodded.

"Do you remember Izzie?"

"One of the interns?"

"Izzie often has difficulty sleeping after a shift at the hospital because her mind's overwhelmed by the day's events. When she can't sleep, Izzie gets up, goes to the kitchen, and bakes. Baking engrosses her and is more productive than wasting energy struggling to sleep. However, Izzie goes a step further. Her mother was a baker and Izzie wants to replicate her mother's recipes from memory. She often spends the night engrossed in recreating the exact taste. While sleep might be Izzie's preferred option, baking is more productive than ruminating, and offers an additional benefit. Her need for power is satisfied by the satiated sighs of roommates enjoying a homemade breakfast."

Dr. Aye looked at Harriett and assigned some homework. "I want you to comprise a list of distracting behaviors that you can reference whenever you want to stop thinking and start doing."

"A list sounds so mechanical and contrived."

"It is contrived," agreed Dr. Aye. "That's why it works. When you're in emotional mind, devising options is difficult. Having the list available facilitates your transition into wise mind. The list should contain proven behaviors that you know will keep you engrossed in what you're doing."

"I like jogging because I stay focused on my pace and forget about what's bothering me. Only lately, I've been so tired that even walking is hard."

"Does walking distract you as much as jogging?"

Harriett winced at the memory of her walk on the day she lunged. "I couldn't stop dwelling and worrying about even the smallest things."

"Then put jogging on your list and eliminate walking."

"But I can't abandon what I'm doing every time I want to avoid thinking! That would be irresponsible."

"And why I recommend having a list," replied her counselor. "A repertoire of behaviors increases the likelihood of success. If one behavior isn't feasible or not working, move to the next option. What else might be on your list?"

Harriett thought about activities that she found engrossing. "I used to love reading, but now my mind wanders so much that I can't focus."

"When you find your mind wandering, tell yourself to 'Stop Thinking! Start Doing!' and challenge yourself to stay involved in the book for at least a few more pages before moving on to a different option. Remember, learning to make wiser choices is similar to developing good habits. Both require desire, dedication, and discipline."

Then Dr. Aye asked a question that made a shiver run down

Harriett's spine.

"Can you devise a distracting behavior that involves people?"

"I've been avoiding people as much as possible, including my own family!"

"Because?"

"People make me feel vulnerable and exposed. I'm afraid they'll ask about the lunge."

"How's avoidance been working for you?"

"Not good," she admitted. "I have too much time to dwell on the devastation I've caused." Dispirited tears glazed her eyes.

"Your tears highlight an important reason to include people on your list—relationships fill time. Relationships also satisfy the need to feel connected, and satisfying a need is what produces energy."

Harriett reached for a pillow tucked into the corner of the loveseat. Her hands kneaded the cushion as if it were a ball of dough.

"I know what I'm asking is hard. Would you like to know what makes you resist becoming involved with people?" asked Dr. Aye.

Harriett continued squeezing the pillow, her head bent and lips pouting.

"Your resistance is due to low energy. Socializing is demanding, and people with low energy tend to think isolating will conserve their energy by alleviating the pressure to be cordial, affable and, in your case—explain your behavior. I suggest you change your perspective. Rather than thinking of people as companions you must entertain, consider them distractions that are facilitating your recovery."

Harriett continued to squeeze the pillow.

"Now would be a good time to use the Tolerate skill," advised Dr. Aye. "Is there an option that involves people and also feels safe?"

Harriett set aside the pillow and endured her feelings long enough to consider alternative behaviors. "I could call my friends from college who don't know that I lost it with Jake."

"That's a good option and this week's homework assignment includes at least one call to a friend. Continue expanding your list of distractions and practice other ways to Stop Thinking, Start Doing."

"When would be a good time to use Stop Thinking, Start Doing?"

Dr. Aye's silence challenged Harriett to construct her own example. Her thoughts focused on the children. *I spend hours dwelling on the distress I've caused them and that makes me too ashamed to spend time with them.*

She looked at her counselor. "I wish I could stop feeling so ashamed around Matt and Katie."

"When the thoughts that make you feel ashamed enter your head, picture a big red stop sign—make it humungous! Imagine a crossing guard holding up the sign shouting, 'Stop Thinking! Start Doing!' Then, grab your list of distractions and choose one. If the first behavior doesn't engross you, keep moving through the list until you find an option that works. Remember to stay aware of the difference between a thought and a feeling, and continue practicing the Tolerate skill."

Sarcasm permeated Harriett's response, "Is that all?"

"For now."

7

How Self-Evaluation
Facilitates Wants and Motivates Behavior

Harriett walked to her car, her mind filled with a mosaic of images. Today's session added roller coasters, Yoda, and a television character to the mix of batteries, engines, and trucks. She was tempted to share the images with her friends, certain they'd have a good laugh.

Would they even believe me?

She formulated a provocative question to ask at the next cocktail party. "Excuse me, but my counselor thinks I'm a bright-yellow Hummer. What kind of truck are you?"

Visualizing the perplexed look on people's faces, she emitted a wry laugh. "Their reaction might merit more than a mere mention in the newspaper's police log."

Harriett pictured the headline: "Woman who lunged at husband claims she's a truck!"

Chuckling, she pulled into the high school parking lot to wait for Matt and Katie. Her quiet laughter became a groan when she heard a tap at the car window and looked up into the face of Karla Nicholson, the school's guidance counselor.

The abrupt shift in feelings echoed Dr. Aye's earlier observation, "Feelings are transient and change as the situation changes."

"Roll down the window," Karla mouthed.

And right now, I feel trapped!

85

She pushed the button that operated the window on the driver's side and watched as both the window and her sense of well-being disappeared. "Hello, Karla, nice to see you." She knew her greeting sounded as wooden as it was perfunctory.

"Harriett! I've been meaning to call ever since I saw your name in the paper. Is everything okay?"

Harriett fantasized her answer. *No Karla, everything is NOT okay. I went to see a counselor because my life's in ruins and her solution is for me to distract myself by imagining that I'm a truck!*

Instead, Harriett opted for an ambiguous shrug. Unfortunately, it didn't appease the woman's desire to be of service.

"You know, Harriett. Talking to someone is always good when we're feeling stressed out."

This time her fantasized response was somewhat derisive. *Oh, is that what I am, stressed out? What a relief! I'll just go home and take a warm bath. I'm sure that will wash away all my stress.*

Eager to remove herself from the awkward situation, Harriett resorted to an automatic response born from a sense of propriety. "Thank you, Karla. That's a good idea. Do you have anyone you'd recommend?"

"I have several. However, the name that keeps coming up around school is Dr. Aye."

Harriett blinked hard and covered her surprise with an obligatory nod, accompanied by the equally obligatory, "Thanks."

Please, she prayed, *there must be a way to stop this woman's prattling.*

A burst of bodies sprang from the doorways, followed by a shrill whistle announcing the start of after-school activities. Distracted, Karla looked at her watch, "Oops! Gotta go."

Karla touched Harriett's arm and gave her a long, searching look. "Take care of yourself."

Relieved, Harriett watched Karla blend into the throng of parents, teachers, and students.

"Do I have the strength to take care of myself?" she asked. The question made her recall Dr. Aye's reference to energy. "Can the skills really give me the energy I need to fix my life?"

A picture of the Energizer bunny appeared before her eyes, but she wasn't particularly surprised. She'd grown used to odd pictures popping into her mind ever since Dr. Aye explained about pictures and wants.

According to Dr. Aye, I should figure out a behavior that helps me achieve the picture inside my head. Therefore, if I want to be the Energizer bunny, I guess that means I have to behave in ways that get me energized.

The obvious behaviors seemed to be ones that used the skills, but could they really fix all that she'd broken?

"My success with the Tolerate skill does support Dr. Aye's hypothesis," Harriett conceded. "And maybe the skills can help in the short term, but...." Her voice trailed off as she chewed on her ambivalence.

"What other choice do I have but to try?"

An image of Yoda replaced the one of the Energizer bunny.

"Yoda would say my choices are to do or not do."

Doing nothing didn't seem like a wise option, especially if Jake was serious about removing Matt and Katie from the house. Harriett's stomach heaved every time she thought of losing her children.

She was suddenly conscious of the song playing on the car's radio—*I Will Survive* by Gloria Gaynor. It was her favorite song and the lyrics seemed to epitomize her dilemma. She sang along, unaware that singing had distracted her attention from thoughts of losing her children. When she realized she'd just used a skill, Harriett was impressed. *Maybe I should give these skills a chance. I'll add listening to music to my list of distracting behaviors, but I refuse to watch shows about murder!*

A few nights later, Harriett found herself alone in the kitchen, and decided to take a risk by asking herself a self-evaluation question. "How is avoiding Jake getting me what I want?"

After analyzing both her thoughts and feelings, she was able to answer, "It's not, because what I want is to know why Jake was at the Crowne Plaza with Julie."

The answer prompted another self-evaluation question. "So what do I have to do to get what I want?"

Harriett made a choice to tolerate her discomfort around Jake long enough to change her behavior and go after what she wanted. While fearful, she knew engaging her husband in a conversation was the only way to achieve what she wanted. *I guess I could hire a detective, but that seems a bit extreme...*

She decided to wait until the kids were in bed before approaching her husband, and kept her attention off the worry about Jake's response by strategizing her behaviors. *Rather than confront him, I'll broach the subject with gentle finesse. First, I'll ask about his day, then about seminars at the Crowne Plaza, and finally I'll introduce the topic of Julie.*

When Harriett entered Jake's study and found him alone, she asked, "Do you have a minute?"

Jake glanced up from the monitor of his laptop and nodded.

He looks so tired and drained. I don't have the heart or desire to mention the trollop's name. Instead, Harriett asked, "How do you get yourself back under control when you're upset?"

Jake seemed puzzled, but treated the question seriously enough to consider his answer. "I don't know...I guess I go for a run or surf the web like I'm doing now."

Alarm bells clanged inside her head. "Does that mean you're upset right now?"

"Of course I'm upset! I'm worried about you and the kids...I'm worried about money...I'm worried about work...I've been telling you for weeks that life seems so, I don't know, tedious—a different worry, but the same stress."

Harriett felt an instinctive urge to run before the situation worsened, but an image emerged that helped her tolerate the urge. She saw herself closing the damper on her emotional mind. The picture enabled her to choose a wiser behavior.

I may still have to sound the retreat, she acknowledged; but her fear seemed a little more tolerable, and she was able summon the energy to forge ahead.

Holding her breath, she asked, "So how do you cope?"

The question was open-ended and gave Jake the opportunity to talk about Julie. Harriett felt her nails digging into the palms of her hands.

"I cope by putting one foot in front of the other. It's all I know," Jake replied with a shrug.

No mention of Julie!

Harriett's hands relaxed.

She sat down beside her husband and buried her head into the familiar crook of his shoulder. She breathed in his spicy scent and luxuriated in the hope that things would be all right. She stroked his face, feeling herself melt into a sense of contented well-being.

"Don't," said Jake, brushing her hand from his cheek and moving to the far side of the couch.

Harriett's head fell onto the back of the sofa, no longer supported by the sturdiness of her husband's arm.

Gathering his computer, Jake mumbled, "I've got work to do on this brief. Don't wait up."

Harriett watched Jake's back, along with her hope, disappear through the door, leaving behind a wake of despair. Sobs racked her body as tears poured from her eyes. Jake's behavior confirmed her worst fears. *He no longer wants me! What if he decides he doesn't want this life! What if he takes the kids away from me! Will he demand I vacate the house! Where will I go! What will I do!*

Panic besieged her and her crying intensified. Suddenly, a memory surfaced in some far off corner of her brain and developed into a picture of Dr. Aye holding a bright-red stop sign, mouthing the words, "Stop thinking! Start doing!"

"Am I hallucinating?" Harriett worried aloud. She knew the thought was inane, *but who else has pictures of their counselor floating within their mind?*

"Stop thinking! Start doing!"

"Okay! Okay!" The best course of action was to comply. Maybe then that annoying New York accent would stop reverberating between her ears.

Harriett got off the couch and searched for the television's remote control. Sitting down on the sofa, she pushed on the power, scanned through the program guide, and found a movie on the Lifetime channel about a woman's desperate search to find her kidnapped child. Settling deeper into the couch, she tried to distract herself from thoughts of Jake.

In deference to Yoda, she drew a mental line through the word "tried" and focused her attention on the unfolding drama. It was difficult, but doable. Her eyes became heavy as the voices of the characters blended into a soft, synchronized harmony.

Harriett awoke at one in the morning, astonished that she had fallen asleep. She unfolded herself from the comfortable, velvety softness of the sofa, intending to go upstairs, but reluctant to climb into bed next to Jake.

Looking down at the couch, she considered her options and repositioned herself back into its welcoming warmth. "This seems wiser." She lulled herself back to sleep by humming the words, "I'll survive. I will survive."

The next morning, still pleased about her success with the Stop Thinking, Start Doing skill, Harriett stepped into the shower and used her energy to take stock of her circumstances. *I'm still very disturbed by Jake's behavior, but I think the only way to fix the situation with him is to fix me.*

Squirting shampoo into her hair, she massaged it into her scalp while analyzing the feelings associated with her thoughts. *I'm scared to death, but I hate the way I felt last night and the way I've been feeling these past months. I guess I just have to accept that my road to recovery is going to occur one choice at a time—the choice to use a skill and then utilize that success as the motivation to make the next choice. My choices might not always get me what I want, but at least I'll be in control of how I handle the situation.*

She rinsed away the shampoo and applied conditioner.

I guess you could say I've already walked a few steps on my journey.

As she moved into the stream of water, she was overcome with a ghastly realization that overshadowed all previous thoughts—*I'm on a journey to nowhere!*

Harriett stood motionless under the water as negativity washed over her entire body. She sighed and stepped out of the shower feeling grubbier than ever.

Dragging herself down the stairs, she tried to recapture her energy, but that hideous phrase, *journey to nowhere,* kept echoing inside her head.

She walked into the kitchen and found her daughter sitting alone and looking forlorn. Somehow, Harriett rallied enough to ask what was wrong.

"Everything," Katie replied.

Ordinarily, the catastrophic tone of her daughter's voice would bring a smile to Harriett's lips, but today Katie's misery was a reflection of her own. Feeling defeated, Harriett turned to retreat into the solitude of her bedroom, but stopped when she saw Dr. Aye's business card sitting by the phone. The sight caused her to remember the week's homework assignment—to resume her role as a supportive mother.

How is turning my back on Katie's misery behaving like a supportive mother? Evaluating her answer, Harriett concluded, *I've got to at least try...*

A new picture developed in her mind and the subject matter was shopping. Katie had been begging for a trip to the mall in search of some new spring clothes and shopping was an activity she and her daughter loved to share. However, since the debacle with Jake, Harriett refused to step foot into a place as populated as the mall, fearful of bumping into someone who knew about the lunge. Her inability to spend quality time with her daughter increased Harriett's sense of shame and helplessness.

Well, that stops now! Katie's an excellent student and missing a day of school to spend time with me will be fine. In fact, it's more than fine! It will be a well-deserved mental health day for us both!

"Katie, how would you like to skip school and spend the day shopping?"

Her daughter's joyful response brought tears of happiness to

Harriett's eyes and made the trip up the stairs significantly easier than the previous trip down.

Rummaging in her closet for her favorite pair of shopping shoes, Harriett kept herself distracted by planning ways to employ the skills while at the mall.

I'm still apprehensive about seeing someone, but I know I want to be a supportive mother more than I want to hide from people and I'm determined to use my skills to get what I want!

Recalling the glow of anticipation emanating from her daughter's eyes also quelled some of Harriett's trepidation.

Tolerating her fear of seeing a familiar face long enough to park the car, Harriett locked the door, and walked into the mall's entrance. Each time she caught herself worrying over Jake or dwelling on how her life was falling apart, she reminded herself to stop thinking and start doing. She used her daughter as a distraction by engaging in their favorite pastime— gossiping about tabloid reports regarding the recent fashion *faux pas* of the stars.

Harriett watched Katie's gloom fade into contented delight and offered a silent prayer of gratitude that shopping had momentarily distracted her and her daughter away from their respective misery. *I can't erase all her heartache, but at least by changing my behavior, I helped make Katie's world a little less miserable.*

The thought made Harriett feel more empowered and, on some level, she knew the feeling stemmed from the satisfaction of her need to achieve. Her energy grew when she realized that changing her behavior had also made her feel less isolated and satisfied her need to be connected. *Who would think that a simple activity such as shopping could infuse my life with such quality!*

The thought was positively intoxicating.

The evening past uneventfully, facilitated by Jake's feeble apology for last night's abrupt departure from the study. "I'm up to my eyeballs at work."

While preparing for bed, Harriett compiled the information collected over the week in anticipation of the next day's session with Dr.

Aye. Knowing she'd failed to complete part of her homework assignment by not calling a friend, she hoped her report would appease her counselor.

I like the way my feelings change whenever I self-evaluate and choose to use a skill. I wish the changes were bigger, but at least I feel more energized. Except...that's not entirely accurate. The skills stop me from wasting energy on unproductive behaviors like crying over Jake's rejection or worrying who I might meet at the mall, but I don't see how I can maintain my marriage by distracting my thoughts away from what's wrong with my marriage.

Her mind flashed to an image of an ostrich with its head in the sand. *The same applies to the Tolerate skill. At what point does tolerating my emotions rise to the level of ignoring my emotions?*

Harriett sighed, turned off the bedside lamp, and slid in bed next to her sleeping husband. *Jake blames work, but I think he's also exploiting the lunge as a way to avoid me.* Harriett's thoughts fanned her smoldering resentment. *I'm certain there's more to his remoteness than just work and a fear of knives!*

Her agitation grew, making sleep impossible. Finally, after twenty minutes of tossing and turning, Harriett made a choice—*Enough! I had a good day with Katie and I will not allow unproductive thinking to sap my energy!*

She rolled over and switched on the small television she sometimes used to fall asleep. Unfortunately, no show successfully distracted her mind away from her negative thoughts. She scrolled listlessly through the channel guide until *Grey's Anatomy* appeared.

"Too bad Mother wasn't a baker," she muttered under her breath. "I could really benefit from Izzie's method of distraction."

Then, with seemingly little effort, Harriett's wise mind developed a creative option to add to her list of distracting behaviors. She extracted her body from the tangled bedsheets and relocated to the family computer in search of an innovative way to make brownies.

8

Skill #3
Where R U Living?

"You've obviously been working hard," observed Dr. Aye. "I'm impressed, even if you didn't complete all your homework."

Harriett flushed at the compliment and breathed a sigh of relief that perfection wasn't a prerequisite for impressing her counselor. *Mother's reaction would be to ignore what I did and focus on what I didn't do.*

Thoughts about her mother turned Harriett's pleasure into chagrin. *I've spent my entire life looking for my mother's approval and now I want the same thing from my counselor!*

She considered sharing her thoughts with Dr. Aye, but was afraid doing so would raise the issue of perfectionism.

"Something doesn't make sense," she said. "If I keep tolerating my problems or distracting myself from them, how will my problems get fixed?"

"Think of the Energizer bunny. The bunny needs a certain amount of energy before she's able to bang her drums, move her feet, and start walking. You told me the two skills helped conserve some energy, which means you've begun charging your battery. While you might not be moving your feet, you're certainly banging your drums! Today I'll teach you a third skill that also helps conserve energy. The other six skills focus on finding behaviors that productively move you towards where you want to be."

Journey to nowhere echoed in her mind. "I still feel so confused and helpless."

"Be patient. Focus on charging your battery before you think about where you want to go."

"I can't wait to hear the name of the next skill."

Studying her client, Dr. Aye asked, "Was that sarcasm or are you serious?"

Harriett heard the challenge to self-evaluate. "A little of both," she confessed. "Sometimes I wonder how you developed your approach to counseling."

"I've already told you."

"You've told me a lot of things. I may not remember them all, but I think I'd remember how you came to be so...," Harriett struggled for a polite adjective.

"Quirky?"

The blunt response pricked at Harriett's sense of etiquette and made her blush.

Dr. Aye proffered a philosophical shrug. "If being quirky helps me achieve what I want, then quirky I will be."

"What do you want?" Challenging her counselor to self-evaluate felt good.

Dr. Aye's response was quick and concise, "To teach my clients how to live a quality life."

"How does being quirky help you achieve what you want?"

"You appear to be getting the hang of asking self-evaluation questions," observed Dr. Aye. "My approach seems quirky because it's a unique combination of my personality and my experiences. Does that sound familiar?"

"At our first session, you said wants come from the combination of a unique personality coupled with a unique set of life experiences."

Dr. Aye nodded. "Like you, I have pictures inside my head that represent my wants and I've found behaviors that match those pictures. The behaviors may be quirky, but they get me what I want. If they didn't, I'd have to choose different behaviors."

"And self-evaluation questions are what help you make a different choice?"

Again, Dr. Aye nodded. "Self-evaluation is how we develop pictures that are uniquely ours. Having the pictures increases the odds of living a quality life."

Recalling the success she'd felt at the mall, Harriett asked, "Is your definition of a quality life one where I'm attaining everything I want?"

"No."

"No? I thought I was learning how to achieve what I want!"

"You're learning strategies that *increase* the likelihood of getting what you want," qualified Dr. Aye. "All behavior is a risk because nothing in life is guaranteed. My strategies make living a quality life more achievable and that includes learning to manage the frustration associated with not attaining your wants."

"Then what do you define as a quality life?"

"A quality life means having the clarity to understand your needs and how they provoke your wants, the willingness to problem-solve ways to achieve your wants, the resolve to go after what you want, and the capacity to self-evaluate when the results are not what you intended. Living a quality life requires wisdom to know when to change your behavior, but sometimes the wiser option is to change what you want rather than become a slave to your pictures."

Is she telling me to give up on my marriage because it's too broken to fix?

The thought made Harriett defiant. "I have no intention of tearing up the picture of my marriage!"

"Nor did I ask you to," replied Dr. Aye. She scrutinized her client in thoughtful silence. "May I ask a question?"

The query was unnerving. *When does this woman ever seek permission to ask a question?*

Dubious but curious, Harriett nodded.

"Last week you broached the topic of perfectionism, and I'd like to continue the discussion. Would that be okay?"

"Are you giving me a choice?" Harriett responded dryly.

"The choice is always yours."

Harriett hesitated. *What am I afraid of? I'm fine with always doing my best. What can this woman possibly say to make me think otherwise?* Her second nod was more dubious than the first.

"Essence is a word I coined to describe the attributes that most accurately depict a person's unique perspective on life—a perspective derived from a unique personality combined with the messages we've heard from our unique set of life experiences. Our essence determines our need profile. When we behave in ways that honor our essence, our needs are satisfied, our success identity is reinforced and our quality of life improves."

Dr. Aye's use of "unique" reminded Harriett of the vanilla essence she added to give her French toast a unique taste.

"Are you saying my essence is to be perfect?" she asked, uncertain if that would be good or bad.

"I think your essence is about wanting to please the people who are important in your life," corrected Dr. Aye. "Each time you behave in ways that are consistent with your essence, you satisfy your need to feel loved, powerful, in control, and happy."

"That's a good thing, right?"

"There's nothing particularly good or bad about an essence. Your essence is simply your perspective on life. How you behave on your essence is what adds or detracts from the quality of your life."

Harriett chewed her bottom lip, attempting to absorb the concept. The success she'd felt at the mall seemed consistent with what Dr. Aye defined as her essence; yet, something wasn't resonating.

Jake's "sterling" character implies an essence that wants to be dependable, honest and sincere. That translates into behaviors that avoid tarnishing his wedding vow—not cheating on me with some trollop!

Consternation clouded her face, prompting Dr. Aye to ask, "What's on your mind?"

Loath to voice her fears about the affair, Harriett responded,

"Two things—why would people behave in ways that don't honor their essence and what does my essence have to do with perfectionism?"

"Two very good questions and both have the same answer. I don't think people consciously choose to dishonor their essence, but I do think that the messages heard throughout life sometimes create distorted pictures inside our heads. Distorted pictures hamper our ability to honor our essence."

Dr. Aye paused and Harriett tensed, knowing there was more to come.

"I think your life experiences have resulted in messages that reinforce your want to please the people who are important to you. These experiences have taught you to honor your essence with behaviors that avoid disappointing the people you love. Unfortunately, you've developed a distorted belief in your capacity to shield people from disappointment and think their feelings are dependent on your ability to be perfect. The only pictures inside your head are ones that depict you behaving flawlessly. You've become a slave to your essence because no behavior can ever satisfy the distorted pictures inside your head. Your want to be perfect is consuming your energy and blinding you to the actual impact your behavior has on yourself and others."

Stunned, Harriett fell back into the loveseat, searching for ways to impugn Dr. Aye's hypothesis. When she found what she was searching for, she smiled in smug satisfaction. "What would stop me from behaving flawlessly?"

"How do you know when your behavior is flawless?"

"When it's perfect," she pronounced, certain she was stating the obvious.

"How do you define perfect?"

"When I determine there are no flaws," she replied, infuriated by the curious look on her soon-to-be ex-counselor's face. "What is *your* problem with *my* being flawless?"

"Go back to the homework you did in third grade. Did you think it was flawless?"

Harriett sensed a trap. "Yes." Her response was curt, but contained an inflection that ended with, "and sooooo?"

"What caused your disappointment?"

"I wasn't disappointed until my mother pointed out a problem with my penmanship."

The trap sprang shut with a resounding, *SNAP!*

"Your definition of perfection is based on a perspective of the world that is uniquely yours and that means your standards are uniquely different from anyone else. The external world will never perceive the situation the same as you. While your standards might come close to matching another person's standards, there will always be a mismatch that leaves one of you feeling disappointed. The consequence of a unique essence is what makes perfection an illusion."

Harriett struggled with the idea. *At first, I liked hearing that I was unique, but now it sounds like being unique means always being disappointed.*

Puzzled, she asked, "If I will always be unique, then won't I always be disappointed, even when I'm achieving everything I want?"

"Yes," replied Dr. Aye. "Which is why living a quality life doesn't mean making perfect choices. Living a quality life means making choices that maximize the positive feelings and minimize the negative feelings. When you distort the pictures inside your head to ones that include only perfect choices, you waste energy on an insatiable want to attain an unattainable illusion. Your behaviors no longer reinforce your success identity. Worse, your behaviors lead to a failure identity that depletes your energy, leaves you feeling demoralized, and robs you of a quality life."

Harriett looked down and picked at a fingernail, evaluating what she'd heard. The thought of being a slave to her essence made her feel inadequate.

Dr. Aye continued. "My strategies help you recoup the energy you waste by being a slave to your essence. The skills help control the emotions provoked by distorted thinking long enough to choose wiser behaviors."

Dr. Aye's words mollified some of Harriett's inadequacy. Lifting her head, she asked, "Does that mean the skills will help me be in control of my essence rather than my essence controlling me?"

While uncertain, she felt hopeful and even a bit excited. *How can that be, when I've just heard such awful news?*

"I do have one caveat," said Dr. Aye. "A quality life necessitates behaving in ways that are socially and morally responsible."

Harriett's thoughts returned to Jake. *I wonder what made him stop living a quality life and is there a way I can get him to change?*

Then she recalled Dr. Aye's belief that the only behavior we can change is our own. *If I want Jake's behavior to change, then I have to start by changing mine and I guess that means developing less distorted pictures.*

Harriett's face reflected the depth of her concentration, intensity of her evaluation and the finality of her choice. Looking into her counselor's eyes, she said, "Please teach me the next skill."

Dr. Aye's eyes held Harriett's in a long assessing stare.

No longer on a journey to nowhere, Harriett knew the time had come to walk towards a quality life.

"You make me believe I have the capacity to change. I know I have to work hard, but I feel motivated and ready. So please teach me the next skill," she repeated.

Satisfied, Dr. Aye obliged.

"The third skill is called Where R U Living and focuses on thoughts. We can live in three different places—the past, the present, and the future. Living in all three places requires energy, but only one place uses energy productively. Would you like to guess where?"

"Just tell me," objected Harriett, eager to learn the skill.

"Living in the past is unproductive because we waste energy thinking about ways to change what cannot be changed."

"Like replaying the night I lunged at Jake?"

"How do you feel when you replay that night?"

Harriett's shudder was louder than her single word, "Awful."

"Elaborate on awful."

"Sad, embarrassed, helpless, hopeless..."

"Are those feelings motivating?"

"They motivate me to crawl inside a hole!"

"Is that what you want?"

"No, I'm tired of feeling depressed."

"The outcome of living in the past is typically symptomatic of depression because you squander valuable energy by dwelling on things you can't change. Living in the future also wastes energy because you're worrying about things that haven't occurred. Worry produces feelings similar to the panic you felt when you worried that Matt's unexcused absences might shatter his dreams."

"But worrying is what motivates me!" The skeptical look on her counselor's face made Harriett elaborate, "I use my worry about Matt getting to school on time as a way to plan ahead and avoid a crisis."

"Planning is not the same as worrying—planning is a behavior, worrying is a thought. Like all behavior, you *do* your planning in the present, but you worry about the future. Planning is a productive use of energy because you walk into the future you want, not the future you're worrying about."

"Just because you make a plan, doesn't mean you'll get what you want." Her sullen tone mirrored thoughts of how her husband's behavior had ruined her plans to confront him about Julie.

"Unfortunately, there are no guarantees in life, Nevertheless, worry doesn't make life more predictable, nor can worry guard against unforeseen situations. Worry's only function is the unproductive use of energy."

Harriett's continued protests provoked a poignant example.

"Passengers on the planes that flew into the World Trade Center on 9/11 were probably worried about something—maybe worried the plane would be late or perhaps worried about the outcome of a scheduled meeting. Every ounce of their collective worry had absolutely no effect on their future."

The room was quiet as counselor and client digested the implications of both the example and the point.

"The most productive use of energy occurs in the present. The present affords us the opportunity to behave in ways that have a higher likelihood of making a positive impact on the future."

Dr. Aye expanded on her example of 9/11. "After the disaster, people criticized Mayor Giuliani for his lack of preparedness. He discusses the value of preparedness in his book, *Leadership*. While he concedes he was ill prepared for the surprise attack, he credits disaster planning for his ability to stabilize the situation. Preparedness enables a faster and more efficient response to the inevitable unexpectedness of the future. Embrace the credo—*expect the best, but plan for the worst.*"

The credo made Harriett gasp. "Are you saying you want me to plan for the demise of my marriage?"

"I'm saying use your energy to learn from the past and plan in the present for the future you want. Use Where R U Living to stop dwelling on the past or worrying about the future, and start achieving what you want by doing in the present."

Harriett was unable to contain her distress. "What if there's nothing you can do? Nothing I do is going to fix the situation with Jake!"

Sobs racked her body, vanquishing her excitement, motivation, and finally, her hope.

"I understand your distress, but can't accept your premise," replied her counselor. "As human beings, we're always behaving. Your inability to identify ways to fix the situation with Jake is because you're trying to change the past...and remember what Yoda says about trying."

Dr. Aye offered her client a gentle smile of encouragement. "Let's focus on something you can do in the present that might nudge you towards the future you want."

The silence between counselor and client lengthened as Harriett quieted her sobs and evaluated her options.

"I think I'll make Jake, Matt, and Katie a nice dinner. Perhaps that will regain a semblance of family unity and make me feel less guilty about the dinner I ruined. Only...," she flashed a weary smile. "This time I'll hide the knives."

"How do you feel when you think you might regain a semblance of family unity?"

"Definitely more hopeful. And maybe even a bit powerful because there's something I can do that might improve the situation." Baffled, Harriett asked, "Why wasn't I able to plan a dinner without your help?"

"I pushed you into wise mind where you used your energy productively. Once you identified ways to improve your situation, you evaluated your options and chose the one that maximized the pros and minimized the cons."

Harriett nodded in agreement.

"Oh, Harriett, you disappointed me!"

"Pardon?"

"You didn't ask the question I was certain you would."

"What question?"

"Wouldn't I rathah choose the behaveah that has zero cons?" The answer mimicked Harriett's distinct Boston accent.

Harriett groaned before retorting, "That would be the perfect choice and you've already chastised how it's egotistical and distorted to strive for perfection."

"I know what I said, but I'm more interested in what you say."

An unexpected insight gave Harriett the incentive to continue walking her walk. *I'm becoming savvy to this woman's tactics! Her irreverent mocking of my perfectionism is a challenge to evaluate my perspective on the topic.*

Acknowledging the challenge, Harriett evaluated her thoughts and shared her conclusion. "A choice that maximizes the pros and minimizes the cons means accepting that all choices have good and bad points."

"You've just alluded to another skill," hinted Dr. Aye. "However, I worked you hard today, so let's table that discussion until our next session."

While reaching for a business card, Dr. Aye urged her client to consider ways to use the new skill in tandem with the Stop Thinking, Start Doing skill. "Combining the two skills is a good way to maximize the conservation of your energy"

Harriett fixed her eyes on the picture of the swans as she deliberated her options. Then she realized—*That's what I did when I was in the kitchen strategizing ways to confront Jake about Julie!*

Pleased with her inherent ability to behave wisely, Harriett replied, "When I catch myself dwelling on the past or worrying about the future, I can use the stop sign to stop thinking and start doing something that distracts me from my unproductive thoughts."

"Your homework is to practice all your skills and make dinner for your family."

"I'd rather you teach me that other skill."

"Patience, my dear, patience."

9

Making a Plan Increases
the Likelihood of Success

Harriett opened the car windows and breathed in the warmth of a sun-filled day. *If only there was a way to turn this feeling into an elixir that I could drink to cure my woes!*

She chuckled. *I suppose I could think of the skills as an elixir that cures people of emotional mind.*

Reviewing the day's session, she evaluated her reactions. *I may not fully agree that I have a distorted perspective of perfection, but I do know I want to be comfortable in my own skin. I can see what Dr. Aye means by wasting energy. I haven't felt calm or in control for a long while. If the skills help me feel more peaceful, then I agree using the skills is worth the hard work.*

Her thoughts focused on self-evaluation. While the questions made her think (not feel) she was the little white ball in a game of question-and-answer ping-pong, Harriett did appreciate how asking the questions facilitated self-awareness.

In a way, gaining self-awareness is like being on a scavenger hunt. The objective of a scavenger hunt is to find a list of items by paying attention to clues. The items on my list are my needs; the pictures in my head are the clues, and self-evaluation questions force me to pay attention to what the clues mean. The hunt requires hard work, but winning the game is worth the effort!

Harriett pictured a trophy inscribed with the words "A Quality Life" and the satisfaction she felt was amplified by the memory of Katie's face while sitting at the kitchen table.

My daughter satisfies my love and belonging need, and I told Dr. Aye I wanted to be a supportive mother. When I asked how turning my back on Katie's misery was behaving like a supportive mother, the answer forced me to evaluate the likelihood of satisfying my need. Paying attention to the answer provided evidence that I was ignoring the clue because I was NOT behaving like a supportive mother.

The fragrant smells of spring were intoxicating enough to distract Harriett away from thoughts of Katie and Dr. Aye.

"I'll show Dr. Aye! I'll use a big stop sign to stop thinking about the session and distract myself by heading home, making some iced tea and working in the garden. These fragrant smells are a clue that summer's just around the corner..." The picture she'd described during her first counseling session re-emerged. "And I need to pay attention and start hunting for ways to make it glorious!"

While the thought felt invigorating, the chronic worry over Jake and Julie tempered her enthusiasm and provided another reminder of the day's session. *I heard what Dr. Aye said about worry being an unproductive waste of energy, but staying focused in the present feels strange.*

"That's why you need to practice," intoned her counselor's voice.

Harriett nodded in agreement.

She progressed through the week, feeling her energy level rise and noticing how practicing the skills required increasingly less effort. Harriett also noticed how self-evaluation encouraged her to take control over her feelings.

Pleased, she decided to keep listening to Dr. Aye's "pearls of wisdom," even when a chance encounter tested her commitment...

Standing at the counter, waiting to collect her clothes from the dry cleaner, Harriett heard a beep announcing the entrance of another patron. Turning, her stomach tightened as one of the volunteers from the food bank waved a greeting.

Oh no! What if she asks about the lunge?

Worried about what to say, Harriett failed to hear the woman's innocuous question about a fund drive, and confounded the situation by commenting on the weather.

"Excuse me?" replied the volunteer, obviously confused by the obtuse response.

Cringing, Harriett stuttered an inept explanation and rushed out of the cleaners, leaving the laundry behind. Creeping back into the store, she muttered an apology, retrieved the clothes, and beat a hasty retreat. Throwing the laundry into the backseat, she berated her incompetence— *On top of everything else, now I have to worry what everyone in the cleaner thinks!*

Driving aimlessly through the streets of Bayview, Harriett searched for somewhere safe to hide—a place devoid of prying eyes, people demanding her attention or judging her every move. She approached an intersection and stopped at the flashing red stop light, dwelling on what had happened. A stop sign on the side of the road captured her attention.

"Stop thinking, start doing," she chanted and leaned across the center console to turn on the radio. She pushed the buttons in a vain attempt to find a distracting song, but her thoughts ricocheted between the past and the future. *What can I do? I have to stay focused on the road!*

Her thoughts continued to bounce backwards and forwards, leaving her paralyzed with indecision.

HONK!

Harriett looked into the rearview mirror and saw the annoyed faces of impatient motorists urging her to go.

"I've got to *do* something!"

Pulling to the side of the road, she ordered herself to live in the present. Thankfully, wise mind devised a plan. *I'll drive to Dunkin' Donuts, buy a coffee and newspaper, and go down to the beach.*

Harriett made the plan more specific by reminding herself to use the drive-through as a way to avoid another chance meeting.

Feeling calmer, she focused her attention onto driving and arrived at the beach without further incident. The soft rhythmic sounds of waves splashing against the shoreline provided the comfort she sought and gave her enough energy to plan a more productive reaction to an unexpected encounter.

During the car ride home, she evaluated her failures as well as her successes and learned two useful pieces of information—using the skills had prevented a bad situation from getting worse and planning for the future mitigated her incompetence by making her feel more prepared.

What Harriett couldn't anticipate was how she'd implement her new plan on the very next day...

Passing the strip mall that housed the local supermarket, Harriett thought, *Ever since that stupid lunge, grocery-shopping takes twice as long because I have to drive an extra twenty minutes to avoid people I know.* Her thoughts made her feel annoyed.

"Who says you have to drive an extra twenty minutes?" she asked, pleased at how the self-evaluation question seemed to roll off her tongue.

"Me," she replied.

The answer made Harriett briefly reconsider her choice, but she changed her mind at the last minute. *I can't be worried about anyone bombarding me with curious questions. I want to focus all my energy on preparing tonight's dinner and completing my homework for Dr. Aye.*

She realized that driving an extra twenty minutes was her choice, and the realization abated some of her annoyance.

Pushing her cart through the sliding doors of the larger, more anonymous store, Harriett saw a yellow stack of neatly arranged fruit and decided to add a bit of zing to her chicken recipe. She moved towards the pile of lemons and stopped short. Directly ahead was the exceptionally nosy receptionist who worked at Matt and Katie's orthodontist. The sight made her gulp. *My future's arrived and it's up to me to take control of the present!*

Taking a deep breath, Harriett enacted her plan. Maintaining her position, she proffered a polite smile. Even if it was a bit vacant, Harriett knew smiling was a better option than reversing her cart and running away. She spent a few minutes tolerating the receptionist's inconsequential conversation before raising her wrist to look at her watch.

"Oh dear, look at the time. I've got to go." She tendered a cheery wave as she moved past the woman, celebrating her minor triumph over fear.

Choosing her lemons, Harriett sighed in relief. *Thank goodness she didn't ask any intrusive questions.*

The thought made her worry over future encounters.

Stop! Celebrate this victory before worrying about the next failure.

Reaching inside her purse, she pulled out her shopping list and used food shopping as a distraction. Feeling energized, she drove home determined to have a perfect family dinner.

Dr. Aye's face flashed before her eyes, mouthing the word, "Perfect?"

Harriett eradicated the image by focusing on the dinner plans. A smug giggle escaped her lips. "I just completed part of my homework! I combined Where R U Living with Stop Thinking, Start Doing, and distracted myself away from that maddening woman!"

In the distance, Harriett heard the Energizer bunny clanging her drums.

Much to everyone's surprise and relief, dinner went smoothly. Harriett worked to stay focused in the moment rather than retreat into memories of the past, and was pleased when Jake contributed to the conversation by asking about soccer schedules and Katie's plans for spring break.

At least he's involved enough to promise Katie he'll drive her and her friends to the Civic Center for that concert she's been raving about.

Harriett cleared the dishes and reflected on what made the evening a success, albeit small. *Instead of worrying about the outcome of dinner, I brought myself back to the present by reading the recipes for lemon chicken and stuffed mushrooms (no beef Stroganoff, thank you). I also stopped myself from dwelling over that failed dinner by fashioning my own disaster plan! Both tactics helped me use my energy productively instead of getting myself all worked up over things I can't control.*

Harriett's disaster plan included some preplanned self-evaluation questions to ask in case she found herself dwelling or worrying while at the dinner table. As a mother, she appreciated how self-evaluation could help Matt and Katie become independent thinkers. She'd speculated how self-evaluation might even help them take more responsibility for their behavior; and planned to stay focused in the present, pay attention to the dinner conversation, and look for an opportunity to sneak in a self-evaluation question.

Her plan came to fruition when Matt and Katie complained about the high school's new policy to breathalyze any student entering a school dance. Harriett responded to Matt's assertion that the policy was in violation of his civil rights by asking, "What evidence is there to support what you're saying?" She wondered if Matt's slacked jaw and blank stare resembled the way she looked in Dr. Aye's office.

Katie defended her brother's position by announcing she'd researched constitutional protection against unusual searches and seizures under the Fourth Amendment and intended to write a paper on the topic as her final assignment in American history. Harriett validated Katie's creativity and asked what pros and cons she planned to use to support her assumptions.

Alone in the kitchen, Harriett smiled over how closely the scene at dinner matched the picture inside her head. The resulting feelings were positive and she considered which of her needs had been satisfied. "The obvious answer is love and belonging. That's a no-brainer."

Yet, there seemed to be more. "I feel a small surge of power when I realize that my behavior made the dinner a success."

She lifted a half-filled glass of leftover lemonade and toasted another of Dr. Aye's "pearls"—one behavior has the capacity to satisfy multiple needs, but only if you have a clear picture of what you want.

The next morning, Harriett awoke to Jake's whispered, "Honey?" He was obviously trying to tell her something without totally disturbing her slumber. "I'll be a little late tonight. Don't wait dinner."

Harriett struggled to sit up, wiping the sleep from her eyes. She opened her mouth, intending to confront him on what was becoming an increasingly frequent wake-up call. "Another late night? That's three so far this week!"

"So, what's your point?"

The defensiveness in her husband's voice weakened her intent. "I'm just worried about you."

Jake's look was inscrutable and his response vague, "Maybe things will quiet down after I win this case. I'll see you tonight."

Harriett got the kids off to school, put on her gardening gloves, and went outside to yank at the dead undergrowth left from the desiccating winter winds. Deception and betrayal filled her thoughts and she felt her frustration build.

Finally, she stood up, brushed her dusty hands on her jeans. "Enough dwelling! Stop wasting your energy and start doing something more productive." She marched inside, picked up the phone and called Peggy, one of her friends from college. *I can always count on Peggy to be a fun distraction.*

The sound of Peggy's voice swept away some of the cloying thoughts and infused Harriett with enough energy to lace up her running shoes and head out for a jog. She left the potting soil and garden tools smack in the middle of the yard, defying anyone to comment on the unfinished chore. Running past the debris, she shouted, "Perfectionist? I don't think so!"

She jogged through treelined streets, past the steepled white church, and over the bridge leading to the west side of town. Her thoughts focused on her essence and she worked to find other experiences in her past that reinforced her want to do her best.

She conjured a memory of her wedding. *Mother and I spent hours searching for the perfect place card to adorn the dinner tables. We were so pleased to find one designed to accommodate a fresh flower. The effect was perfect—soft and elegant. I decided to handprint the names of the guests because I wanted to add a personal touch to the occasion.*

Her feet pounded the pavement as the vividness of the memory intensified. *I practiced for days with that silly calligraphy pen...all because I wanted the perfect blend of lines and swirls! What a waste!*

Intermittent panting interrupted the evenness of her breathing.

Mother said the cards looked amateurish and rushed new cards to the printers. I was so annoyed at her for making an arbitrary decision about MY wedding!

A cramp in her side forced her to stop. She bent over, waiting for the pain to subside.

As always, Mother was right. The printed cards were perfect and so much better than my sloppy attempt at calligraphy.

The memory triggered feelings similar to those she experienced as a third-grader. Unhappy with the feelings, Harriett brought herself back to the present by resuming her run. She kept herself in the present by engrossing her mind in the task of placing one foot in front of the other and felt the feelings wane.

Another "pearl" entered her mind—*feelings are transient.*

Harriett purposely ignored the gardening paraphernalia and tolerated the resulting discomfort long enough to take a shower and dry her hair, imagining the stunned look on her counselor's face as she recounted her victory over perfectionism. Dr. Aye's antics often made her groan, but Harriett continued looking for ways to win her approval. *Does that make me a slave to my essence?*

Sometimes, distinguishing between wanting to do her best and feeling driven to be perfect could be difficult. However, the day's efforts emboldened Harriett to push the envelope...

When she heard Jake's car pull into the garage, she greeted him with a hug and expressed concern over the toll his late nights were having on him and the family. Holding her breath, she waited in fearful anticipation of another rejection.

Jake rubbed his eyes. "This case is sapping me dry. And worrying about you and the kids only makes things worse." He looked resigned and dejected. "I can't seem to reconcile your behavior."

His words aroused an anger that caused another out-of-body episode, only this episode played out somewhat differently.

Instead of lunging, Harriett chanted, *Tolerate, just tolerate,* and endured the resentment provoked by Jake's words long enough to find a wiser behavior.

"I don't know how many times I can say I'm sorry. Please tell me what else I can do."

"I guess you just need to keep doing what you're doing. You seem a little less withdrawn and more in control of yourself."

Again, she tolerated her anger and augmented the skill by paying attention to the positive part of Jake's message. *At least he's not rejecting me or issuing more mandates.*

Then Harriett made a plan. Even though she was certain Jake was using the case and the lunge as an excuse for his behavior, she decided to accept his excuse, terminate the discussion, and wait to process her thoughts and feelings with Dr. Aye. She diverted the conversation onto the children, blissfully naïve of the unintended consequences associated with her choice...

The next night, Harriett capitalized on the energy conserved by avoiding a fight and planned another dinner. *I haven't done stir-fry in awhile and it's a meal we all enjoy. Although...that darned wok leaves so much greasy splatter on the backsplash.*

"No matter what I do, the position's always wrong," she muttered, but a change in thinking brightened her mood. *I'll tolerate my annoyance and create a different picture inside my head! I'll picture Matt using the muscles he's developed as a goalkeeper to scrub the backsplash until it shines!*

She pulled out the wok, pleased she'd planned a behavior that would get what she wanted—a tasty meal made with less annoyance.

Harriett stepped back and evaluated the heaping platter of pork, rice, and vegetables. "Everything looks so crisp and fresh. The white rice makes a nice backdrop for the vibrant colors of the vegetables."

Remembering to put the chopping knife back into the knife block, she called her family into dinner. Only this time, harmony did not take a seat. Jake was too preoccupied to engage in conversation, Katie sulked because brown rice contained more fiber, and Matt announced plans to meet his goalkeeping coach immediately after dinner. To make matters worse, there was no opportunity to sneak in another of her planned self-evaluation questions. The family's interaction was limited and laborious, and Harriett felt herself withdraw in weary defeat.

She stood alone in the kitchen and assessed the meal. "That was certainly *NOT* the picture I had in my head." Dwelling on her inadequacies, she hunted for the Windex and paper towel to wipe away the greasy remnants of a failed dinner.

Harriett walked towards the stairway, still ruminating, but intent on using one skill to accomplish two tasks—reading would distract her thoughts away from the night's failed dinner, and she would use the distraction to prepare herself for this month's book club. *I want to experiment with Dr. Aye's suggestion to tolerate being among people long enough to use the women at book club as a distraction.*

Jake's voice calling from his study made her stop. *Dear Lord, I'm in no mood to talk to him.*

"Can you come in here a second? I need to ask you something," requested Jake.

Harriett entered the study, wishing she could retreat to her bedroom, but knowing it'd be wiser to tend to her husband.

"I hope we're not busy Saturday night. I forgot to tell you at dinner that I made plans to drive into Boston and entertain a new client. He and his wife are a nice couple and I thought it'd be a chance to do something different."

At first, Harriett was relieved. *He wants to spend time with me!*

Relief turned to worry as she wondered what they'd talk about during the hour-long ride up to Boston.

Stop! Where are you living?

The future was the obvious answer.

What can you do to get back to the present?

Harriett urged her brain to think, but her mind was blank. She heard Jake calling from afar, his tone urgent.

"Harriett? Harriett! You're worrying me! What's going on?"

Shaking her head slightly, Harriett looked at her husband. "Pardon?"

"Where did you go?"

"What do you mean?"

"You zoned out and for a moment, you looked like you did that other night. Are you okay?"

She briefly contemplated screaming, "No! You're driving me crazy!"

Wisely, Harriett chose a different behavior. She sighed and made a quiet observation. "First of all, I'm obviously not okay, so I understand why you would be worried. However, I don't intend to go after you with a knife. But Jake, there's so much about my life that I don't understand and we really do need to talk."

Jake's reply was guarded. "About what?"

Should I confront him about Julie? Recalling the disastrous outcome of her previous attempt, Harriett concluded, *I don't have the resiliency to rebound from another failure. Besides, I just tried using the Where R U Living skill and couldn't. I need more practice.*

Instead of confronting Jake, Harriett chose a safer option. "I don't understand why it's so important that I look perfect for the dinner you're talking about," she replied.

Jake seemed genuinely concerned, but confused. "What?"

"Oh, never mind," she recanted, hoping to prevent an escalation.

Regrettably, Jake persisted in prolonging the exchange. "You said first of all."

"Pardon?"

"You said 'first of all' when I asked if you were okay. Does that mean there's more?"

"I was thinking about something Dr. Aye taught me this week."

"Is she helping you?"

Harriett felt caught in a vortex of negative energy. Worry over

Jake's late nights, residual anger left by the unresolved discussion earlier in the week, annoyance about the evening's failed dinner, compounded by the ever-present fear of losing everything she held dear—all grew into a mounting agitation that was impossible to tolerate.

One misstep and he expects me to fix everything that's broken in our marriage. Ms. Perfect makes one mistake and now I'm in danger of losing everything. That's not fair! She stomped her foot, resentful that she was the only one working to improve the situation.

Why doesn't Jake feel responsible for making me so upset? Doesn't he realize how coming home late, distancing himself from the kids and complaining about boredom makes me insecure? How can he not understand how terribly hurt I am by last week's rejection? Why isn't he honoring his essence!

Harriett looked at her husband, willed herself to avoid an argument and answered his question. "I don't know."

"Because," Jake continued, unaware that his next words were about to unleash the fury she'd been working to keep under control. "I hope Dr. Aye can figure out what your problem is."

"My problem," exploded from her mouth. "My problem? Did it ever occur to you that maybe you're my problem?"

Harriett saw the look on Jake's face turn to fear. She turned and fled the scene before further calamity ensued. Once again, she went seeking somewhere safe to hide; but in her heart, she knew the truth—there was no safe refuge from her erratic emotions.

Later, much later, Harriett collected herself enough to let Jake know she was all right, but wanted to sleep in the guest bedroom. "I need some time to think about what to tell Dr. Aye," she explained, hoping her words would appease her husband enough to dissuade him from taking Matt and Katie away.

Thankfully, Jake concurred, but insisted he would be in charge of getting the kids to school in the morning.

The house felt empty as she sat at the kitchen table the next morning, reliving the night's events and feeling utterly dejected. *What's wrong with me? I thought things were getting better. I really believed I could keep my emotions under control. What made me forget how to use the skills? All that yelling and carrying on must have reminded Jake of the night I lost it. No wonder my poor husband's scared of me. I'm scared of me!*

Slowly, she trudged up the stairs to dress for the day's counseling session. In her hand, Harriett held a list she'd comprised in the wee hours of the morning; detailing the things she'd learned over the past weeks:

- ❖ There are four needs—love and belonging, freedom, power, and fun.
- ❖ Needs are represented by pictures (wants) inside our head.
- ❖ Self-evaluation determines if what we are doing is getting us what we want.
- ❖ The most pragmatic way to feel better is by changing how we behave and the only behavior we can change is our own.
- ❖ Skills help control emotions long enough to find different ways to behave, but how we behave is our choice.
- ❖ We use energy productively when we behave wisely instead of acting emotionally, and this motivates us to continue hunting for new ways to satisfy our needs.
- ❖ Behaving wisely honors the uniqueness of our essence and creates a success identity.

Even after the exhaustive review, Harriett remained uncertain how to answer Jake's question, "Is Dr. Aye helping?"

10

Skill #4
How Do You Spell ASSuME?

"Hi, Harriett," Dr. Aye called through the open doorway. "Come in."

Harriett marched into the office and walked to the oversized chair across the room. *I want to sit as far from this woman as possible!*

"Oh my! There's no sense asking about your week. The answer's written all over your face."

"It was a disaster," Harriett confirmed.

"Tell me about it."

"Last night…," she began. "…and we haven't spoken since. I keep wondering what happened, but don't understand why everything fell to pieces when the beginning of the week went so well. All I know is that talking to you confuses me more than it helps."

"How does that make you feel?"

"Mad and scared!" Harriett hoped her tone of voice made her sound emphatic.

"Good…"

"See!" she interrupted, barely able to contain her anger. "With you, everything's *good*. You're just like Pollyanna!" Her face contorted into an angry sneer.

"I've been called many things, but none have likened me to Pollyanna."

"How else do you explain why every other word out of your mouth is 'good'?" This time, her pronunciation was purposely disparaging.

"Do you want an answer or are you too upset to listen?"

Harriett's raw emotions made hearing the challenge to self-evaluate impossible. "I assume it's because everything in your life is good. That's why you can't possibly understand how atrocious I feel!"

"Oh, Harriett," admonished Dr. Aye. "How do you spell assume?"

The question fueled her agitation. *I'm tired of being treated like a schoolgirl!*

Adopting a bored expression, she recited, "A-S-S-U-M-E. There, have I passed the test?"

"Are you familiar with the common wisdom that to assume makes an ass out of you and me?"

"That's offensive and classless!" Her indignation made her sound haughty, but Harriett didn't care. Worse, Dr. Aye seemed unfazed.

"You might find the question offensive, but jumping to a conclusion without gathering the data to support your assumption certainly makes you look foolish and uniformed."

"I am not jumping to a conclusion! I just don't think you really understand my situation. Last night Jake reiterated his threat to rob me of my children!" Harriett opened her purse, pulled out the list she'd compiled and shoved it at Dr. Aye. "You want me to listen to what you say and I have! But you've failed to hear what I'm saying!"

"What are you saying?"

"That my life's in shambles and you can't possibly understand."

"Understand what?"

"My pain!" Sobs muffled her response.

Dr. Aye sat quietly, watching tears form rivulets on her client's cheeks.

The ensuing silence gave Harriett a moment to quiet her frayed nerves. Reaching for the box of tissues, she pulled out one after another. Eventually, she looked up at her counselor, gave a final blow and wiped her nose. "I'm sorry. I know you want to help, but I just feel so lost."

"There's no need to be sorry. You're right. No one can understand your pain as well as you. Nevertheless, your willingness to stay committed is how you'll find your way. From my perspective, you've been doing a great job." Dr. Aye chuckled as she glanced down at the catalog of points. "Your list proves it, even if it also proves that I talk a bit too much!"

Then she explained. "You obviously comprehend the concepts on an intellectual basis and are consciously working to adapt them into your life. However, enacting the skills without constant awareness and vigilance requires more practice."

She placed the paper atop the credenza and offered a smile of encouragement. "I have every confidence in your ability."

"There you go again, being Pollyanna."

"So why not call me Dr. Polly?"

Harriett's laugh was thin. "I can think of a lot of names to call you, but Dr. Polly is just too far fetched!"

Despite being upset, Harriett was surprised by how much she valued Dr. Aye's confidence. Dabbing at the residual tears, she asked, "Why did you say I looked foolish when I made an assumption about your life being good?"

"Assuming my life is better than yours, sets you up for a wealth of negative feelings that may or may not be valid. What evidence do you have to support your hypothesis?"

Dr. Aye's question sounded eerily similar to the self-evaluation question Harriett had posed to Matt earlier in the week.

"I guess I just made an assumption," she admitted. "Are you saying that when I assume, I'm judging?"

"Actually, it's even worse because you were judging the pros of my life against the cons of your life. That's the equivalent of comparing apples to oranges, and misery is the inevitable consequence of that type of comparison."

"I doubt you've ever lunged after your husband with a knife!"

"How do you know?" asked Dr. Aye.

"Have you?" she persisted.

"There may have been times when I've thought about it. What do you think stopped me?"

Harriett considered the question. "Wise mind?"

"Can you elaborate?"

Intent on proving herself worthy of her counselor's confidence, Harriett's brow furrowed in concentration. "You might have felt mad enough to lunge, but you didn't behave on your feelings. You tolerated your feelings long enough to figure out another way to behave." Comprehension filled the creases in her face. "That's why you say the skills are universal!"

"What makes you *assume* I don't use them as much as I urge others to use them," queried Dr. Aye. "I walk the same walk I ask of all my clients. The only difference between you and me is that I'm more practiced. With practice, your ability to use the skills will become easier, faster, and more intuitive."

Insistent, Harriett again asked, "But have you ever used the Tolerate skill to stop yourself from attacking your husband?"

Dr. Aye shrugged. "Sometimes I tolerate, other times I distract. Sometimes I use Where R U Living..."

The careless delivery made Harriett laugh. Only this time, her laughter contained genuine mirth. "I don't think I want to live with your husband!"

"As I said, you incur the risk of looking foolish whenever you fail to verify an assumption. Besides," added Dr. Aye. "If the assumption's invalid, then the associated emotion is invalid, and that's a waste of energy."

"What's the alternative?"

"Behave wisely by invoking the skill I call How Do You Spell ASSuME. Rather than acting emotionally on an unverified assumption, gather the data required to validate or invalidate your hypothesis."

"Jake collects evidence to defend his position on a legal case."

Dr. Aye offered a different example. "The business community collects evidence by performing due diligence—gathering information to evaluate the feasibility of a prospective business decision. Most business leaders agree that due diligence requires time and effort, but they also agree that troublesome situations are usually the result of improper due diligence."

Harriett pictured Lady Justice holding her scales. "Are you saying this new skill allows me to counterbalance emotional mind by adding weight to reasonable mind?"

Prompted by her counselor's puzzled expression, Harriett

elaborated. "If wise mind is a ratio of reasonable mind and emotional mind, then adding data increases the proportion of reasonable mind to emotional mind. Isn't that another way to control emotions long enough to behave more wisely?"

"I never thought of it that way. But...yes, I suppose that's one way to look at it."

"Is there another way?"

"If you're processing information to support or invalidate your assumption, where are you living?"

"In the present?" Dr. Aye's nod provoked another insight. "You really don't care what skill I use..."

"...only that you use a skill," finished Dr. Aye.

"I once had a client who likened the skills to tools that he stored in a toolbox. He took the toolbox wherever he went and opened his box whenever he encountered a situation that required fixing. Sometimes the situation needed only one tool, but often the best outcome required a combination of tools. How you use the skills is your choice, as long as you combine them in ways that work for you. Then, when the situation's rectified, you pack up your toolbox and have it ready for the next situation."

"I like the concept of the toolbox, but prefer to call this new skill, *Don't Assume.*" Thinking how she might apply the skill, Harriett hypothesized, "I can see how obtaining additional information is wiser than jumping to a conclusion."

"People often say that knowledge is power; however, I consider knowledge empowering."

"What's the difference?" Harriett asked.

"See if you can identify the difference within the context of needs."

"I suppose...," Harriett paused to collect her thoughts. "Obtaining knowledge is another form of achievement and achievement represents the power need." Her face brightened. "Oh! My need for power is also satisfied when I use my knowledge to make a positive difference on the situation!" She sat back in self-satisfied contentment.

"Are you feeling better?"

Harriett looked into her counselor's eyes and smiled. "Define better."

Dr. Aye bowed her head. "*Touché.*"

Settling into the oversized chair, Harriett admitted, "I'm not sure what I'm feeling. The week was so confusing. I felt energized when I used the skills correctly, but then felt so inept when they didn't work with Jake."

"You experienced the emotional dysregulation we discussed in a previous session. The high you felt earlier in the week fostered an unrealistic expectation regarding your skillfulness and left you ill-prepared for the low you experienced with Jake."

"But you tell me to enjoy my highs! You also tell me to focus on my successes because they provide the motivation to change my behavior."

"And did you?"

"Pardon?"

"Did you change your behavior based on your success earlier in the week?"

"Yes, but I failed miserably at the end of the week!"

"Do I care?"

Attila the Hun replaced the image of Pollyanna. "No, you only care that I do the homework and practice the skills so we can evaluate the results."

"Increasing your skills repertoire gives you more options to control your feelings and change your behavior. Use the How Do You Spell ASSuME skill to avoid wasting energy on errant emotions."

"But how can I check out an assumption without admitting that I jumped to a conclusion?"

"An assumption is nothing more than a thought, and thoughts don't get us into trouble," reminded Dr. Aye.

"Assumptions are a natural byproduct of combining information learned in the past with information received in the present. The best way to avoid trouble is to suspend judgment on an assumption long enough to gather information about your assumption. When you gather the data and pay attention to how the information influences your assumption, your behavior is likely to be more wise. All behavior is a risk, but wise behavior minimizes the risk."

When her client seemed to struggle with the concept, Dr. Aye offered an example. "Tell me what you do just prior to proceeding through an intersection after the traffic light turns green."

"I step on the gas pedal."

"Perhaps, but I suspect you also do something else."

"I don't know what you mean."

"Most of us check out our assumption that other motorists also stop at a red light."

Harriett shrugged her shoulders. "Of course I look both ways before I go!"

"What about Matt? How often do you remind him to look both ways before he moves through an intersection?"

Harriett frowned. "He usually just assumes it's safe."

"Your reminder cautions him to suspend judgment long enough to check out the validity of his assumption that a green light means it's safe to proceed. By looking both ways and paying attention to the information he receives, your son is able to make a more informed choice and behave wisely. The choice to proceed through the intersection still entails risk, but using How Do You Spell ASSuME minimizes the risk. Encouraging Matt to apply the skill is how you help him become a quality driver."

"In the same way you encourage me to apply the skills to live a quality life," Harriett concluded.

"When it comes to driving, you've had years of practice proceeding safely through an intersection. Your experience makes looking both ways an ingrained behavior that no longer feels odd. The same rationale applies to my skills—the more you practice, the more ingrained they become."

"Sometimes I get so overwhelmed." Fresh tears made Harriett reach for another tissue.

"I understand," soothed Dr. Aye. "You're a novice in the same way Matt's a novice driver. Learning the skills is like opening a driver's manual for the first time. At first, asking self-evaluation questions feels odd and you need constant reminders to use the skills. With practice and experience, this new approach to navigating through life becomes rote. And don't forget, you can always refer to the manual whenever you need a refresher."

Harriett plucked at the damp tissue in her hand.

"And," continued her counselor, "as you become more familiar with the concepts and increasingly certain of your ability, you'll begin adapting what you've learned in ways that work for you. In fact, that occurred earlier in this session. Do you know when?"

"Not really."

"Your observation that information changes the ratio of reasonable mind to emotional mind offered me a different perspective. Soon you'll be taking control of these sessions and challenging me to keep up."

"Really?" Harriett's longing was palpable.

Dr. Aye nodded. "And when that happens, I get to sit back, watch you reap the rewards of your hard work, and enjoy the wonderment of all you discover."

Harriett continued to cry softly until, after awhile, she wiped her tears and offered a rueful smile. "At this rate, I'll have to pay extra for using up all your tissues."

"Tissues are included at no extra charge," assured her counselor. "If you have the energy, I'd like to emphasize two important aspects of the How Do You Spell ASSuME skill."

Despite her weariness, Harriett nodded.

"Earlier, you worried over how to check out an assumption without revealing you'd jumped to a conclusion. The obvious way to check out an assumption is to ask a question, but there's a way to phrase the question that doesn't place you at risk for looking foolish."

Harriett was intrigued. Referring back to her assumption that Dr. Aye's life was always good, she searched for ways to obtain information without blatantly comparing her counselor's life to her own. Unable to formulate a suitable question, she asked, "Aren't the only logical questions ones that ask if my assumption's valid or why my assumption isn't valid?"

"Those types of questions focus on the conclusion you've already reached and force a comparison between your perspective and the other person's perspective. Since our uniqueness makes our opinion of the situation different from the other person's opinion, questions that force a comparison typically make the other person feel judged and defensive. Rather than acquiring new information, questions that focus on your conclusion often result in escalated emotions that provoke unproductive arguments that waste energy."

"Then how do I check out an assumption without revealing my assumption?"

"The most expedient way to obtain new information is to ask questions that don't make the other person feel defensive. In most cases, you can achieve what you want by rephrasing a 'why' question into a 'what' question. Asking 'why' often makes people defensive. Asking 'what' is more productive because the word doesn't provoke as much emotion. 'What' questions also allow you to conceal your thoughts on a situation until you have the information you need to check out your assumption."

Sensing Harriett's protest, Dr. Aye asked, "What happens when you ask Matt or Katie why they did whatever they did?"

Harriett remembered Katie's reply when asked why she had treated the new sweater so carelessly. Her daughter had shrugged an indifferent, "I don't know," that was more annoying than the damage done to the sweater.

"The question made Katie feel judged and caused a reflexive desire to defend against the emotion," explained Dr. Aye. "The easiest way to defend against negative feelings is to shut down. 'I don't know' is non-responsive and stonewalls the conversation by pleading ignorance. 'What' elicits less emotion and enables more reasonable mind to enter the equation. There is a greater opportunity to obtain the information you require."

"But you can still get the same answer,"

"Yes, but that sets up your next question."

"Which is?"

"I understand you might not know, but *what* might be the reason?"

Discerning her client's continued doubt, Dr. Aye asked, "When I say your behavior will get you what you want, how do you usually respond?"

"I don't know what I want!"

"Paint me a picture of what you want to achieve in counseling."

"I want to figure out why I lost it with Jake so I can have my family back." Endeavoring to practice the new skill, Harriett rephrased the statement. "I want to figure out *what* made me lose it with Jake."

"And if you figured that out, *what* would you have?"

Harriett pondered the question. "I'm not sure why, but maybe peace?"

"Change the *why* to *what*."

"That's easy...I'm not sure what made me say peace. But, how does that help? I still feel lost and confused."

"*What* might be some reasons people want peace?"

"To feel less confused?"

"Or maybe less conflicted or maybe less scared?"

"Or maybe less angry..." *That's exactly what I want—to be less angry!* Harriett leaned forward in the chair, excited by the realization.

"The quality of information garnered from 'what' questions will always be higher because 'what' questions are self-evaluation questions," observed Dr. Aye.

Harriett opened her mouth, about to argue that "why" questions might produce the same response. Before she could speak, Dr. Aye remarked that "why" might have produced the same response.

"How do you do that?"

"Do what?"

"Answer my question before I've even formulated it."

"Would you believe I can read minds?" Smiling at the absurdity of her reply, Dr. Aye pointed to her bookcase and directed Harriett's gaze to the middle shelf where there was a plaque inscribed with a phrase popularized by Ram Dass—*Be here now.*

"The words remind me to stay focused long enough to pay attention to the information broadcasted by my clients. Paying attention is a key aspect of the How Do You Spell ASSuME skill. Don't bother checking an assumption if you're not willing to suspend judgment long enough to pay attention to the answer and combine what you learn in the present with information you've learned in the past."

Redirecting Harriett's attention back to her, Dr. Aye explained, "That's how I was able to answer your question before you asked. I paid attention to your body language and combined that information with the fact that many clients have asked a similar question in the past."

"Doesn't that mean you were behaving on an assumption?"

"Sure, but what's the risk?"

"You could be wrong."

"We incur the risk of being wrong whenever we behave on an assumption. However, is there an upside to taking a risk?"

The smug smile on her counselor's face made Harriett indignant. *The woman's mocking my need to be perfect!*

Realizing she'd made an assumption, Harriett swallowed a quick retort and waited in cautious silence. She watched as Dr. Aye's smug smile transformed into a triumphant grin.

"The upside is that I look like a rock star whose awesome capabilities fill my client with wonder!"

Phew, using the skill just saved me from looking foolish!

Rolling her eyes, Harriett remained silent.

Dr. Aye equivocated. "Well, perhaps the upside is that I created another teachable moment."

Harriett's sigh was long and loud. "Which is?"

"We are always behaving on our assumptions and that means we're always vulnerable to unwise behavior. All behavior is a risk, but the best way to minimize the risk is to suspend judgment on an assumption long enough to gather the data required to behave as wisely as possible."

The words produced an onslaught of tears. "You make everything sound so simple! I don't think you understand how badly I want to feel better. The things you want me to do are *hard!*" Harriett reached for another tissue.

"Harriett, I've never misled you. The skills are simple to learn, but applying them to your life requires effort. I know how badly you want to feel better because I see how hard you're working."

"But do you really understand?"

"What do you want me to understand?"

"That I feel like a failure for letting everyone down! My family, my friends, my mother, even my grandfather! These are the most important people in my life and now I feel like an outcast."

"Is that what you think or feel?"

"I know it's what I think, but I still feel horrid!" Despair permeated her words and she cradled her head in her arms. She watched tears form dark splotches on her beige slacks. "I wish you could just give me a pill."

"What type of pill?"

Harriett spoke into her lap, "A pill to make me feel less sad and anxious."

"Those pills do exist and I do refer clients for a medication evaluation if I think their emotional dysregulation impedes their ability to practice the skills."

Harriett remained hunched over, watching the splotches grow. Despite her despair, she felt the intensity of her counselor's gaze.

"Frankly, I'm undecided about your capacity," said Dr. Aye. "However, you've told me you're not in any immediate danger of hurting yourself or others. Is that still true?"

Harriett lifted her head. "I don't want to hurt myself or anybody else, but what happened last night really scared me."

"Then we'll proceed as planned, as long as you promise to alert someone if your thoughts change."

Harriett nodded her compliance.

"Does what happened to you make more sense after our discussion about emotional dysregulation and assumptions?"

"I think so," she replied, wiping her tears for the umpteenth time.

"Since the first part of the week went so well, I assumed that the worst was behind me. I see how that was unrealistic and why I felt so let down by what happened at the end of the week. I wasted energy dwelling over the injustice of life instead of conserving my energy by using a skill. When I encountered Jake in the study, I had no energy left to cope. That's why my emotions became erratic. First, I was elated that Jake wanted to spend time with me, but then I got scared. It was just like your description of an emotional roller coaster—my feelings were thrown in one direction and then in another."

Harriett flopped backwards into the chair, her face etched in exhaustion.

"Good work, only you left out the most important part. What's the good news?"

Harriett struggled to sit upright. "Good news? I told you my emotions plummeted and I lost control! That's why I think I need medication! I couldn't use a skill!"

"You did use a skill," corrected her counselor. "You used Where R U Living when you were dwelling and again when you were worrying. I understand you might have wanted the skill to be more effective, but that's a matter of practice. I also understand how you might think you lost control when your emotions plummeted but, in reality, you remained in control long enough to chose a behavior safer than lunging after Jake with a knife—you ran away. That's the good news."

"Running away is not my idea of being in control of my emotions!"

"Is it better than lunging after Jake with a knife?"

"Yes, but..."

"Don't 'yes, but' me! I think you did fine. You even used a skill without knowing it."

Harriett's eyebrows rose in puzzlement.

"We'll discuss that next week. For now, answer me this—what made you run away from Jake?"

"I didn't want to lose it again."

"Exactly. You behaved in a way that got you what you wanted."

"I still don't see how that's good news! Will I always have to run away in order to avoid losing it?"

"No, but at least you have an option; and don't forget, wise mind created the option. The likelihood of finding other options increases as you become more adept at using the skills to make an even smoother transition into wise mind."

Dr. Aye paused before asking, "In retrospect, what were some other options?"

Harriett looked at her counselor and contemplated the question. "I guess I could have given him an inconsequential response when he said he hoped you were helping. Saying something like, 'I hope so too,' might have averted the disaster."

The alternative seemed so obvious.

Why, she wondered, but realized she already knew the answer. *Right now, I'm in wise mind. Last night I was in emotional mind.*

"What stopped you from choosing that option?" asked Dr. Aye.

"I got so angry because Jake was putting all the blame on me when..."

"When what?" Dr. Aye gently probed.

"Please don't ask," Harriett begged. "I don't want to talk about it." She held her breath and willed herself not to flinch under the scrutiny of her counselor's measured stare.

Finally, Dr. Aye nodded, "I won't push as long as there's no physical abuse occurring."

"Oh, no! Jake would never hit me!"

Although Harriett's reaction seemed to mollify Dr. Aye's concern, it came with a caveat. "Just remember, I walk the same walk I'm teaching you. That means I assume nothing."

"I assure you no one is getting physically hurt, but isn't emotional abuse just as hurtful?" asked Harriett.

"Absolutely, and shouldn't be tolerated. However, physical abuse is more dangerous and more urgent to address."

Harriett pledged to notify her counselor if the situation changed.

Dr. Aye repeated her previous question. "What stopped you from answering Jake's question with an inconsequential response?"

"I wasn't in wise mind and got even more upset when I tried to use Where R U Living and failed. Running out of the room and avoiding Jake for the rest of the night were my only options."

"That's not entirely accurate," countered Dr. Aye. "Based on today's evidence, I know that you used at least two other skills to transition back to wise mind and both helped you create other options."

"What evidence?"

Dr. Aye turned towards the credenza, retrieved Harriett's list with her right hand and pointed with her left. "This evidence!"

Harriett smiled. *She looks like a district attorney proving her case.*

"These pearls of wisdom are proof you used a skill. Which one?"

Harriett considered the question. "I think I used Stop Thinking, Start Doing because reflecting back on previous sessions distracted me from dwelling on Jake."

"Perhaps you used Tolerate because you were able to endure your negative feelings long enough to produce the list."

"I suppose I also used Where R U Living because writing in the present was better than dwelling on the past, even if the past had just occurred," added Harriett. *I guess I do have an innate ability to use these skills when I feel overwhelmed.*

Feeling more confident, she asked, "You said I used two skills?"

"You tolerated your negative feelings long enough to persevere."

Again, Dr. Aye turned towards the credenza. Only this time, she opened a drawer, rifled through her files and handed Harriett a piece of paper decorated with frogs.

PERSEVERANCE – POEM: FROGS
Author Unknown

Two frogs fell in a deep bowl.
One was an optimistic soul,
But the other took the gloomy view.

"We shall drown," and he cried adieu.
So with a last despairing cry,
he flung up his legs and said goodbye.
The other frog quoted with a merry grin,
"I can't get out, but I won't give in!"
I just swim around till my strength is spent,
then will I die the more content.
Bravely he swam till it would seem,
his struggles began to churn the cream.
On top of the butter at last he stopped,
and out of the bowl he gaily hopped.
What is the moral? 'Tis easily found—
if you can't hop out, keep swimming around.

"The second frog survived by behaving differently on his feelings... And so can you! Achieving a quality life is an ongoing journey, not a destination. We progress through the journey one change in behavior at a time. Today's evidence indicates several successes. I suggest you focus on them and use them to persevere through your journey."

Studying her client, Dr. Aye nodded in satisfaction. "This has been a good session."

Somewhat surprised, Harriett agreed. *What made it good when I came into the office so upset*? Realizing the answer lay in her feelings, she replied, "I don't feel as confused, hopeless, or helpless."

"Convert those feelings into more positive emotions."

"Pardon?"

"Instead of 'confused, hopeless and helpless,' substitute 'more certain, more hopeful and more self-reliant.'"

"Why...," she began. Remembering the day's lesson, Harriett self-corrected. "What's the difference?"

Dr. Aye's smile was enigmatic. "We'll discuss that another time. For now, I want you to spend the week challenging yourself to use each of the skills and apply them across different situations. I also want you to suspend judgment on your assumptions long enough to check them out. Remember to ask 'what' questions and pay attention to what you learn. And," she instructed. "Eliminate 'try' from your vocabulary. You used the word several times today, but I graciously overlooked your *faux pas*."

"I've just decided that your name isn't Dr. Polly. It's Attila the Hun!"

Dr. Aye puffed out her chest. "Do you know what makes me proud to wear that title?"

Harriett shook her head in weary surrender. "No, but I'm not really surprised."

"Attila the Hun united his subjects, creating one of the most formidable and feared armies Asia has ever seen. Some say '*atil*' is the Hunic word for iron will. My goal is to instill that same ferocity in all my clients."

Will this woman ever allow me to have the last word?

11

Using Information to Make Wiser Choices

Harriett frowned in annoyance as she watched the stop sign slowly arc away from the side of the school bus. "Great, now I'll be late for this week's appointment with Dr. Aye." She tapped impatiently on the Jeep's steering wheel and waited for the bus to discharge its passengers.

Then Harriett made a choice. "I'll tolerate my annoyance and stay focused in the present. Instead of worrying about being late, I'll use the time to review the data I collected from doing my homework."

She recalled how she'd left last week's session motivated to reconcile with her husband. Calling Jake from the parking lot outside Dr. Aye's office, she asked if they could meet for dinner.

Jake's reply was a curt, "Why?"

"I'd like to talk about last night."

Despite his reluctance, Jake agreed.

Next, she'd gone home, typed up her list of pearls and prepared two copies to use as an agenda for the night's dinner conversation.

Harriett heard the bus engine rev and glanced to her left, but the oncoming traffic made passing impossible. Forced to follow as the bus lumbered to the next stop, she continued her retrospective. *I used Where R U Living to stay focused in the present even though I was worried about the outcome of our discussion.*

She'd met Jake at one of the bistros that dotted the Providence waterfront and waited until they were at the table before delivering a well-rehearsed apology.

"Jake, I'm really sorry about last night."

"So am I."

"The reason I ran away was because I was upset and I didn't want to risk doing anything crazy."

"And running away from me isn't crazy?"

"Not as crazy as coming after you with a knife."

Jake grudgingly conceded the point and listened as Harriett highlighted the concept of self-evaluation and the rationale behind the skills. She also explained what made it hard to gauge if Dr. Aye was helping and vowed to continue attending the weekly sessions.

Jake remained skeptical. "Why does Dr. Aye think her skills can guarantee my safety and the safety of the kids?"

"She can't guarantee anything. But learning to control my emotions long enough to change my behavior gives me a better chance of acting more rationally when I'm upset."

Jake sighed, agreeing the theory sounded good. "But I need more evidence," he stipulated.

His stipulation made her prickly, but she tolerated the feeling long enough to parry with an inconsequential, "I understand."

Watching another gaggle of youngsters rush off the bus, Harriett recalled how her wise choice had reduced the tension and allowed the conversation to continue without conflict.

I'm especially pleased at the number of "what" questions I inserted into the conversation.

However, one exchange had produced a decidedly unfavorable outcome...

"Jake, I can understand you being tense around me, but what's making you so edgy with the kids?"

"It's not just you and the kids. I told you, I'm worried about most everything."

Harriett persevered. "I understand you're worried, but what makes you worried about the kids?"

Jake responded with another deep sigh. "They seem to require so much time and attention. I never thought raising teenagers would be so demanding. I feel like we spend more time fixing their mistakes than enjoying their company."

Curbing her impulse to correct Jake's misuse of "feel," Harriett affirmed her husband's observation. "I think that too and the thought makes me feel sad. However, no one said raising children stops when they enter high school. I guess the best we can do is maintain a united front if we want to survive these next years." Flashing a tentative smile, she leaned across the table and gave Jake's hand a gentle squeeze. "We've done a pretty decent job to this point."

The school bus veered right and she darted left, pleased to pass the slow moving vehicle. However, the maneuver did not distract from the memory of Jake's reaction to her touch.

Stiffening, Jake had pulled his hand away and then tried to cover his response by reaching for the glass next to her hand. His eyes darted across the restaurant, looking everywhere but at his wife.

The image of Julie invaded Harriett's brain, making her feel alone and afraid. Working hard not to make an assumption, she'd managed to choke back her fear long enough to ask, "What's wrong?"

Jake's answer was evasive. "I guess I'm just tired." His eyes met hers, but the connection did little to close the gap between them. "I'm glad we're not fighting, but can we please finish our meal in peace?"

After dinner, she'd taken a solitary walk along the water's edge, bought an ice cream and sat down on a nearby bench. She used the chocolate gelato as a sweet distraction to stay in wise mind and assessed the dinner's outcome. Pleased she'd controlled her emotions after Jake short-circuited the conversation, Harriett credited her success to suspending judgment on Jake's behavior. Instead, she'd used the information wisely and tabled the discussion until she could solicit the input of her friends, rationalizing that she was foolish not to seek the advice of her closest confidents.

Harriett's assessment of the week continued as she crossed the rickety bridge that divided the east and west sides of town. The clattering of the car's wheels resonated the rattling of her nerves as she struggled to resolve a growing conflict.

"Why didn't I call my friends?"

Harriett rephrased the question. "What stopped me from calling my friends?"

The answer was simple—shame.

Stopping at a red light, she made a conscious choice to continue chronicling the week's successes rather than focus on the failures.

I'm so glad I made the choice to honor my commitment to chair the garden club's flower show. Attending this week's meeting was a major achievement, especially when I knew I'd be seeing people for the first time since "the lunge." Instead of avoiding the situation, I tolerated my discomfort, used Where R U Living to stay focused in the present, and made a plan that helped me integrate myself back into the community!

Her pleasure increased as she recalled how she'd entered the crowded hall, intent on tolerating her worry over people staring. Challenging herself to check out the assumption, she scrutinized the room and paid attention to the fact that nobody was gawking. Indeed, no one seemed particularly interested in why she'd gone after her husband with a knife! The information caused her to lower her estimate of the number of people reading the police logs.

Resolute, she'd walked towards the two people she knew would make her feel safe—Sarah and Gill, the owners of the local bakery. Both personified kindness and acceptance, and Gill was infamous for his dry wit. She'd purposely planned to capitalize on the couple's affability and spent several minutes enjoying their lively banter. The tactic was a successful distraction that occupied her mind until it was time to begin the meeting.

Nervous but in control, Harriett had taken her place at the head of the table, called the meeting to order and steadily plowed through another agenda. An argument over the flower show's venue threatened to derail her progress, but the skills kept her on track.

After listening to several minutes of useless bickering, she'd stood up and said, "Enough!" Her firm tone demanded attention. That's when the situation became dicey, because an immediate silence ensued as people turned and waited.

A voice inside her head screamed, *Oh no, look at what you've done! You've made yourself the focus of attention!*

She'd stood frozen, feeling trapped and uncertain.

Run! The voice insisted, fueling her panic and causing her to gasp for air. Then she heard a different voice and this one commanded her to "Stop!"

The memory made Harriett smile as she waited for the traffic light to turn green. *I know the voice was mine, but I distinctly heard a New York twang!*

She'd somehow tolerated her panic, taken a deep breath and whispered, "Please let this work."

Gathering her wits, she'd resumed her seat and proffered a soft admonishment. "Look, we all want the same thing—to make this a perfect event. But since we each have a different definition of perfection, I suggest we come up with some excellent options that we can discuss."

The meeting continued and the group seemed pleased with the outcome. More importantly, she'd achieved her goal—to remain in control and not give people a reason to gossip.

The traffic signal switched from red to green. Looking left and right, Harriett laughed as she stepped on the gas. *Life feels so much easier when I use the skills!*

In wise mind, her perception of the world seemed clear and vivid. Being in emotional mind reminded her of watching the fog slowly creep across the bay, blanketing the landscape in a dense layer of gray that made everything seem hazy.

"So why is staying in wise mind so hard?" She quickly self-corrected, "What makes staying in wise mind so hard?"

Satisfied with the self-evaluation question, Harriett analyzed the answer. *I'm so accustomed to being in emotional mind that transitioning into wise mind feels odd. I guess I just have to keep practicing. After all, practice makes perfect!*

Again, she smiled, but the thought made her wonder, *Am I as much a slave to perfection as Dr. Aye seems to think?*

Knowing the question was important, but realizing she wasn't ready to cope with the answer, Harriett decided to use her energy differently. *Thinking about the successes I had with the kids is definitely more gratifying!*

Worry over proper supervision had provoked Harriett to refuse Katie's pleas to attend a sleepover party. The mask of disappointment on her daughter's face reminded Harriet of how it felt to be a fifteen-year-old excluded from her clique of girlfriends. Aware that she was making an assumption, Harriett chose to suspend judgment about the supervision and made a phone call to the parents hosting the sleepover. The information she received, combined with the knowledge that Katie was a reasonably responsible teenager, enabled Harriett to risk giving Katie permission—but not without a stern lecture about consequences.

Making her final approach to Dr. Aye's office, Harriett re-experienced the pride she'd felt when the friend's mother called to praise Katie for being well mannered and conscientious. *Dr. Aye would probably say the phone call validated my want to raise Katie to be a responsible teenager and my sense of achievement means I satisfied my need for power.*

Tucking the memory away in her success savings account, Harriett focused on her second success. *Tolerating my emotions long enough to avoid an argument with Matt was even more difficult than suspending judgment on Katie's sleepover.*

The red Saab Matt received for his eighteenth birthday had been the topic of the aborted argument.

Finding the car of his dreams on the driveway made him whoop with joy. I just never realized how quickly the bloom of the moment would fade! I've lost track of how many times Matt's tried to negotiate the rules about using that darned car.

Matt's wrangling reached new heights when he announced he

wanted to drive a group of friends into Providence to see the *Rocky Horror Picture Show* and would return home at four o'clock in the morning. The announcement escalated Jake's growing impatience with the family. He'd stomped out of the house, demanding that Harriett deal with "her son." Jake's behavior had infuriated Harriett more than Matt's ludicrous proposal.

She'd turn towards her son, intending to make him the brunt of her fury. From deep within the recesses of her mind, she heard Dr. Aye's voice admonishing her to use a skill.

Tolerating her wrath long enough to swallow her anger at Jake, Harriett had asked Matt a self-evaluation question. "What did you think your father's response would be to such an outlandish scheme?"

"I guess I'm kind of testing the limits," Matt replied.

Together, they'd devised a more reasonable plan that worked for both Matt and his parents.

Suddenly, Harriett's hands gripped the Jeep's steering wheel. Her thrill of victory vanished as she recalled her ineptness at using the skills during a visit with her mother.

Her mother had called repeatedly to discuss "the lunge," but Harriett had purposely evaded the calls and ignored her mother's messages. Intent on having a heart-to-heart with her daughter, Mother mounted a counterattack by insisting that Granddad talk to Jake. Granddad refused, maintaining he wouldn't interfere in a matter that might impact the day-to-day operations of his law firm. The stalemate continued until Granddad summoned Harriett to Boston, demanding she put an end to "the nonsense."

She'd felt a growing sense of doom as she drove north to Boston, knowing she had no words to make her mother understand. Trying (*sorry, Yoda*) to use distraction, she'd punched the buttons on the car radio, vainly searching for songs to divert her thoughts. Each step up the front stairs of the brownstone had made her foreboding climb higher. As predicted, Mother's worry over the fate of the family was consuming and her "what ifs" intensified the ache in Harriett's clenched teeth.

"Goodness, Harriett, a KNIFE? What if the police had arrested you or Jake decides to divorce you? Imagine how a divorce will affect the firm's partnership! I suggest you learn to wrap up your emotions into a tiny little package and hope he forgives you!"

Nothing Harriett said abated the barrage and she'd retreated into silence, hoping her mother's onslaught would eventually peter out. Unfortunately, Mother interjected a "what if" that was just too hard to tolerate.

"What if people in Providence learn of the debacle? Imagine the havoc on your sister's restaurants!"

Harriett's emotions erupted. "Oh, yes, Mother, let's not forget *THE* restaurants—Faye's gateway into the world of philanthropy. The world you hold in such high esteem!" Bitter tears ran down her face as she sat in her grandfather's lounge, dwelling over the inequities between her sister's life and her own.

It's so unfair! Faye's not the one who works hard to uphold family tradition! Nooo, she's the one whose high school antics made Granddad's hair stand on end. She's not the one who studied to be a lawyer and she's certainly not the one who sacrificed a social life for good grades in college! Faye's the one who treats life with the same reckless disregard that unhinged Mother. How come she gets to have everything I want?

Faye had partied her way through college and met her husband while carousing at a nightclub in Providence. A culinary student at Johnson and Wales, Randy had been a financially struggling, but aspiring chef with big dreams. Through hard work and determination, he'd received international acclaim and many considered him Rhode Island's most successful restaurateur. Part of Harriett's resentment stemmed from her belief that Randy's meteoric rise was due to an infusion of money from her grandfather.

While love for her twin compelled Harriett to acknowledge how perseverance also played a role in Faye's fairytale life, things always seemed to fall perfectly into place for her sister. *Even Faye's inclination to use nannies didn't stop her from raising perfect children! It's just not fair!*

I'm the one who's always made the safer choices, but Faye's the one who grabbed the gold ring!

"Harriett! Are you okay? You haven't heard a word I said!"

The urgency in her mother's voice refocused Harriett's attention. Sighing, she'd responded, "Yes, Mother, I'm fine. It's just that dwelling on the past and worrying about the future hasn't left me any energy to pay attention in the present."

"Pardon?"

Hearing the word made Harriett realize how she'd acquired the annoying habit.

"It's something my counselor would say," she replied.

"How is that going?"

Harriett deflected the question by asking, "Have you ever thought about going to counseling?"

"Once, when your father left," admitted Mother. "But then I got too involved with raising you and your sister and didn't have the luxury of paying someone to listen to me babble about a broken heart."

Her mother's admission was unsettling. "Is that what you think I do with Dr. Aye? Babble?"

"Well, dear, compared to your sister, I find it hard to understand what could make you resort to knives. After all, Jake takes care of all your needs. Faye and Randy have so many commitments that are dependent on the success of the restaurants. However, your sister seems to handle her issues quite well."

Unable to tolerate the injustice, Harriett buried her face in the settee and cried.

"Sweetheart, whatever is the matter?"

"I wish I could just roll up into a carpet and wait for life to pass me by!"

Harriett pulled into the parking lot, remembering how her mother had sat down beside her, administered a slight shake and issued an edict. "Now you listen to me, young lady. You are a Smyth, and Smyths do not allow life to pass them by. It took me a long time to recover from the mistake I made with your father. I worked hard and I expect you to do likewise."

Knowing she lacked the energy to argue, Harriett had swallowed back her tears and prayed for the afternoon to end.

The memory of the visit made her feel depleted. She sat in the parking lot contemplating her mother's transformation from a rebellious hooligan into a pillar of Bostonian society. *I wonder what messages Mother heard that made her become so conservative?*

Sorting through the chronology of her mother's life, Harriett determined the most likely explanation lay in the disastrous ending to her mother's marriage.

My father abandoned Mother and she had no option but to swallow her pride and allow Granddad to take care of us. Mother says she named me after Granny as a way to thank them, but I suspect my name symbolizes Mother's capitulation to a conservative lifestyle—one that avoids pain by shunning the risk of failure. In retrospect, it makes sense that Mother became the family matriarch after Granny's death. Granddad was bereft over losing the love of his life and taking care of Granddad allowed Mother to repay her debt.

Harriett's reflections provoked an intriguing insight. *No wonder I place such a high priority on doing what's proper. I grew up hearing how Mother's laissez-faire attitude shattered her life. Perhaps, the messages I heard were ones that said being perfect is the only way to avoid pain.*

A bitter laugh erupted. "I obviously failed to consider the consequences."

Walking across the parking lot, Harriett wondered how to recount the yin yang of her week to Dr. Aye. Her paced slowed as another failure outweighed her successes.

Dr. Aye will be aghast when she hears how I compared my life to Faye's and made so many assumptions! How do I know if Granddad bankrolled the restaurants? I never asked, I just assumed! Mother seemed to imply that Faye's life was stressful, but I was too miserable to ask what she meant! Maybe Faye's children aren't as perfect as I think. How do I know if Faye's life is a fairytale? I only know what she tells me. We haven't had a heart-to-heart in ages!

148

Guilt assuaged Harriett as she realized how often she'd failed to return her sister's messages.

Feeling more like a beat-up old wreck than a gleaming yellow Hummer, Harriett opened the waiting room door, anticipating a despicable outcome to Dr. Aye's inevitable question, "How was your week?"

12

Skill #5
Stop, Drop, and Roll

"Help me to understand," began Dr. Aye. "You had a fair amount of success with the skills, so what makes you so glum?"

"I'm confused and...," Harriett struggled to encapsulate the reason she felt so drained. "I'm just confused," she repeated. "If I like being in wise mind, why is it still so hard to use the skills? I wasn't able to tolerate my mother's 'what ifs' and I feel terrible for how many assumptions I made about my sister."

"We've already established what makes using the skills hard," reminded Dr. Aye. "And being a slave to perfection makes it even more difficult because you deny yourself the rewards gained from working hard."

The reference to perfection felt like an assault. *I haven't even settled into my seat! Can't this woman at least pretend to care about my feelings before we get down to business?*

"Which feels better, celebrating your successes or dwelling on your failures?"

"But accepting anything less than perfection is hard."

"I have a remedy for that. However, today I want to focus on how you unknowingly used a skill that contributed to your week's success."

"I tried using everything you've taught me!" Harriett winced, knowing there was only one way to erase the frown on Yoda's face. *Stop worrying about what you didn't do and stay focused on what you did!*

"We haven't discussed this new skill," observed Dr. Aye. "However, being unfamiliar with the skills doesn't mean you lack the innate ability to transition into wise mind. The pithy names I've concocted are merely reminders to make the switch. The names aren't as important as knowing the importance of making a conscious choice between emotional mind and wise mind. Assigning names to the process helps make the transition a little easier when you're emotionally overwhelmed." She paused before asking, "Are you ready to learn the next skill?"

Harriett nodded, pleased she'd become attuned to self-evaluation questions. *More importantly, it's become easier to use the answers to make better choices. Not easy, but definitely easier.*

"The name of the skill is Stop, Drop, and Roll," said Dr. Aye and nodded as Harriett opened her mouth to ask a question. "Yes, just like the fire safety technique. Stop, drop, and roll is a safety routine that also helps avoid panic if you catch fire. I've taken the liberty to apply the concept to an emotional fire."

"Emotional fire?"

"Think about your feelings the night you lunged. You said they started as a slow, smoldering burn and then ignited into a burning rage. What happened once your feelings were burning out of control?"

"I lost it."

"Be more descriptive."

"I started acting crazy."

"Doesn't that sound similar to how a person on fire might behave?"

"You mean I panicked?"

Again, Dr. Aye nodded. "You told me you ignored your feelings by clenching your teeth and when that didn't work, you lunged. Ignoring your feelings fueled your emotions in the same way running fuels a fire—both behaviors are a waste of energy. Like a fire, your emotions needed to be contained, not ignored. Stop, Drop, and Roll is a skill that helps contain emotions."

She gave her client a moment to digest the concept and then proceeded. "First, you STOP what you're doing because what you're doing is not likely to achieve what you want."

"You mean I had to stop clenching my teeth, just like the fire victim must stop running?"

"Imagine how difficult it would be to stop running if you were on fire. Resisting the urge to act emotionally is just as hard. Then you must do more than resist, you must DROP the urge. Being on fire makes the urge to run overwhelming, yet the wisest choice is to stop running and drop to the ground. The change in behavior inhibits acting upon the urge."

"I'm confused. What urge should I have dropped—the one to go after Jake with the knife? If so, then why not use the Tolerate skill to tolerate the urge long enough to change my behavior?"

"The urge you drop is the urge to prove you're right and the other person is wrong."

Harriett shook her head in opposition. "But..."

"I understand you wanted Jake to know that he'd made you feel dismissed," interrupted Dr. Aye. "However, using emotional mind to prove your point is a waste of energy. Because what you're really doing is forcing the other person to submit to your will, when the only behavior you can change is your own. The urge you drop is the urge to defend your position, no matter how strongly you believe you're right."

"But you're asking me to do more than drop! You're asking me to capitulate! I thought you were helping me get what I want!"

"What do you want?"

"I want what you just said I wanted! I want Jake to know he's upsetting me!" Harriett's face burned.

"Because he short-circuited the other night's conversation?"

"No! Because he..." she stopped, gathered her wits and willed herself to stay calm. "Look, Dr. Aye, I'm sure it's quite obvious that my husband and I are having issues. Nevertheless, you tell me everything is my choice. Well, it will be *my* choice to tell you what I want, when I want." Harriett's gaze was level and intense.

"My, my, are you setting a limit on me?"

"Pardon?"

"Setting limits is a wonderfully empowering skill. I told you being unfamiliar with the skills doesn't mean you lack the innate ability to use them effectively!"

Harriett's fists balled in anger. *The woman's infuriating! She has a skill for everything!* But then, a second thought emerged. *Maybe that's why she's always in wise mind.*

Taking a deep breath, Harriett unclenched her fists. "Are you going to tell me the name of this new skill, or do you want me to guess?" she asked, her voice oozing sarcasm.

"Neither," replied Dr. Aye. "For now you're going to listen to me explain why dropping the urge to prove you're right isn't the same a capitulating."

"So much for having choices."

"I'll ignore that," scolded her counselor.

"Capitulating means to surrender. Does that sound like something I'd advocate?" asked Dr. Aye.

"No," Harriett grumbled, aware her petulance sounded similar to her son's.

"Forcing someone to submit to your will is aggressive behavior; and the more aggressively you behave, the more you fan the flames of emotion. The wiser choice is to drop the urge to be aggressive and ROLL out an assertive behavior—one that achieves what you want in a way that respects the needs of others."

Mollified, Harriett sat back in her seat and considered ways to adapt the concept. *Intellectually the skill makes sense, but I don't see how I can possibly stop myself when I've already started acting emotionally.*

Then she remembered… "Didn't you say I've successfully used Stop, Drop, and Roll?"

"Many times," affirmed her counselor. "When Jake short-circuited your talk at dinner, you told me you dropped the urge to make him explain, even though you still thought he was wrong. What new behavior did you roll out?"

"I ended the discussion, finished my meal, and used gelato as a distraction."

"Was that a wiser option?"

"Not for my waistline! But yes, even though it was hard to respect Jake's request to end the discussion, my behavior enabled me to keep the situation from getting worse and that's what I wanted."

"What about your behavior when Matt announced he wanted to drive to the movie?"

Harriett replayed the scene through the lens of Stop, Drop, and Roll. "I was about to yell at Matt, when I was really mad at Jake. That would have been aggressive. Instead, I closed my mouth and dropped the urge to make Matt the brunt of my anger. Then I rolled out a self-evaluation question." Puzzled, she asked, "Are you saying a self-evaluation question is the equivalent of an assertive behavior?"

"That depends on how you pose the question and when you ask," replied Dr. Aye. "I'll cover the topic when I teach you about setting limits. For now, humor me with one more example of how you used Stop, Drop, and Roll."

A picture of herself at the committee meeting popped into Harriett's mind. "When I was feeling panicked, I stopped what I was about to do—run for the nearest exit."

"What made you stop?"

"Running would have made the situation worse by giving people even more reason to gossip."

"And what you wanted was to avoid giving people more reason to gossip?"

"Of course! It just never occurred to me that I dropped the urge to make people understand my discomfort. In fact, I was standing at the head of the table and made myself drop down into the chair. My change in behavior curbed the urge to run and...," she realized, "I asserted myself by using a soft, controlled voice to tell the committee what I wanted."

"Any more?" prompted Dr. Aye.

"Last week you said running out of Jake's study constituted a success. You were referring to Stop, Drop, and Roll because the behavior to run out of the room didn't fuel my emotional fire as much as continuing the fight. Jake knew I was upset, only my behavior wasn't as aggressive as the night I lunged."

The grin on Harriett's face caused her counselor to ask, "What's so funny?"

"I haven't used a single tissue!"

"What's changed?"

Harriett found the self-evaluation question easy to answer. "I think I'm beginning to understand what you mean when you say the only behavior I can change is my own. Instead of blaming Jake or using his behavior as an excuse to act emotionally, I'm supposed to use a skill and change my behavior to one that's more consistent with what I want. What's changed is that I don't feel as helpless or hopeless. This week I became more actively involved in taking back control of my life and I like the outcome."

Harriett thought about the Energizer bunny. "Perhaps I'm gaining enough energy to get my feet moving in the right direction."

"How do you feel when you think you're moving in the right direction?"

"I feel good...," she began, aware of the insipidness of the adjective. "I feel less anxious, more controlled and more empowered."

"Wow!"

"Yeah, wow!"

"So, now what?"

"Can you teach me one of those other skills?"

"No, I think you need to go away and practice the one you just learned. I also want you to check out all those assumptions you made about your sister."

Harriett sighed. *Did I really think this woman was done imitating Attila the Hun?*

"AND, I want you to practice suspending judgment and paying attention. Both concepts helped facilitate your successes with Jake and with Katie. You paid attention to Jake's behavior in the restaurant and suspended judgment on what it meant. You also paid attention when you noticed the look on Katie's face..."

Harriett finished the sentence, "...and suspended judgment long enough to obtain more information!"

Silence filled the room as Harriett watched a pensive look form on her counselor's face. Worried, she asked, "Did I say something wrong?"

Dr. Aye shook her head. "No, I was contemplating if you're ready to learn about a frustration signal."

"Pardon?"

"A frustration signal is a physiological feeling that warns you of a mismatch between the current situation and the pictures inside your head. Frustration signals are similar to signals found at railroad crossings—both warn you to stop, pay attention, and be mindful of a potentially dangerous situation. A railroad signal warns that a train is coming; but, until you stop, pay attention, and assess the situation, you can't behave wisely. You'd be foolish to ignore the railroad signal and ignoring a frustration signal is equally foolish. Paying attention to a frustration signal makes transitioning into wise mind easier. The quicker you heed the warning and identify its meaning, the faster you can change your behavior and avoid the train that might be coming down *your* tracks."

"What do you mean by a physiological feeling?"

"A physiological feeling is the disconcertion you experience when you think something about a situation isn't right, but you can't ascertain what's wrong. For instance, I describe the feeling as a pit inside my belly. Some say their hearts are in their mouths, while others feel confused. My Italian ancestors use the word, '*agida*' and the Yiddish counterpart is '*mishegas*.' One of my favorite descriptions came from a man who described the feeling as '*balagan*'—an utter and complete fiasco."

Harriett struggled to identify a feeling that described her frustration signal.

"You often use a specific word that many use to describe a frustration signal. In fact, we've used the word several times throughout this session."

Dr. Aye responded to Harriett's perplexed look by pulling her hands apart as if she were stretching taffy. "Come on, think! *Streeeetch* that brain of yours," she coaxed. Then she relented. "Might the word be panic?"

"Of course! I've always judged my panic as something to fear or ignore! You're saying to acknowledge my panic and use it as a warning that something's wrong."

Harriett's excitement grew.

"I have a choice! I can allow my panic to control me or I can use it as an ally cautioning me to tolerate the feeling long enough to suspend judgment, pay attention, and change my behavior based on what I learn. That puts me in control of my panic!"

"That's exactly what you did during your committee meeting," observed Dr. Aye.

A profound sadness intruded upon Harriett's excitement. "I wish I'd known about these skills before I went after Jake with that knife. Things would be so different."

"Where are you living?"

The command hurled her thoughts into the present and reminded her of how easy it was to become involved in unproductive thinking. Looking to her counselor for guidance, Harriett asked, "What makes staying in wise mind so difficult when the alternative feels so much worse?"

"As emotional beings, we are always emoting. I teach the skills to all my clients, present them at seminars, share them with friends, and practice them twenty-four hours a day, seven days a week. Yet, I'm constantly vulnerable to emotional mind."

Dr. Aye reminded Harriett about the rationale for self-evaluation and the purpose of the skills. "The goal isn't to eliminate our feelings—the goal is to acknowledge them, accept them, and to use our energy to control them. Pay attention when your frustration signal starts clanging. Use the feeling as a reminder to open your skills toolbox."

Harriett stared down at her folded hands resting quietly on her lap, contemplating how she might behave differently on her panic.

"I have one more suggestion for this week's homework."

Harriett looked up.

"Drop the urge to be perfect and roll out behaviors designed to infuse your life with excellence."

Dr. Aye put up her hands, warding off her client's protests. "I understand doing so will be hard. However, next week's skill will make things a bit easier."

Harriett was doubtful. "I think this will be the hardest homework you've ever assigned."

"Remember, I only request a single attempt."

Rising from the loveseat, Harriett walked towards the door. *I feel like I can handle one try.*

Realizing she'd committed two grievous errors, she cast a nervous look over her shoulder and amended her thought. *I think I can handle changing my behavior at least once!*

Feeling energized, Harriett stepped across the threshold, ready to tackle the week.

13

Paying Attention and Suspending Judgment

THOUGHTS...FEELINGS...ENERGY...THOUGHTS...FEELINGS...

The cadence of her thoughts matched the rhythm of Harriett's footsteps as she strode towards the Jeep. Sliding into the driver's seat, she turned the ignition and heard the engine roar to life. *Just like me! I'm roaring with energy!*

"Well..., perhaps not roaring, but I'm certainly feeling better!"

"Define better," she challenged, as she backed the car out of the parking space, shifted into drive, and continued her self-evaluation.

Do I really believe all behavior is a choice when, for most of my life, I've felt like a puppet and other people are the puppet masters pulling on my strings?

"Whoops," she cautioned aloud. "Be careful—that was a thought."

Differentiating between a thought and feeling was becoming routine.

"And I certainly don't like the feeling provoked by the thought of other people yanking on my strings!"

Dr. Aye's voice reverberated inside her brain. "So, whaad can you do?"

Neither the New York twang nor the self-evaluation question sounded peculiar.

"Change my behavior," she replied, aiming her response at a spot over her right shoulder. "But, why must I be the one to change when it's everyone else's behavior that makes me feel bad? I agree changing my behavior feels better, but if everyone else wouldn't make me feel bad, there would be no reason to change."

Although she was specifically referring to Jake, Harriett could extrapolate the question to people like her mother, her children, the members of the garden club, and even to her neighbor, Phil!

"How would Dr. Aye answer the question?"

"First she'd tell me to substitute why with whaad."

While flippant, Harriett knew the answer was accurate.

"When Dr. Aye says the only behavior I can change is my own, she means that I am responsible for finding ways to lessen the impact other people have on my feelings because I'm the only one who can control my feelings."

Her head shook in rueful awareness. "No wonder I've been feeling helpless and out of control! I've been wasting energy angering over people who pull my strings rather than using my energy to cut the strings!"

Her self-evaluation completed, Harriett pulled into the garage with her mind made up. *This week I intend to use my energy productively by concocting a new recipe for lemonade! I will stay focused in the present, suspend judgment, pay attention, and behave wisely.*

Vroom! The yellow Hummer had reappeared!

Walking into the kitchen, she glanced at the microwave's digital clock, discovered she had time before the kids came home, and made a choice...

She tolerated her discomfort, picked up the telephone, and dialed Faye's number.

"Well, hello, stranger!" Her twin's voice replicated her own. "I wasn't going to answer, but then I saw your number. What's up? You've been ducking me for weeks. Is everything okay?"

Tears pricked her eyelids as Harriett acknowledged the concern in her sister's voice. "Oh, Faye, I know I've been acting strange, but I don't know how to explain."

"When have you ever had to explain anything to me? Did you forget that I love you?"

Faye's nonjudgmental acceptance felt like a balm and the two sisters used mindless chitchat to resume their special connection. Eventually, Harriett felt brave enough to check out some of her assumptions.

"Faye, can I ask you a question?"

"Of course. Do you need something?"

"No, no. I just want to check out something I've been wondering. Were you always sure that Randy was the love of your life?"

"Sure?" Faye repeated with a laugh. "I wasn't sure! I was scared out of my mind! I wasn't even sure if the marriage would last!"

"But, you never said anything. I thought we told each other everything!"

A question niggled within the recesses of her mind. *So how come you haven't confided your worry about the affair?*

Faye hesitated before answering. "Your thoughts about Randy have always been somewhat...transparent. You were so critical after finding out he was a chef and not a lawyer that I couldn't risk sharing my worries with you. That would have made you and Mother even more determined to break us up, and I was too vulnerable to risk another lecture on family values and tradition. I needed to talk to someone who could listen and not judge."

Faye's admission made Harriett feel ashamed. "Oh, Faye! Can you ever forgive me?"

"Forgive you? For what?" Her sister's confusion traveled through the phone lines.

"For failing you!"

"Harriett, what in the world are you talking about? You didn't fail me! Why are you beating yourself up for something in the past? It happened. Life isn't perfect. Get over it. I did."

Faye's words sounded eerily similar to Dr. Aye's and filled Harriett with wary suspicion. *Could Dr. Aye be the "someone" who'd listened to Faye's fears without judging her behavior?*

Feeling betrayed, Harriett was tempted to end the call. However, she quickly realized that emotional mind was making her thoughts absurd. *For goodness sake, Faye's been married over fifteen years! I doubt Dr. Aye was even in practice!*

Then Harriett remembered... "Faye weren't you in counseling once?"

She held her breath, determined to suspend judgment and tolerate her suspicions.

"Yes, don't you remember? It was after the first restaurant failed. I wanted to start a family, but Randy and I were financially strapped. We started fighting and decided we needed some help."

"Did it help?"

"Sure, it helped—once Randy figured out he was wrong!" Her sister's voice became serious. "I think counseling helped us realize we had to tolerate each other's differences and figure out a way to work together to get what we wanted."

Faye's words intensified Harriett's wariness, and she worked hard to suspend judgment rather than behave on her assumption. *I'll check out my suspicions next week when I see Dr. Aye.*

She kept herself focused in the present by changing the topic. "I've been thinking I should invite Mother and Granddad to my house for the traditional Smyth family Easter extravaganza. What do you think?"

"No can do, Sis. Randy's scheduled a family vacation at Little Dix Bay in the British Virgin Islands."

Harriett opened her mouth to protest her sister's rejection of family tradition, then recalled Faye's earlier comment about needing someone to listen.

Stop, she silently commanded and closed her mouth. *Don't give in to the urge to prove to your sister that she's wrong. Roll out a new behavior—suspend judgment until you have more information.*

Wisely, Harriett asked, "What made you decide to go away at Easter?"

"Randy and I have been arguing more than usual. That typically means life's getting too hectic. We've learned to use arguing as a signal to slow down and take a chill pill. What better place to chill than in the BVI?"

Faye's admission escalated Harriett's suspicions about Dr. Aye. Her finger hovered over the phone's "off" button; but once again, she made a wiser choice.

Tolerate, just tolerate, she chanted to herself, and immediately felt less overwhelmed. Her thinking cleared, allowing the creativity of wise mind to penetrate her consciousness. *Even if Faye's been a client of Dr. Aye's, the fault lies with Dr. Aye for not telling me.*

A different behavioral option emerged. *Instead of hanging up on Faye, I could check out my assumption by asking the name of her counselor.*

Harriett wondered if wise mind held any other creative options.

"Harriett?"

Her sister's voice interrupted her thoughts.

"I'm sorry, Faye, I didn't hear what you said."

"I was saying that we really need some family time, but convincing two adolescents to spend spring recess with their parents is difficult, so we bribed them with a trip to a tropical resort. The chef at Little Dix is a friend of Randy's and he got us a great rate. My two little brats could care less about foregoing Easter with relatives!" Faye giggled as she confessed, "And neither do I. The resort boasts about being an instantaneous retreat from a fast-paced life and comes complete with beachfront cottages and a spa. I have this image of behaving like an island girl for a week."

Faye's voice went taut. "I'm a little worried about Randy. He had chest pains last week that the doctor attributes to high cholesterol and stress. The recession's affected the restaurants and I'm hoping this vacation will distract him from his woes."

Relieved she hadn't acted on her suspicions, Harriett asked, "Are you sure everything's okay? If you need me to help out, you know you just have to ask."

"Believe me, sister dear, your willingness to spend Easter with Mother and Granddad is a godsend that relieves me of one more worry. I hate to think of those two alone in Boston. Besides, I won't have to fret about you brandishing weapons. Knowing Mother, she'll lock up every knife in the house the moment she steps through your door!"

Harriett gasped at Faye's cavalier reference to the lunge. Again, she worked hard and used Stop, Drop, and Roll to curb the urge to scream at her sister's insensitivity, hang up the phone, and retreat in injured disgrace.

Instead, Harriett rolled out a less aggressive, more assertive behavior. "I don't appreciate your humor." She allowed her cool tone to indicate her displeasure with Faye's remark, but became even more annoyed when her sister laughed.

"Oh, come on! Lighten up on that supercilious attitude! Do you really think you're the only woman who's been frustrated by her husband's behavior? Trust me—you've earned my admiration. I bet Jake will think twice before he complains about your cooking. My friends say you're their role model!"

Harriett astonished herself by joining in her sister's laughter. She hung up the phone, feeling pleased. *Mission accomplished! I used my skills to check out my assumptions, and letting go of some of my guilt certainly feels good! It's amazing how Faye's irreverence always gives me a different perspective. I've missed her.*

Harriett acknowledged how her behavior was responsible for the self-imposed exile, as well as the reconnection with her sister. *Dr. Aye would say I feel pleased because I behaved in a way that satisfied my need for love and belonging.*

Harriett recalled her confusion when Dr. Aye first described the interrelationship of needs, wants, and behaviors. *What seemed so incomprehensible now seems so logical.*

"What's changed?" The self-evaluation question was automatic and the answer felt seamless. "My willingness to work hard and to practice."

In addition to feeling pleased, Harriett's ability to tolerate her discomfort long enough to call her sister had garnered new information about "the lunge."

Granted, lunging after Jake was a mistake and I would never recommend solving a problem with weapons—but I'm the one who's elevated what I did to the same degree of abhorrence as Aileen Wuornos. Lunging may have been wrong, but I doubt that anyone would consider me one of America's most infamous female serial killers!

Harriett found herself laughing for the second time in less than an hour. She remembered Dr. Aye's observation that distorted thinking intensifies negative feelings. *Another good reason to check out assumptions!*

As the afternoon progressed, Harriett realized that her ability to laugh and feel pleased meant she was using her energy differently. *I'm not wasting energy by dwelling over my mistakes or by being annoyed at Faye's cavalier attitude. In fact, I'm feeling quite energized!*

She visualized the Energizer bunny, saw her feet moving and fluffy, white tail wagging, and wondered where she was headed...

"Anywhere you want to go!" The answer popped out of her mouth with surprising ease, but her next thought quickly negated her burgeoning excitement. *But I don't know what I want!*

Instead of feeling anxious, Harriett felt irritated.

"So figure it out. Don't waste all this energy! Use it to figure a way out of this mess!"

With dawning insight, Harriett comprehended how her mess included more than just the situation with Jake. *I think my want to be perfect is what's gotten me into trouble. But, who would I be if I weren't perfect?*

The question left her feeling ambivalent, conflicted, and vulnerable. A wave of memories flooded her mind and her ambivalence turned to sadness as she concluded that her quest to be perfect had mostly yielded recollections of failure.

Harriett's thoughts focused on one memory in particular—Katie's first communion. *I should be reminiscing about a day of celebration, but all I remember is being frustrated and annoyed over that damned communion dress!*

She'd spent hours dragging Katie from shop to shop looking for the perfect communion dress that would make her little girl look perfect on her special day. After days of searching, the decision boiled down to two dresses.

"One that Katie loved, and one that I thought perfectly suited her long slender body." Harriett scowled at the memory of her daughter's reaction.

"But, Mom, I love how this dress feels and when I twirl around, there's this really cool swishing sound."

"Oh, Katie, That dress makes you look like a little girl. Wouldn't you rather look like a princess?"

"I think this dress *does* make me look like a princess." Katie's lips twisted into a petulant frown.

I thought I came up with a perfectly acceptable compromise. I suggested we continue searching until we found a dress that made us both think Katie looked like a princess.

They'd settled on a dress that Harriett thought suited Katie almost as well as the original and Katie had reluctantly agreed. *Although, Katie did point out how the dress didn't make the same cool swishing sound.*

The sun had shone brightly on the day of the communion and Katie looked beautiful. Harriett recollected her plan to take an assortment of pictures to commemorate, what she believed was a perfectly delightful event. However, unbeknownst to her, Katie had changed outfits soon after the guests arrived at the celebration party.

"I was so annoyed by Katie's behavior because I thought she'd purposely dismissed all the hard work that went into finding the perfect dress." Harriett gasped. "Did I just say, dismissed? That's the same word I used to describe how Jake made me feel on the night I lunged!"

She felt her chest tighten and recognized the feeling as a prelude to panic.

"Stop," she ordered. "Pay attention to the signal."

Knowing it was time to stop thinking and start doing, she jotted a quick note to the kids, put on her running shoes and went for a jog.

Later in the week, Harriett was sitting at her desk and paying bills. Preoccupied, she heard the phone ring and answered before screening the call. That's when she knew her self-imposed exile was over...

"Harriett? It's Beth. Remember me? One of your dearest friends?"

Harriett's stomach dropped as she listened to Beth's ultimatum.

"You can't avoid us forever, so here's the scoop. I'm planning a girl's night-in and you have a choice—either you come willingly or be prepared to get kidnapped!"

Beth's determination made Harriett smile, and she decided to tolerate her shame long enough to accept her friend's invitation. *I can always back out at the last minute.*

A sudden thought made her ambivalent. *What if Brenda's there?*

Harriett had spent countless hours blaming Brenda for planting seeds of doubt regarding Jake's fidelity. *This whole debacle wouldn't have happened if Brenda had kept quiet about seeing Jake in Warwick!*

Tolerating her ambivalence, Harriett asked, "By the way, who all's going?"

"The usual suspects—you, me, Lissa, Sharon and Tricia. Brenda took the kids to her mother's for the week."

Relieved, Harriett thanked her friend for the invite and hung up the phone.

She returned to the bills, but a yearning for connectedness impeded her concentration. *Just because Jake's not willing to accommodate my needs, doesn't mean I can't paint myself a different picture of how to satisfy this yearning.*

Pictures of her four closest confidents developed in her mind.

Only now, I have to be willing to change my behavior to get what I want!

In addition to reaffirming her commitment to Beth, Harriett made a commitment to herself. "I am going to continue using the skills and make my pictures a reality! Eventually, I'll have to cope with Brenda; but for now, this is a good plan." She grinned when she realized her friend's company would also distract her from dwelling.

Returning to the computer, she scrutinized the bank's online billing statement and, once again, she felt her chest tighten. *There should be more money in this account!*

She panicked as Julie's face replaced the picture of her friends. Inside her head, alarm bells clanged.

"Be careful. Don't leap to any assumptions."

She clicked on the account number and held her breath, waiting for the details to appear. Scanning down the itemized list, her eyes lit on a particular entry.

"One hundred-seventy-four dollars and thirty-eight cents," she recited.

Suspicious, she clicked on the blue highlight to gather more information and immediately felt foolish because the charge was for the pool supplies she'd ordered over the phone. "That's what I get for assuming the charge was for a hotel room. What a waste of energy!"

As anticipated, Harriett's loyal friends facilitated her reentry into the group by studiously avoiding any mention of the lunge as they sat around Brenda's kitchen table, enjoying a meal of chili, crusty bread, and wine. Harriett picked at her food, appreciating their efforts to ignore the elephant in the room. Finally, she took the plunge and asked, "So, what do you want to know?"

For one excruciatingly long moment, there was a stunned silence. Then Tricia, known for her slapstick humor, decreed, "Everything! But first, to hell with the wine—what we need is a really strong martini!"

Tricia's pronouncement broke the ice and the conversation flowed into a superbly cathartic experience. While all her friends had questions, Lissa's query was most disconcerting. "You've been mad at Jake before, what made this time different?"

At first, Harriett felt herself withdraw. *I know there's no reason to be ashamed if Jake's having an affair, but if I voice my fears out loud, I'm afraid they'll somehow become real and I don't think I have enough energy to cope with that much pain.*

She looked at her friends and saw their concern, yet she was loath to share.

"What do you want from your marriages?"

Harriett's question surprised her as much as it did her friends.

Tricia's response rescued the situation. "Besides money and hot sex?"

A chorus of groaning and "yeah rights" followed, but once her friends concentrated on the question, Harriett found their input enlightening.

"I want to feel special," declared Lissa.

"And appreciated," added Beth.

"I feel insecure when Tim discounts my opinions," admitted Sharon. "I think he's being disrespectful and that makes me feel unneeded and unloved."

Her admission provoked a murmur of agreement.

Acting as the group's spokesperson, Tricia summarized. "I guess what we're saying is that we want a partnership with someone who's a stud, respects us, loves us, and makes us feel special." Then she quipped, "Anyone know where to find this man?"

Harriett sat in quiet contentment while her slightly tipsy comrades engaged in a game of one-upmanship over whose husband had disrespected whom the most. She listened to entertaining and funny accounts of the consequences caused by a husband's shockingly disrespectful behavior. Peals of laughter erupted as each story became more and more outrageous, until the discussion degenerated into an affable dispute over which wife had been most egregiously "dissed."

Cloaked in the comfort of her friends' laughter, Harriett assessed the state of her own marriage. *Jake's dismissal of my Stroganoff epitomized the lack of respect I've been sensing over these past months and I really don't know what's changed.*

In the beginning, theirs was a true partnership. Jake worked hard to master the law and became the financial provider, while she'd worked equally hard to ease him of the day-to-day pressures associated with maintaining a home and fulfilling family and social obligations. The joint decision to have children added to their life and, despite the ever-growing complexity, their alliance grew stronger. *Jake's been there whenever things become too difficult and vice versa. I've always been at Jake's side whenever he needs my support.*

Harriett suddenly wondered if Jake would agree with her assumption, especially in the one area of their life where the alliance paled—sex.

I was a virgin when I met Jake. How foolish I was to think he'd teach me everything I needed to know and all I had to do was follow his lead.

Initially, they'd made love on a regular basis but, even in the beginning, their sex lacked the passion and satisfaction she read about in magazines or listened to her friends swoon over. She shuddered at the long ago memory of discussing her concerns with Faye who immediately advised her to have a heart-to-heart with Jake.

"My god, Harriett! You've got to tell him how you feel! I don't care how much you love each other—life's too short to spend the next fifty years wondering what you're missing."

"But what would I say? Honey, I love you, but the sex is terrible?"

"No, but I can't imagine that Jake would want you to be unhappy. If he's not aware of how you feel, how can he make you feel better? Try starting the conversation by asking him what you can do to make his love life more exciting. Maybe then he'll ask how he can make your toes curl!"

She'd taken her sister's advice and tentatively broached the topic one morning over breakfast.

"Jake? Can I ask you something?"

"Of course, my beloved. What's up?"

"Do you ever think about sex?"

Pretending to be Groucho Marx, Jake wiggled his eyebrows and replied, "Only all the time."

"Please, Jake, I'm serious. I worry that I'm not experienced enough for you and I want to make sure I'm making you happy."

Harriett remembered how her husband's normally affable nature turned guarded. "Why? Are you unhappy? Am I not satisfying you?"

"Oh, no, everything's great. It's just that...oh, never mind."

Throughout the years, I've tried to get him to talk, but I can't seem to make Jake understand how lackluster our lovemaking's become. Even before the lunge, I felt like he barely knew I was in the bed. Now, forget about skyrockets and fireworks, I'd be happy with a night of snuggling and intimate conversation!

"Care to share?"

Tricia's question shook Harriett out of her reverie. "Pardon?"

"You have this faraway look on your face. Are you okay?"

Harriett administered a mental shake. "I'm fine—just a little overwhelmed by how good it feels to be back in the fold."

Sharon came from behind to give her a gentle squeeze. "It's good to have you back. We've missed you."

For a moment, Harriett was tempted to share what was really on her mind, but didn't want to spoil the group's genial mood. Instead, she adopted a false bravado. "So, let's celebrate. Tricia! Another round of Cosmos! Only make them weak so we can all find our way home!"

Later that evening, she lay in bed listening to Jake's soft, even breathing and sorted through her hodgepodge of thoughts. Under the cover of darkness, she risked challenging her preexisting assumptions regarding both her sex life and her marriage.

Was Faye right? Have I spent the last twenty years wondering what I've missed? Okay, so sex with Jake doesn't measure up to the rapture in an R-rated movie or how those woman on Oprah describe their orgasms, but is that a reason to dismiss how good Jake makes me feel in other ways? He's forever complimenting me and bragging about my cooking abilities, and he tolerates (oh, that's a spoof on words) my want to be perfect.

In countless ways, her husband was available to build her self-esteem and foster a sense of well-being. *Jake makes me feel valued, valuable and, most importantly, he treats me like his equal.*

Filled with ambivalence, she gazed out onto the moonlit water and wondered, *Is that enough? If I have doubts, does that mean Jake's been wondering the same thing? Might that be what's pushed him to Julie? Is he trying to recapture what he's missed for the last twenty years?*

Harriett thought about the need profile that Dr. Aye believed motivates people's wants. *All my friends have the same need to feel connected to their husbands, but each of us wants to satisfy the need differently. Beth said she wanted her marriage to contain laughter, yet*

Tricia seemed to want someone who could act as a stabilizing influence when she goes off on one of her harebrained tangents!

Harriett smiled, secretly wishing she could enjoy life with the same lighthearted silliness as her friend.

"So, what stops you?" Her lips formed the self-evaluation question with ease, but answering the question required effort.

"Dr. Aye would reference my slavish devotion to perfection. After all, how can I enjoy what I have if I'm always focused on what's wrong?"

Harriett dared to apply this logic to her marriage. *If I'm always harping on the imperfections, maybe the message Jake's heard is that nothing he does or says is good enough, including sex. Maybe he's given up trying to please me or worse, maybe he's given up on everything about our marriage!*

She thrashed around the bed, searching for a comfortable position. *Is it possible that by trying to be perfect, I've actually driven a wedge between us? Does he feel disrespected? Is that why he's been grumpy and distant? Am I the one responsible for the affair? Is that why Katie changed out of her communion dress? Did I place my want for perfection over my daughter's need to be happy? Have I become such a slave to my essence that I've suborned my quality of life!*

Wave after wave of unanswered questions deluged her mind and she swam hard to stay ahead of the avalanche of emotions.

STOP! she screamed inwardly. *DROP the urge to beat yourself up. ROLL out a new behavior.*

Harriett struggled to the edge of the bed, reached across the end table, switched on the reading lamp, opened the bureau drawer, and pulled out her journal. Still working to remain calm, she propped up her pillow, leaned back, placed the journal against her bent knees and became engrossed in composing a list of questions she planned to ask at tomorrow's session with Dr. Aye. She wrote furiously, almost without thought, until her breathing slowed and her eyelids drooped.

As sleep descended upon her, Harriett thought her final thought. *I'm glad my toolbox was in the bedroom.*

14

Skill #6
Accept Doesn't Mean Agree

Settling comfortably into her customary spot on the waiting room sofa, Harriett reviewed the points she intended to discuss with Dr. Aye.

I want her to know that I do see some light at the end of the tunnel and that my perspective of the world seems a little clearer. I still feel like (oops, another thought) the weight of the world is resting on my shoulders, but at least I'm less fearful of succumbing to the burden. She smiled as a picture of Atlas holding his celestial sphere developed in her mind. *Only my Atlas is a ninety-eight-pound weakling and the look on his face is one of doubt rather than confidence!*

"...and I want to work on changing the picture to one where I have more muscle and fewer worry lines."

Harriett's description made Dr. Aye laugh. "I've never had a client verbalize their wants quite so vividly. Nevertheless, the behaviors required to match that picture are well within your grasp..."

"I know," Harriett interrupted. "All I have to do is self-evaluate and practice the skills."

Reaching into her purse, Harriett pulled out her journal and placed it on her lap. In the wee hours of the morning, she'd decided the time had come to consider her role in the seeming demise of her marriage.

"I've begun to suspect that my want to be perfect is diminishing the quality of my relationships." Looking down, she opened the journal and

175

read one of the prepared questions. "Do you think I have a distorted belief around perfection that is driving a wedge between me and Jake?"

"Let me ask you a question before we discuss yours," replied Dr. Aye. "How ready are you to trust me?"

"I'm not sure," answered Harriett, surprised by the frankness of her response. "Granted, I'm feeling marginally better and I can even acknowledge the power of the skills. However, your emphasis on self-evaluation and skills training sometimes makes me think you underestimate the complexity of what you want me to do and overestimate my capacity to work hard. That makes it difficult to fully trust you."

"Because?"

"How do I know you won't make a mistake and push me too far? I understand the purpose of self-evaluation is to make me uncomfortable enough to change my behavior, but sometimes you make me so uncomfortable that I'm on the brink of exploding. You always manage to pull me back, but how do I know you won't make a mistake?"

Her eyes implored Dr. Aye to allay her fears.

"You don't."

Frustration swirled within her. *Why can't this woman just once reassure me that everything will be all right?*

"Your question epitomizes the meaning of trust because trust requires a leap of faith—faith that even though I'm not perfect, I'll do my best to provide excellent care."

Harriett elicited a dispirited sigh, certain the reference to perfection was more about her than her counselor. "Are you saying I'm afraid to trust people because I expect them to be perfect, yet know they won't be?"

"That's one side of the trust coin. I suspect the other side will be more difficult for you to accept."

Dr. Aye's soft voice made Harriett lean forward, intent on capturing every word.

"You're afraid to trust that people will love you even if you're not perfect."

Harriett slumped backwards into the loveseat. Random words

floated through her mind—*Needs...Wants...Essence...Messages.* The words coalesced into a single, cogent thought—*All my life, I've operated under the assumption that people loved me because I did my best. Somehow, I've distorted that assumption into the belief that being loved is contingent upon being perfect. Ergo, imperfect means unlovable.*

Harriett struggled to grasp the implication. Again, her eyes implored Dr. Aye to rescue her and again, her counselor challenged her to look inward.

Tolerating her negative feelings, Harriett applied the newfound insight to her original question—*Have my distortions driven a wedge between Jake and me?*

Wise mind helped her disseminate the answer.

If I can't trust Jake to love anything less than perfection, then how do I know he's not the one feeling mistrusted and unloved? If I'm so busy judging the meaning of perfect, doesn't that mean I've stopped listening to what Jake thinks? Maybe he's the one feeling disrespected!

Harriett applied a similar logic to Katie's communion dress.

I was so busy finding the perfect dress that I didn't listen to what my daughter wanted. No wonder she changed out of the dress so quickly. It wasn't the dress she wanted—it was the dress her mother wanted!

Her subsequent wail made her anguish obvious. "What do I do now?"

"Learn another skill," replied Dr. Aye.

Harriett's eyes glistened with tears of frustration. Reaching for the box of tissues, she lamented, "Every time I think I'm making progress, something forces me to backtrack."

"Do you know the song by Joe South, 'I Never Promised You a Rose Garden'?" Dr. Aye refreshed her client's memory by humming the words, *"Along with the sunshine there's gotta be a little rain sometime..."*

Then she observed, "You're at a point where your ability to trust me becomes essential. You must trust that I will walk with you into the sunshine. I won't pull you nor will I push. I'll just walk alongside you."

Harriett rubbed her lips with her index finger. "I remember you once told me that you'd be my keeper of hope until I could hope for myself.

I keep getting these little glimmers of hope and then become disappointed when they're dashed. You're asking me to persevere through the rain until I find my rainbow."

Dr. Aye shifted in her seat. "I think we've had one too many metaphors for this session! Let's change gears and learn the next skill."

"Can I ask you one more question about trust?" Too nervous to wait for an answer, Harriett blurted, "Has my sister ever been a client?"

"What makes you ask?"

"Faye said something that reminded me of your skills and I don't think I could trust you if I knew you'd seen my sister and not told me."

"Does that sound like something I'd do?"

Harriett heard the challenge to self-evaluate. Studying the look on her counselor's face, she concluded that, while Dr. Aye might be a bit quirky, she was also straightforward and honest. *In fact, I think I'm almost ready to take that leap of faith. I just hope this woman's there to catch me!*

Harriett explained how the phone call with her sister had provoked the question. "Faye talked about tolerating and working together to get what she and her husband wanted. She also said there's no such thing as a perfect way, only a way that works for their marriage. For a moment, I thought I was talking to you and that made me wonder if you were the one who taught Faye those lessons."

"Remember what I've said about the skills being inherent. Your sister sounds proficient at using the skills to her advantage. In fact, her comments sound a lot like the Accept Doesn't Mean Agree skill."

Harriett felt a familiar pang of jealously that arose anytime she thought Faye was the more competent twin. However, she ordered herself to STOP! *Stop wasting your energy on unproductive sibling rivalry!*

She redirected her energy and paid attention as Dr. Aye taught the next skill.

"The Accept Doesn't Mean Agree skill focuses on your thoughts about a situation. The goal is to accept the situation, even though you don't necessarily agree with the situation."

Harriett thought the concept sounded ludicrous. "Why would I do that?"

"Accepting the situation frees up the energy wasted agitating over something that's beyond your control. Rather than resisting or rejecting the situation, accept the situation and use the energy more productively—work to lessen the impact the situation has on you."

"I understand the first part—accept, but what do you mean by don't agree?"

"Accepting a situation doesn't mean you've abdicated your thoughts and feelings. You're still entitled to disagree."

Dr. Aye clarified the difference by referring to her client's past. "Go back to your thoughts about being a puppet on a string."

"The thought made me agitated and I wanted people to stop pulling my strings. I felt more powerful when I accepted that I was responsible for cutting the strings."

She stared at the picture of the swans and quietly evaluated how the new skill fit into her toolbox. Turning back towards her counselor, Harriett shared her analysis. "Accept Doesn't Mean Agree seems to contain elements of suspending judgment, dropping urges and tolerating."

"The skills are cumulative," reiterated Dr. Aye. "Understanding one helps facilitate the use of another."

Settling into the loveseat, Harriett listened as Dr. Aye explained the origins of Accept Doesn't Mean Agree.

"I derived the skill from one of the rules taught in improvisational acting."

"How can improv have rules?"

"I know, talk about an oxymoron! Nonetheless, I once knew someone who took a college course on the techniques associated with improvisational acting. His grade was based on the number of rules he avoided breaking while performing a skit."

"OKAY...?"

Dr. Aye grinned. "Why, Harriett! Your skepticism exemplifies Accept Doesn't Mean Agree."

"Pardon?"

"Your intonation was equivalent to saying, 'I accept your premise, but don't really agree. However, I'll suspend judgment and keep silent until I hear more.'"

"The way *you* said that reminds me of the Tolerate skill!" she retorted, a bit annoyed by her counselor's teasing. "However, I am beginning to understand what you mean about the skills being interconnected. The more I know how they work, the more empowered I feel to apply them in different ways and in different combinations, depending upon the situation. I also get why you've given the skills such pithy names. It makes controlling emotions seem a little less overwhelming."

"I'll choose to accept your observation about the names, even though I don't agree with how it's stated."

"But, you're the one that called them pithy!"

"Yes, but they're my names. You calling them pithy is like someone calling your dog ugly. You might accept that your dog is ugly, but you don't have to agree when someone makes a rude comment!"

Dr. Aye waited for the anticipated moan before continuing.

"*Yes, And* is a rule in improvisational acting that stipulates an actor must accept a scene, no matter if she agrees or disagrees. Suppose there are two actors involved in a skit. The first actor embellishes the scene before handing the scene off to the second actor. The second actor must accept the scene, even if she disagrees with the embellishments because rejecting the scene stops the forward progress of the skit. Essentially, the second actor must say, *Yes, I accept the scene despite disagreeing with your interpretation*. Once the second actor takes ownership, she can work to improve the scene. In other words, *And now watch while I make this skit even better*."

Responding to Harriett's ongoing skepticism, Dr. Aye elaborated. "Let's pretend the first actor sets the scene in Alaska but is wearing a hula skirt when she relinquishes the skit. The second actor doesn't agree with the Alaskan setting, but accepts the scene and begins regaling the audience with an outrageous account about making the skirt while on a Club Med vacation. Her behavior allows her to switch to a setting of her choice. Wasting energy by rejecting the scene would have denied the audience of a good laugh."

"I think I understand, but how does the skill apply to my want to be perfect?"

"Your question epitomizes using Accept Doesn't Mean Agree *incorrectly*."

Harriett remained baffled.

"The reason the rule isn't called *Yes, But* is because *but* negates the validity of the preceding words. Picture a drawbridge. *But* is the equivalent of opening the bridge and creating a gap in the flow of information. From a skills perspective, *but* inhibits the flow of information into reasonable mind. *And* keeps the two sides of the bridge connected."

Dr. Aye reminded Harriett about the scales of justice. "*And* adds weight to reasonable mind, which then counterbalances emotional mind."

At her counselor's request, Harriett revised her previous question. "I think I understand *and* how does the skill apply to my want to be perfect?"

"Can you differentiate the feelings provoked by the two versions of the question?"

After repeating both questions, Harriett slowly nodded her head. "The first question sounds tentative and somewhat pessimistic. The second sounds more confident and hopeful. In fact, I'm more inclined to consider ways to apply the skill rather than waiting for you to answer the question."

"This week's homework is to tolerate the frustration you feel when someone doesn't perform up to your standards..."

Harriett pushed herself upright. "Like dying Easter eggs?"

Dr. Aye stared blankly. "You lost me."

"Every year I insist that we dye Easter eggs as a family. I know that sounds silly, considering Matt and Katie are beyond the age of believing in the Easter bunny. Nevertheless, I think maintaining holiday tradition is important; so every year, I buy a dye kit, boil the eggs, and check them for cracks."

A deep sigh accompanied the rest of her narrative. "And every year, Matt and Jake moan and groan over the event. Inevitably, dying the eggs degenerates into a competition over who can make the ugliest egg. They torment me until I finally give up, dump the whole mess into the garbage, buy more supplies, and dye my own eggs."

"You do this every year?"

"Yes."

"And every year ends the same way?"

"Pretty much."

"And you continue to do this...why?"

"Because every year I hope they'll make pretty eggs."

"But...,"

Harriett wondered if the choice of word was intentional. "I know—whose behavior can I change."

"And...,"

"This year you want me to accept ugly eggs even though I don't agree."

"That's only the first half of the skill!"

"But why do I have to accept ugly Easter eggs!"

Silence filled the room as Dr. Aye's penetrating stare challenged Harriett to self-evaluate the question.

"*But* hampers my ability to find ways to make the situation better."

"What makes Jake and Matt participate in the first place?"

"They love to torment me!"

"That sounds like an assumption. Might there be another explanation?"

"Such as?"

"Oh, no, sweetie, the time's come for you to take a more active role in problem-solving your situation. Use a skill to transition into wise mind."

Harriett chose to tolerate her muddle of emotions, including her frustration with her counselor. She felt herself transition into wise mind long enough to consider alternative explanations.

"Maybe they know the event is important to me but have a different perspective on its purpose."

"Meaning?"

"Maybe their goal is to participate in a family occasion, not to have perfectly dyed Easter eggs. But does that make me wrong to want pretty eggs?" She stumbled over her choice of words.

Dr. Aye assured Harriett that eliminating *but* from her vocabulary wasn't a requirement for using Accept Doesn't Mean Agree. "However, the more you pay attention to your choice of words, the more aware you'll become of the energy gained by substituting *and*."

"Am I wrong to want pretty eggs?" Harriett repeated.

"The concept of right and wrong isn't germane. Remind me again, what makes dying the eggs important to you? Is your goal to have pretty eggs?"

"No. Being around the table with all of us participating in the same event matches the picture I have of a family, and that makes me happy."

"Jake and Matt's behaviors seem consistent with your image—they're seated 'round the table and they're participating. So what makes you unhappy?"

"The eggs are ugly!"

"Is your family together?"

"Yes, but can't I have both a happy family and perfect eggs?"

"Answer the question using Accept Doesn't Mean Agree."

Harriett pondered her dilemma. "I know what you want me to do, but I'm not sure how it helps."

Reasonable mind acknowledged her inappropriate use of *but*. Yet, emotional mind completed the thought—*AND I don't care.*

Harriett felt her lips purse into a petulant pout, knowing the silence in the room was another challenge to self-evaluate. She stared at the computer monitor sitting atop the credenza and watched the screen saver flash pictures of Monet's water lily pond. As one image faded into the next, Harriett saw her reflection in the blankness of the screen, and a sheepish smile replaced the pout. *I look like a spoiled brat!*

Turning towards her counselor, Harriett accepted the challenge. "I guess I can accept that to have a happy family means I have to tolerate ugly eggs. Instead of becoming frustrated and throwing the eggs in the trash, I can use my energy to..."

"Make egg salad?"

"Or wrap the eggs in those little plastic films that adhere with a hair dryer."

Dr. shrugged. "Whatever works."

Harriett's smile widened. "Hey, they're my eggs!"

"You're absolutely right as long as you can tell me how wrapped Easter eggs are an example of Accept Doesn't Mean Agree."

"I can accept that my family doesn't value pretty Easter eggs, even though I don't agree AND I can embellish on the situation by smiling whenever I hear the guys whoop at making me groan, because their whoops reaffirm my want to have a happy family. I can also remember my smiles while I use the hair dryer to convert ugly eggs into pretty eggs."

"How is this productive use of energy?"

"Instead of wasting my energy agitating over Jake and Matt's behavior, I am being productive by making the situation better."

"For who?"

"For me!"

"Certainly not for me! I hate those little plastic films and would rather eat egg salad. Nonetheless, your application of the skill is spot on."

Another lengthy silence filled the room as Harriett sat lost in thought.

"What are you thinking about?"

"The whole notion of perfection," she replied. "Frankly, I'm confused."

"About what?"

"This week I was thinking how I wouldn't have to use these skills if everyone would just behave correctly."

"Correctly is subjective. Correct according to whom?"

"Correct according to what they committed," Harriett yelled. Her nostrils flared and her hands clutched around the tapestry pillow adorning the loveseat.

Dr. Aye studied her client. "Who isn't behaving according to what they committed?"

"My husband," she replied, her anger accentuated by tendons stretched across her slim neck. Her chest heaved as a series of short gasps made her breathing labored.

"Are you ready to talk?"

Working to control her emotions, Harriett ran her palm down the pillow and focused on the material's rough texture. Looking down at the pillow, she answered in a small voice. "I guess I have to."

"No, Harriett. All behavior is a choice and you will choose to talk when you're ready."

"But when will I be ready?"

"When the discomfort of remaining silent outweighs the discomfort of talking."

Dr. Aye watched indecision wash across her client's face. "You told me you're safe. I can wait until you're ready, but I'll always check in. I assume nothing."

Her counselor's words provoked tears of gratitude. Bowing her head even deeper into the pillow, Harriett whispered a muted, "Thank you."

"Remember what I said earlier—my job is to walk alongside you, not in front where I have to pull or behind where I have to push."

Laughing softly, Dr. Aye remarked that there was a time when she was happy to have someone push and pull her along.

The comment distracted Harriett from her wretchedness and she lifted her head. "When?"

"When I was trekking up a mountain in Uganda's Bwindi forest. Climbing that mountain was the hardest thing I've ever done, but I persevered because I wanted to see the gorillas living at the top of the mountain. About halfway up, I realized I needed help. The guide walking beside me suggested a second guide. The first guide stayed in front and pulled me up the mountain, while the second stayed behind me and pushed me up the mountain. I nicknamed them Push and Pull. Without their assistance, I would have missed a truly glorious adventure."

Although absorbing, Harriett wondered why Dr. Aye chose to tell her about the adventure.

Her counselor shrugged, tilting her head to one side. "What might be my point?"

Contemplating the story, Harriett postulated, "Accepting our imperfections gives us the opportunity to seek the help we need to attain what we want?"

"Accepting our imperfections also provides the opportunity to form productive partnerships."

Harriett's head snapped backwards. Startled, she asked, "Did you use that word on purpose?"

"What makes you ask?"

Harriett recounted the "night in" with her friends. "Until recently, I've always thought my marriage was a partnership and I'm afraid my perfectionism is making Jake want to dissolve the partnership."

"Help me to understand. You say you've always had a partnership with Jake—a partnership that's been successful despite your vulnerability to perfectionism. What's changed?"

Again, Harriett resisted. She knew her behavior was erratic, yet she was afraid to confess her fears. An almost imperceptible shift in the client-counselor relationship emerged as she listened to Dr. Aye assign the week's homework.

"I want you to do three things. First, practice the Accept Doesn't Mean Agree skill. Second, ponder how not talking about your fears helps to address your fears. Finally, spend some time assessing how much you trust me."

The brusqueness in her counselor's voice made Harriett uncomfortable. She opened her mouth to interrupt, but Dr. Aye curtailed her objection.

"The quality of this relationship is predicated on trust. If you don't trust me, then how can you trust that what I teach works? Are you ready to take that leap of faith? Are you ready to make a commitment—not to me, but to yourself?"

Dr. Aye held up her hands, warding off Harriett's protests. "I don't care about the answer as long as it's genuine. I'm a tough old broad and I'll handle anything you throw at me."

Stunned, Harriett extricated herself from the loveseat. *This woman's throwing down the gauntlet and daring me to pick it up! She's challenging me to take more responsibility for my behavior instead of blaming Jake and everyone else!*

Harriett stood in the middle of the office, fingering a garland of twisted beads that dangled from her neck and feeling decidedly uncomfortable. A flash of insight burst around her.

She wants me to feel uncomfortable! The more uncomfortable I feel, the more motivated I'll be to rock my Hummer out of the mud! She's daring me to change my behavior as a way to achieve what I want—to give Atlas more muscle and fewer worry lines.

Harriett nodded in agreement. "Yes, Dr. Aye, you truly are a tough old broad." Grinning, she added, "<u>AND</u> crafty as well!"

15

Challenging Past Messages

Harriett's plan was to leave Dr. Aye's office and tolerate her emotions long enough to resume marketing at the local grocery. However, conflicting reactions to the day's session made her head ache. *I feel too raw to risk bumping into anyone, even though my ability to tolerate unexpected encounters is getting better. Therefore, I choose to do my marketing across town!*

Acknowledging that the choice was hers felt empowering. *I might not agree that it's the best choice AND I accept that it's the best I can do.*

She drove towards the supermarket, intent on investing the energy she'd saved from not agitating over her inability to shop at the local market.

I'm going to suspend judgment on Dr. Aye's feedback AND spend the next twenty minutes unraveling what I learned.

A soft ping interrupted her reflections. Glancing down at the car's dashboard, she saw an amber light illuminating one of the gauges and realized she'd better stop at the Mobil station for gas.

Harriett recalled the analogy of wise mind being like a car's engine. *When I first met Dr. Aye, my wise mind was flooded with too much emotional gas.*

Mimicking her counselor's question, she asked, "What's changed?"

"I guess I can accept that things are better, even though I don't agree that anything's changed between Jake and me."

Remembering to keep her mental drawbridge in the closed position, Harriett completed the answer. "AND I can make the situation better by using my energy to figure out what to do about my marriage!"

She turned right off the highway and continued her evaluation while waiting in line at the busy pumps. *Why am I unable to trust that I'm worthy of Jake's or anyone's love?*

The question was provocative, yet deciphering her response felt as painful as poking a sensitive tooth. She substituted "what" for "why" and asked, "What do I think about my inability to trust that I'm worthy of being loved?"

Rephrasing the question provided emotional distance, allowing her to tolerate the pain and examine her thoughts. Inexplicably, they focused on her sister.

I've always lived in Faye's shadow. It doesn't matter that we're mirror images. Faye's always managed to outshine me. Her clothes hang a little straighter, her hair's more lustrous and her personality's more outgoing. People call Faye the gregarious twin. She's even got the more exciting namesake—Faye Dunaway, Mother's favorite actress!

Mother always laughs how our names reflect her two lives. Naming Faye after a leading-lady with a sensual reputation reminds Mother of being a rebellious hellion. Naming me after Granny is a constant reminder of why remaining steadfast and loyal to tradition is important.

In Harriett's mind, life was a constant struggle to step outside the shadow cast by her sister. *My solution's always been to make people marvel over my competency and commitment in the same way Faye impresses them with her gregariousness.*

Moving to the front of the line, Harriett turned off the car's engine and considered other options. *For starters, I could stop comparing myself to Faye.*

Opening the driver's door, she stepped onto the pavement and walked towards the pumps. *I guess I could also stop making people marvel.*

However, this option caused her to ask the same question she'd posed after the phone conversation with her sister. "Who would I be if I wasn't perfect?"

Harriett expanded on the question as she inserted her credit card into the pump's console. "Would I simply fade from the scene, eclipsed by Faye's expansiveness?"

Feeling defiant, she wrenched the nozzle from the pump.

Maybe I like being a conformist! Granny was a conformist and everybody loved her!

Harriett idolized her namesake, even if her grandmother's reputation was more about stalwart conservatism than steamy, sensuous charm. *My entire life's been devoted to upholding the honor of being Granny's namesake.*

Her next thoughts made her doubt her devotion. *Perhaps I've taken the distinction a bit too seriously. Sometimes I think my conservatism's made me an anachronism. I've spent so much energy upholding Granny's reputation, maybe I've become a relic of the past. My friends accuse me of not believing in the woman's movement and laugh that the only television shows I watch are ones with happy endings. At book club, they roll their eyes and groan at my naïve interpretation of the book.*

Harriett recalled how one of the law firm's female partners once commented that she seemed awfully unsophisticated given her and Jake's socioeconomic bracket.

"But that's not true!" She stamped her foot on the asphalt. "I've watched *Oprah* and *Dr. Phil!* I just don't happen to agree with their more enlightened perspective of the world. Am I not entitled to my opinion?"

Or maybe..., I'm afraid to risk blazing new trails and feel safer walking down a more conventional path. The thought refuted her image of a bright-yellow Hummer.

I like that I'm known for my competency and commitment, but does this mean I'm afraid people wouldn't notice me if I adopted some of Faye's joie de vive?

"Obviously that's the message I've been listening to AND I'm tired of listening to that message!"

She shoved the nozzle into the tank. Against the steady click of pumping gas, Harriett decided to conduct an experiment that would challenge the message. "I'm going to change my approach to Easter and analyze the outcome."

She developed a protocol that methodically used each of the skills to control her emotions regarding perfectionism long enough to change her behavior. "AND, if I don't like the results, I can always change my behavior back to what it was."

Satisfied, she squeezed the last drops of fuel into the tank, replaced the gas cap, returned the nozzle to the pump, printed her receipt, and got back into her vehicle.

Harriett's first opportunity to enact her plan came while shopping for a new tablecloth. After trudging to four stores in search of one that perfectly complemented the color of the dining room walls, she found herself standing in the middle of Home Goods, agonizing over the quandary. The folly of her behavior became apparent when she asked a self-evaluation question, "Will my family love me less if the tablecloth doesn't match the walls?"

Harriett shook her head at the absurdity, turned around, and resolutely marched out the store. As the glass door closed behind her, she gave herself a mental pat on the back for using Stop, Drop, and Roll.

She awarded a second pat when she resisted the urge to traipse to a different market after learning the brand of ham she cooked for Easter was not available. Instead, Harriett accepted the butcher's apology (even though his reasoning for stocking a different brand seemed a bit misconstrued), tolerated her annoyance and suspended judgment long enough to conclude that the difference in quality between brands didn't warrant a car ride through three towns and across two bridges!

Harriett's *coupe de grace* came after discovering two cracked eggs among the dozen she'd boiled in preparation for dying Easter eggs. She resisted the urge to omit them from the others and set a basket of twelve eggs in front of her family.

Matt gave his mother a puzzled look. "Do you want to dye the cracked ones?"

Blithely, Harriett replied, "I don't care, Matt. The choice is yours."

Tolerating her frustration at the sorry sight of blotchy brown eggs accumulating on the kitchen table, she declared Jake's egg the frontrunner in the ugliest egg competition.

"Hey!" said Matt. "I didn't know it was a competition. What's the prize?"

"The winner gets to gloat over making Mom moan and groan the loudest."

Harriett watched her family enthusiastically reach into the basket of eggs and listened to their good-humored banter.

Afterwards, she was shocked to see a single pink egg sitting amongst its mottled companions. Picking the egg out of the basket, Harriett turned it from side to side. "Matt, Katie, Jake," she read, noticing how each family member had emphasized their point with a heart.

The simple token made her eyes moist. She looked down at a basket filled with love, dabbed her eyes, and decided to make her counselor a container of egg salad!

She gave Matt and Katie an extra long bedtime hug, thanked them for the egg and headed for the bedroom to thank Jake for making the event fun.

"Harriett, dying Easter eggs is fun. You're the only one who stresses over ugly eggs. It was good watching you smile and relax a little."

Unable to resist the urge, she shot back. "You won't say that when the Easter baskets are filled with ugly eggs!"

Jake shrugged. "Pretty or ugly, the eggs will be perfect because we made them together."

Harriett looked at the man who'd been her partner for almost twenty years. She so badly wanted to put her arms around him and tell him how scared she was to lose him. *Is now the time? Has the discomfort of not changing my behavior begun to feel worse than the discomfort associated with doing something different?*

Risking a rejection, Harriett tolerated her fear and reached for her husband.

Jake's responding hug felt familiar, safe, and secure.

Harriett hid her face in his chest and asked, "Jake, can you love me even if I'm not perfect?" She held her breath and worked hard to suspend judgment on the answer.

Jake seemed surprised by the question. He took a step backwards and gave her a puzzled look. "Perfect? Who ever said you were perfect?"

She stared back. "Isn't that what makes you love me?"

"No, Harriett, I love you for trying to be perfect."

A sigh preempted his next words and Harriett's heart lurched.

"But living up to your impossibly high standards has become too hard. I don't know what's changed, but lately I feel like all I do is fail. That's what made dying the eggs so enjoyable. Tonight was the first time in a long while that I felt like I was making you happy."

Harriett stood before her husband, speechless and immobilized by the fear of what might follow.

"I'm sorry I failed you so badly that you needed to come at me with a knife."

No mention of Julie, she chortled in silent celebration. Overwhelmed with relief, she chastised herself for being so foolish. *I should have checked out my assumption a long time ago! He's not having an affair! He's just tired of me wasting my energy trying to be perfect! That's something I know I can fix!*

Busy reveling, Harriett failed to notice Jake turn away. He was almost out the door before she realized that he was leaving.

"Where are you going?"

"I think I'll sleep in the guest bedroom tonight."

"But why?"

Jake turned and considered her question. He opened his mouth, closed it, shrugged his shoulders, and said he needed time alone with his thoughts. Without waiting for a response, he turned and disappeared through the door.

Harriett stared at the empty doorway in shocked bewilderment, not knowing what to think or what to do. However, she knew what she felt—helpless and...

Angry! Yes, damn it! I feel angry! I risked being vulnerable and this is what I get in return? I assumed Jake would be warm, comforting, and reassuring!

The word "ASS" kept flashing through her mind, fueling her anger, and tempting her to rush after Jake, yelling for him to make everything right.

"Whose behavior can you change?" Her counselor's voice asked the question, but it was Harriett who shouted an angry response, "Mine!"

She marched to the nightstand, determined to maintain a semblance of control. "I refuse to waste another ounce of energy on that man."

Intent on distracting herself away from her angry thoughts, Harriett picked up the phone and punched the keys. She paced around the room, impatiently waiting for someone to answer.

"Faye," she said, the moment she heard her sister's voice. "You said I could come to you if I needed anything and I need you to distract me from what I'd like to do to my husband!"

"Slow down! I can barely understand you," instructed Faye. "First of all, I'm glad you've finally realized that I'm more than a pretty face! And second, I'm glad you decided that talking to me is a whole lot safer than lunging after Jake!" Adopting a more serious tone, Faye asked, "How can I help?"

Afterwards, Harriett knew she'd made the right choice to confide in her sister. Sharing her fears about an affair and unburdening her misery felt good.

Tired and drained, she decided to go downstairs, make a cup of tea, and think about the options she'd discussed with Faye. She glanced down the hall at the guest bedroom's closed door and hesitated—*Do I dare?*

The hard work she'd done to control her emotions helped Harriett choose the wisest course of action. She continued down the stairs, promising to have a frank discussion with her counselor. *I've collected enough information to assess the current situation and I've determined it's intolerable!*

While her choice didn't obliterate the fear and anxiety, her feelings seemed less overwhelming.

As she sat at the kitchen table, drinking her tea, Harriett made another choice. *Realistically, I can't eradicate my anger at Jake, but I can use my anger as motivation to claw my way out of this predicament.*

She resolved to avoid wasting energy by dwelling and worrying over her husband's rejection. Instead, she vowed to stay firmly in the present until her next session with Dr. Aye, and renewed her commitment to her experiment.

When Harriett found herself stuck amongst a mass of vehicles, she chose to tolerate her annoyance over the construction of a new bridge that was creating a quagmire in Bayview's traffic. Instead, she distracted herself by surveying the reactions of the other drivers.

Shaking her head, she watched as one woman rolled down her window and shouted obscenities at the workers on the bridge.

"They'd better be careful. She looks ready to jump out of her car and pummel them with her handbag!" Inching her way to the traffic light, Harriett wondered how lunging after Jake was any worse than the woman's behavior.

She gave the steering wheel a sudden twist to the left. "To hell with what people think!" She turned into the parking lot of the local market. "There's no reason to sit in this traffic just so I can avoid a chance encounter in the grocery store!"

Harriett pulled the Jeep into an empty space, turned off the ignition, and boldly advanced towards the store's entrance. Halfway across the lot, she stopped. *I'm not wearing any makeup!*

Ambivalent, she weighed her options—retreat or persist onward.

"Tolerate, just tolerate," she chanted, and a different realization emerged—*Anyone I meet will just have to tolerate me!*

Defiant, Harriett continued moving forward; but, at the last minute, dug inside her purse for a pair of sunglasses. "Okay. I accept I'm not as courageous as I'd like to be *AND* I refuse to waste energy by running away!"

Harriett's foray into the world of productive energy continued during a shift at the food bank. Her love of volunteering was more comprehensible when considered within the context of Dr. Aye's explanation of needs.

To some extent, volunteering satisfies all my needs. My need to feel connected is satisfied because I'm able to be among people with similar altruistic values. The antics of both the volunteers and the patrons certainly satisfy my need for fun! Volunteering even satisfies my need for power and freedom. I get to use my organizational talents in ways that feel rewarding. Plus, I'm free to choose times that best suite my schedule.

Viewing volunteerism through a needs filter explained why the want to be a volunteer improved her quality of life. *It doesn't matter that others barely acknowledge my efforts, nor do I care that I don't receive a salary. My behavior is consistent with what I want—to make a difference in people's lives!*

Hanging her coat on the dilapidated coat rack, Harriett affirmed that she did make a difference. *Besides, I never worry about being perfect and don't go home dwelling on my mistakes. I just stay focused on what's important—the people I serve.*

So, when she found herself embroiled in a power struggle with another volunteer over the proper allotment of toilet paper, Harriett chose not to waste her energy trying to prove she was right and Eric was wrong. She stopped arguing, dropped the urge to explain why her way of thinking made more sense, and rolled out a new behavior—she laughed.

Eric scowled, flummoxed by her behavior.

"Eric, do you realize we're arguing over toilet paper? If the poor man needs an extra roll, I'll gladly spring for the cost!"

Disgruntled, Eric protested. "It's not about toilet paper, it's about policy!"

"I understand," she reassured. "And I appreciate your commitment to the food bank's financial needs." She continued in a tone oozing conspiracy, "Just this one time...," she stopped and pretended to scan the room looking for whistle-blowers. "Let's have a small revolt."

With a laugh, Eric tossed the man his extra roll of paper and, for a moment, the two volunteers shared a connectedness that Harriett found disturbing.

When was the last time I felt close to Jake? I spend so much time worrying over how to please my husband that I've forgotten how to laugh with my husband.

The thought made her sad, both for Jake and for herself.

Harriett left the food bank, motivated to continue practicing the skills and considered how to apply them to other areas of her life. The answer was obvious—*MOTHER!*

Too energized to wait until she got home, she pulled out her cell phone, intending to confirm the plans for Easter. She pushed the programmed code that automatically dialed her mother's number and was startled when her mother's face appeared in the phone's monitor. "Oh, that's right. Matt downloaded pictures to go with all the numbers in my phone. I guess the time's come to embrace the twenty-first century!"

The Friday morning before Easter, Harriett opened the garage door and backed the Jeep onto the driveway, determined to make the weekend work out the way she wanted. She reached up to adjust the rear view mirror and spoke directly to her reflection. "And that means using the skills to control your emotions, no matter what anyone does, thinks, or says!"

She'd arranged to drive to Boston, collect her mother, and bring her back to Rhode Island for the Easter weekend. Granddad would drive down on Saturday evening and then drive Mother home after Easter dinner.

Am I ready to spend so much time alone with Mother when our last encounter was a fiasco?

"Stop," she instructed and resolved to stay focused in the present. She leaned forward and tuned the radio to an FM station. Cruising down the highway, singing at the top of her lungs, Harriett became aware of the lyrics. *"As long as I know how to love, I know I'll stay alive. I will survive!"* Again, her favorite song provoked reflections...

Maybe I've become a little sidetracked, but I certainly know how to love and, for the most part, I like the way I behave.

It took her a moment to realize she'd used the Accept Doesn't Mean Agree skill. Instead of agitating over her inability to be perfect, she'd accepted her mistakes and used the resulting energy to validate her successes.

"Awesome," she affirmed, imitating the lingo of her kids' generation.

However, reconciling the mistakes caused by being a slave to her essence was difficult. *I hate to think I'm the reason Jake's become disengaged from our marriage or that Katie didn't enjoy her communion.*

Once again, her thoughts provoked a sadness that she worked hard to dispel. "Careful, Don't start chastising yourself for things you've done in the past. You can't change the past or worry about the consequences. What you *can* do is learn from the past and use the information in the present to figure out new ways to honor you essence. *And* that can start right here, right now! I'm a grown woman *and* I want to start behaving like one. I want to take responsibility for my situation *and* that means excuses are no longer an option! Stop wishing your problems away or waiting for someone else to fix them. Start fixing them for yourself!"

Harriett pressed a little harder on the car's accelerator.

Opening the sunroof, she felt the sun warming her face. Spring was in the air and the evidence lay in the budding landscape lining the road. Everywhere she looked, foliage was bursting with new growth. The cacophony of greens, pinks, and whites brought a sigh of pleasure to her lips. *The world's shedding the burden of winter and donning the silky lightness of a new summer frock!*

Harriett's feelings mirrored her thoughts.

"Is it possible," she wondered aloud, "that something as basic as self-evaluation and skills can make such a difference?"

She reached the split in the highway that forced her to choose between turning right into downtown Boston and left towards northern New England.

"That's not the only choice I have to make. I can continue wasting energy by doubting Dr. Aye's concepts or I can stay focused in the present and revel in my newfound energy."

The choice was obvious, as was Harriett's next revelation.

"I'm learning how to take responsibility for how I think, feel, and behave. Rather than insisting everyone play by my rules, I'm learning how to adapt to the situation in ways that make me feel good and in control. *That's* what it really means to accept even though I don't agree."

With dawning comprehension, she continued. "I don't have to succumb to panic whenever a situation isn't to my liking. Instead of wasting my energy panicking, I can use my energy productively by choosing behaviors that make the situation better suited to my needs!"

Harriett composed a buzz phrase to use whenever she heard the clanging of her frustration signal. "From now on, I'm going to chant—*The situation's not going to adapt to you, so figure out how to adapt to the situation!*"

Buoyed by a toolbox filled with skills, she turned right and gunned the car.

On the return trip to Rhode Island, Harriett used her energy to disarm her mother's attempts to pull her into the future, deflecting each "what if" with a preplanned response, "I understand, and I'm working hard to make things better."

"But, Harriett, I've tried to sit here and listen while you tell me about Jake being withdrawn and distant. You and I both know that's not like him. What if he wants a divorce?"

"I understand your concern, but I have no idea what Jake's behavior means, and I refuse to make an assumption. I intend to find out, and when I do, I'll accept the situation, even if I don't like what he says. Somehow, I'll find the energy to make everything work for my family. That's the best I can do."

"I'm sure this weekend's going to be quite awkward. When are you planning to speak with him?"

"Soon, Mother, soon." Stealing her next line from her sister,

Harriett said, "In the meantime, promise me you won't raise the topic or confiscate the knives."

"Harriett!"

She smiled at her mother's dismay, but chose to keep her fears about Julie to herself. *I'm certain no skill can fortify me with enough energy to withstand the onslaught of Mother's hysterics!*

Easter weekend past in a haze of uneventful interactions. Mother was on her best behavior, the kids talked in excited anticipation of the fun they hoped to have while on spring break, and Granddad sighed in contented pleasure when Harriett handed him a piece of lemon meringue pie. She'd been thinking about the recipe ever since she'd painted her picture of power for Dr. Aye.

Harriett especially savored the moment when Mother commented about the ham being "a bit saltier" than the usual brand.

Tolerating her irritation, Harriett replied, "I anticipated the ham being salty and used the sweetness of the baked apples to balance the flavors. I like how the combination works and plan to add the apples to my repertoire of recipes."

Even Jake seemed to shake himself out of his funk long enough to be a congenial host.

Maintaining a façade of normalcy was difficult, especially when Harriett revisited her thoughts about pleasing her husband. Studying Jake from across the table, she couldn't help but compare the feeling of connectedness she'd shared with Eric, to the remoteness that existed between her and Jake. *I've been so worried about pleasing Jake; I've never stopped to ask—when was the last time Jake seemed worried about pleasing me?*

Julie's face accompanied the thought, along with an intense anger. However, Harriett chose to behave wisely and opted for an unspoken truce for the remainder of the weekend.

I know I have to find another way to behave on my anger, but for now my best option is to tolerate the anger long enough to survive the weekend. Then I'll ask Dr. Aye to help me find a more productive way to cope with my anger...and with Julie!

The plan didn't dispel Harriett's anger or her fear, but knowing that the plan was her choice did mitigate some of the negative impact Jake's behavior had on her feelings.

In the quiet aftermath of a hectic weekend, Harriett evaluated the data collected from her experiment. "Using the skills makes me feel more confident and competent, but does that mean I'm ready to abandon my quest for perfection?"

Her answer was a resounding, "Yes!"

But..., was she ready to trust that people would love her despite her imperfections?

"I'm not as certain of that answer," she admitted.

Nonetheless, Harriett was ready to take a leap of faith in herself as well as with her counselor. *Facing my fear is the only way I can conquer my fear and the only way to face my fear is to change my behavior.*

Harriett smiled at the image of her and Dr. Aye holding hands while cliff diving off one of the cliffs that dotted the Narragansett coastline.

16

Skill #7
The Best Defense is a Good Offense

Harriett waited in eager anticipation for Dr. Aye's call into the office. *I can't believe I'm actually looking forward to today's session.*

Learning how to self-evaluate made it easier to understand why she'd found the initial sessions with Dr. Aye so threatening. *I was unaware of what I truly thought or felt, so how could I possibly feel comfortable sharing myself with another person. Self-evaluation helps me learn about myself and accept who I am.*

"Well, well," marveled Dr. Aye, "someone's been working hard."

The words filled Harriett with satisfaction.

I still want Dr. Aye to think of me as a worthy client. Only now, I've changed my behavior to get what I want. Instead of being perfect, I've learned that being an excellent client is how to make my counselor marvel. The best part is that being an excellent client makes the achievement of my power need so much easier—not easy, but certainly easier!

"I still think I'm climbing Mount Everest."

"How close are you to the summit?" asked Dr. Aye.

"I'd evaluate my progress to be about halfway."

"Based on what?"

"I know I'm more in control of my thoughts, feelings and behaviors; but, I wish the feelings were less conflicted. Part of me wants to continue

203

climbing and part of me is scared silly."

"What might be your greatest fear?"

"The unknown."

"Where are you living?"

Harriett sighed. "Is everything always related to self-evaluation and the skills?"

"Yes, and let's spend some time discussing how you can become even more proficient."

"Have I learned all the skills?"

"There are three more. However, we mustn't overlook the important data your hard work has yielded regarding some of the subtle aspects of skills training."

Harriett blushed, feeling foolish at the sense of pride evoked by the comment.

"Affirmations are responsible for the sense of pride your feeling," observed Dr. Aye. "When we affirm our hard work, we harness the energy derived from working hard."

"And use it as the wind required to set sail on the next adventure?" Harriett smirked at her wittiness.

"Oh, no," replied her counselor. "I hate when clients start interjecting their own metaphors!"

Dr. Aye exhaled an exaggerated sigh before asking, "Can you identify times in the past weeks where you've harnessed your energy by giving yourself an affirmation?"

Harriett rifled through her memory and found two. "When I marched out of Home Goods and when I settled on the off-brand of ham."

"You also awarded affirmations when you acknowledged how volunteering satisfies your needs and when you were singing the lyrics to your favorite song."

Harriett recalled how both instances made her feel energized and motivated.

"Affirmations promote a success identity because they validate and reinforce our productive use of energy," said Dr. Aye.

"Didn't you tell me a success identity occurs when we actively pursue what we want and focus on the behaviors that got us what we wanted?"

"Yes, and affirmations are the equivalent of focusing on the behavior—only affirmations include an added pat on the back!"

Harriett watched Dr. Aye settle into her chair, aware that her counselor's behavior was a prelude to another pearl of wisdom.

"A message often broadcasted throughout society is that celebrating success is egotistical and arrogant. Granted, arrogance does exist. However, most of us avoid being arrogant by minimizing our successes and amplifying our failures. Amplifying failure is wasted energy because there's no wind created for our sails to harness."

"Are you saying we should ignore our failures?"

"That would be irresponsible," chided Dr. Aye. "There's a wealth of information contained in failure, but focusing on our failures to the exclusion of our successes promotes a failure identity that makes us feel hopeless and powerless."

"Then how do we learn from our mistakes?"

"By acknowledging the failure, accepting the mistake (even if we don't agree), and suspending judgment long enough to self-evaluate both our behavior and the legitimacy of our wants. Then we use our energy to make the situation better."

Harriett thought the concept sounded similar to making lemonade from lemons and Dr. Aye's next words confirmed the thought.

"Our success identity grows stronger each time we take responsibility for our vulnerabilities and affirm our ability to change our behavior. Affirmations satisfy the need for achievement, and the resulting empowerment motivates us to continue working to get what we want."

"What you're saying is that, each time I affirm my choice to make lemonade, my success identity grows stronger," said Harriett. The source of her chronic frustration and fatigue became clearer. "I've spent most of my life identifying with failure rather than affirming my successes. You're saying I can feel better by making more lemonade."

"And savoring the taste," added Dr. Aye.

Holding her hands out in front of her body, Dr. Aye positioned her left hand lower than the right. "Let's use your analogy of a scale—when you first came to me, your scale was decidedly out of balance. Your failure identity outweighed your success identity and the repercussion was an energy drain."

Dr. Aye changed the position of her hands and made the left hand higher than the right. "You've begun adding weight to your success identity and the happy consequence is more energy."

Sitting back in her chair, Dr. Aye assigned some homework. "This week, I want you to grow your success identity. Whenever you experience a failure, use the Accept Doesn't Mean Agree skill to make the situation better. Then, consciously affirm your success."

Harriett evaluated other instances in the past weeks where she'd given herself an affirmation. "I remember affirming my behavior after Matt got up in time for school and again when I didn't run away from the nosy receptionist at the market. Both experiences made me feel successful."

She continued to hunt for other clues, and recalled last week's car ride home from Boston. "I knew I was using my energy productively when I stayed in the present and deflected my mother's worries. Does that constitute an affirmation?"

"Deflecting your mother's worries is the equivalent of setting a limit."

Recalling that, in a previous session, Dr. Aye had referenced setting a limit, Harriett asked, "Is that the seventh skill?"

"The Best Defense Is a Good Offense is a skill that sets limits on the impact another person's behavior has on your feelings. In sports, the best defenses appreciate how success hinges on defending the goal as well as creating offensive opportunities to score points. Football players think in terms of fumbles and interceptions, while soccer players focus on stealing the ball off the opponent's feet. The BDIO skill is especially useful when someone's behavior makes you feel defensive."

"What limit did I set on my mother?"

"What makes you ask?"

"Because I...," she began, but noticed the Cheshire-like grin on her counselor's face. "Hold on a minute! I'm not sure what you're up to, but I sure know that look on your face means I'm about to be hoodwinked!"

"Darn, I was all set to chortle," said Dr. Aye, her lips turned down in a sullen pout.

Adopting her more professional demeanor, Dr. Aye explained. "Posing the question, 'What makes you ask?' enables you to seize the offensive when you've been asked a question that makes you feel defensive. Responding with a question makes it possible to obtain more information regarding the intent of the other person's question."

"How is that setting a limit?"

"Knowing the intent behind the intrusive question allows you to formulate a response that puts you in control of the information you divulge. Being in control limits the impact the other person's behavior has on your feelings."

"Can you give me an example?"

"Your inclination's been to avoid chance meetings out of fear people will ask about the night you lunged. You're allowing others to control your feelings. Let's pretend the worst happens—a nosy neighbor corners you."

Dr. Aye devised a scenario and adopted a cheesy accent. "Hey, babe. Saw the cops bangin' on ya door the other PM. Waz up?"

"Uhm...what makes you ask?"

"Nuthin', just wunderin' what's the skinny?"

The role-play helped Harriett realize the usefulness of the BDIO skill. *Clarifying the subtext behind the question allows me to devise any number of obtuse responses.*

She looked down her nose and gave a haughty answer. "There is no, as you say, skinny. Everything is fine. Thank you for asking."

Dr. Aye clapped her hands. "Great come back! You set a limit on Mr. Nosy while behaving consistent with the messages you've heard about minding your manners."

Giggling just a little, Harriett agreed. "But what if the example were real?"

"What's your version of a real example?"

"My neighbor, Phil. He's a darling, but he's ordained himself as the mayor of the neighborhood. I can easily imagine his answer to the question would be that he's concerned."

"Then respond accordingly. Thank him for his concern and assure him there's no need to be concerned."

"I think I like this new skill!"

"What resonates?"

"I understand how the skill transitions me from emotional to wise mind because setting a limit will relieve some of the pressure I feel to explain myself. I especially like that I have a strategy to cope with the surprise I feel whenever someone poses an unexpectedly intrusive question. Countering with a question gives me extra time to regain my wits, and staying focused long enough to pay attention to the answer provides additional information. I remember what you said about knowledge being empowering."

Harriett leaned against the back of the loveseat, savoring the moment. *Despite the roller coaster ride and the question and answer ping-pong, this woman's helped me become optimistic about improving my quality of life.*

"What are you thinking?" Her counselor's voice was gentle.

"For the first time in a long while, things are beginning to make sense."

"How so?"

"Doing my best will always be an essential part of who I am. Yet, I understand the cost associated with my want to be perfect. Striving for perfection used to be motivating. Now it's a hindrance and I'm tired."

"Tired?"

"I'm tired of placing impossibly high standards on myself and others, and tired of being disappointed and frustrated when those standards aren't achieved or appreciated. I'm tired of overvaluing the opinions of others and, above all, I'm tired of judging myself critically. I'm never satisfied because nothing I do is ever good enough."

"So what do you want?"

"I want to strike a balance between doing my best and accepting my imperfections. I've had a taste of what I want over these past weeks. This weekend was an example and so was the garden club meeting. I want to strive for quality—that's less demoralizing than trying to be perfect. I'm tired of being ashamed because everything I do is wrong."

"Hold on. Who says you've been doing everything wrong?"

"If I'd been doing everything right, I wouldn't be in this situation."

"That's a little black and white."

"Pardon?"

"Thinking everything you do is either all right or all wrong is called All-or-Nothing thinking. All-or-Nothing thinking is based on a perception of the world as *either, or.* Either you're a winner *or* you're a loser. Either you cleaned the house *or* you didn't. There's no provisional, *but.*"

"But..."

Dr. Aye interrupted with a philosophical shrug. "I know, last week I talked about *yes, and.* If you remember, I also noted there's room in our vocabulary for *but. But* provides for the gray in life—you may have lost the battle *but* you won the war. You didn't clean the whole house *but* you cleaned the bathrooms."

Perplexed, Harriett tolerated the feeling and waited to hear more.

"All-or-Nothing thinking makes our failures seem catastrophic, which inevitably leads to feelings of shame. I urge my clients to invoke a do-over when they catch themselves involved in All-or-Nothing thinking."

"A do-over?"

"Have you ever seen *City Slickers*?"

"Isn't that a movie starring Billy Crystal?"

"Billy Crystal's friend is caught having an affair with an employee he worked with at his father-in-law's business. As a result, he loses the girl, his job, his wife, and his children. His life's in shambles and he's ashamed over how totally he failed. Crystal encourages his friend to invoke a do-over and reminds him of playing stickball as a boy. If a batter whiffed the ball, he'd ask for a do-over and got a second chance. Invoking a do-over is like a golfer asking for a mulligan."

Harriett appended her own interpretation. "*But* is the equivalent of giving myself permission to be imperfect. I see how combining the Accept Doesn't Mean Agree skill with a do-over gives me the ability to correct my mistakes."

"The only stipulation is to avoid using *but* as a convenient excuse for not taking responsibility for your mistakes."

"I understand. Using *but* as an excuse is blaming an external reason for my failure and abdicating responsibility for fixing the situation."

Harriett fidgeted in her seat, eager to implement these newfound strategies. "I always think I've mishandled a situation with the kids and then become critical of my ineffectiveness. Instead, I can invoke a do-over as the new behavior to roll out after using the Stop, Drop, and Roll skill! In fact, my options for using these strategies seem endless!"

"The only thing that limits our options is the creativity of wise mind," reminded Dr. Aye. "That's why I don't care what skill you use to transition from emotional mind into wise mind..."

"...only that I use a skill," finished Harriett.

The ensuing silence prompted Dr. Aye to ask, "How are you doing?"

Putting her hand up as Harriett started to respond, she emphasized her question. "I mean how are you *really* doing?"

Was this the time to confess her fears—her fear of being unloved and unwanted...the fear that her illusion of happiness was shattered...the fear that, no matter how hard she worked, life as she knew it was gone?

Harriett studied the woman she'd grown to rely upon as her voice of reason. *How did it happen? A short time ago, I didn't even know her name and now I'm about to trust her with my biggest fears.*

Taking a deep breath, she began...

Afterwards, Dr. Aye sat in thoughtful silence before responding with a soft, "Thank you."

Harriett sniffed into a tissue. "For what?"

"For being brave enough to take a risk."

"What risk?"

"The risk of making yourself vulnerable."

"Vulnerable is a good word for how I feel." She sighed and wiped her tears.

"Feeling vulnerable is terribly unsettling and most of us work hard to avoid the feeling—either by denying, ignoring, minimizing, or perhaps rationalizing the elephant in the room."

Dr. Aye offered her client a gentle smile. "How's that been working for you?"

Harriett shrugged her shoulders. "Not good."

"Would you like to do something else?" Dr. Aye asked, prodding her client to self-evaluate.

"You mean change my behavior? Of course, but how?"

"The same way you've been changing your behavior since we met."

"By using the skills?"

"I mean by using the skills to control your emotions long enough to choose one wise behavior at a time. You did that just now. You accepted the situation instead of wasting energy by resisting, ignoring, or minimizing the elephant in the room. You chose to use your energy more productively by tolerating your vulnerability long enough to risk voicing your fears."

Harriett sank into the loveseat, studied the picture of the swans, and mentally evaluated the concepts she'd come to regard as her lifeline to sanity. *Perhaps I should consider them my recipe for a quality life.*

Looking back at Dr. Aye, she shared the outcome of her self-evaluation. "Voicing my fears required all the skills in my toolbox. However, the one that resonates most is Stop, Drop, and Roll. I stopped what I was doing—ignoring the elephant in the room. I dropped the urge to protect myself from being vulnerable, and rolled out a new behavior—I took a risk and revealed my greatest fear."

"What made you take the risk?"

Harriett turned her thoughts inward. *Was it because ignoring my fear was no longer tolerable? Or, has practicing the skills given me enough energy to face my fear? Perhaps I've developed a clearer picture of what I want and the skills give me the confidence to achieve it.*

Concluding her self-evaluation, Harriett told Dr. Aye what she'd learned. "The picture of what I want is getting clearer, so taking the risk with you didn't feel so daunting. However, the picture's still fuzzy and I think that's what keeps me in a state of ambivalence regarding Jake."

"I have a strategy for coping with ambivalence that's actually an extrapolation of the Tolerate skill," replied Dr. Aye.

"As we've discussed, there is no perfect situation. This means that all situations contain pros and cons. Cons are what provoke negative feelings, including ambivalence. The best way to cope with ambivalence is to create a list of pros and cons."

"But, a list of pros and cons is so rational when..." Harriett stopped, remembering her reaction to the mechanized list of distracting behaviors. "I don't know how it applies to ambivalence, but I do know the goal of everything you teach me is the same."

"Which is?"

"To validate the feeling and then find a way to transition from emotional mind into wise mind."

"Nicely phrased," said Dr. Aye. "My version of a pros and cons list is a little different from the norm."

"What else is new?" Harriett muttered the words under her breath.

"I heard that!"

"You were meant to!"

"I'll choose to tolerate your sarcasm long enough to teach you how to create *my* version of a pros and cons," countered Dr. Aye. "First, list all the behavioral options associated with attaining what you want. Then, create a conventional list of the pros and cons attached to each option and select the option that has the most pros."

"Yes, but...," interrupted Harriett.

"Let me finish and then you can *but* me to death," admonished Dr. Aye. "Next, assign an emotional value to each of the pros and cons associated with the option."

"An emotional value?"

"Each pro receives an emotional value of zero, one, two, or three, based on the degree of positive emotion derived from making the choice. Zero being neutral and three being really, really, really, positive. Then, do the same for each con. Zero being neutral and three being really, really, really, negative. Add up the values. If the pro value adds up to more than the con value, you're almost done."

"Almost? You need a degree in math to use this strategy!"

"Conducting an emotional pros and cons is easier than it sounds and the value gained from the exercise is immeasurable," assured her counselor.

"The final step is to focus on the emotional cons and ask a self-evaluation question—'Can I tolerate the negative emotional cost associated with this choice?'"

"How does that help?"

"Doing an emotional pros and cons clarifies your thoughts and gauges your capacity to tolerate the consequences. If you can tolerate the cons, make the choice. If you can't, then you have two options—either make a different choice or revisit the pictures inside your head. Perhaps they're not really what you want."

"This is so much more than a strategy. It's an approach to life!"

Dr. Aye raised her eyebrows. "I seem to recall telling you that self-evaluation and skills lead to a quality life."

Harriett laughed. "I didn't really believe you."

Dr. Aye concluded the session with a review. "Today I've taught you about affirmations and the BDIO skill. I've also given you three coping strategies: When your thinking becomes black and white, invoke *but;* when you think you've failed, call a do-over; when you're feeling ambivalent, create an emotional pros and cons."

"Any questions?" asked Dr. Aye.

"No *and* I think I'll try..." Harriett quickly amended the statement. "I *will* make a pros and cons regarding the choice to confront Jake."

The picture of Atlas popped into her mind. "The time's come to give Atlas some muscle and that means bulking up my success identity!"

"Good luck."

"Thanks, I'll need it."

Once again, Dr. Aye had the last word—"Good luck requires making good choices."

17

Harnessing Energy

Harriett left the session still ambivalent, but motivated to use what she'd learned. Midway to the car, she realized—*I just used the provisional "but"!*

She stood in place, assessing the effect on her feelings. *Does my ambivalence seem less catastrophic?*

Giving the question a thorough evaluation, she pronounced, "Yes!"

As she made her way towards the Jeep, she focused on the source of her ambivalence—Brenda. *I've been adrift in a sea of ambivalence ever since Brenda's inane question!*

Harriett's feelings morphed into an anger that made her want to throttle her friend.

Wisely, she used the provisional "but" to temper the thought. *Brenda's insinuation may have been the tipping point, but I was well on my way to losing it prior to her comment.*

Invoking the provisional "but" stopped Harriett from using her friend's comment as an excuse for lunging at Jake. *I'm the one responsible for losing it AND I'm the one responsible for fixing what I broke.*

While she managed to accept the first half of the thought, the second part rekindled her ambivalence. *But, what do I want to fix and how do I want to fix it? There are times when I feel a slight gust of wind making my sail flutter and other times when the air feels dank and heavy.*

' Harriett chose to focus on the wind, realizing each gust was the result of using a skill. *This week, I'm going to dedicate myself to harnessing as much energy as I can, AND start taking responsibility for turning my sails in the direction I want to go.*

She dug the keys out of her bag, pressed the remote's unlock button, and opened the car door. Swinging her legs into the Jeep, Harriett recalled something else about the day's session—"*AND,* as I feel my boat cutting through the water, I'll affirm my success!"

She smiled, certain the pithy water analogy was a consequence of her counselor's sardonic humor.

Infused with determination, Harriett started the car and headed for the gym to renew her lapsed membership. She'd decided the tightening of her waistband was more uncomfortable than the discomfort associated with worrying over who she might encounter on the elliptical.

"I suppose I could equate the skills to a workout. Like the skills, each fitness machine serves a specific purpose and I have to choose which machine to use and how much effort to exert. Choosing the wrong machine or expending too little effort won't get me what I want."

The fitness machine analogy caused her to recollect a conversation with Diane, one of the trainer's at the gym. "Diane says consistency and perseverance increase my level of conditioning, which makes me capable of training even harder. I guess that makes Dr. Aye's skills a fitness machine for the mind!"

Harriett imagined her counselor dressed in gym clothes, issuing the same edict Diane often commanded—"Get comfortable with being uncomfortable!"

"At this rate, I'll be in shape to run in next year's Boston marathon!" The words made her gasp. *When was the last time I looked into the future without staring into an abyss? Is it possible that I'm actually optimistic about the future?*

A burgeoning sense of empowerment accompanied her thoughts.

She arrived at the gym, but an unexpected flood had closed the facility. Disappointed, she decided to tolerate the feeling long enough to consider other ways to get a workout. She chose to capitalize on the sun-filled afternoon, went home, and found her running shoes.

Turning left out of the neighborhood, Harriett made her way to the bike path, a fourteen-mile stretch of asphalt that meandered from Providence down to the water at Bristol harbor. The serene beauty of Rhode Island's coves, marshes, and bridges lifted her spirits and added an extra bounce to her step. She divided her energy between maintaining an even rhythm and reflecting on the past weeks.

There's such a difference between reflecting and dwelling. Dwelling makes me feel beat up and demoralized. Reflecting helps me identify the potential hazards to avoid.

She sidestepped a pothole created by the frigid New England winter and smiled as another analogy entered her mind. *The difference between dwelling and reflecting is like traveling down a road filled with potholes. Complaining about the unexpected jarring is valid if I don't know the pothole exists. However, if I continue to ride over the same hole, experience the same annoyance and do nothing, then I have no one to blame but myself. I'm responsible for learning the terrain, identifying the impediments, and choosing to steer clear of the hazard; or I can decide to fix the hazard. Either way the choice is mine.*

Harriett chuckled at her ability to gain insight from everyday life.

A sudden realization startled her out of her complacency. The bike path was a popular route for runners and jogging on it meant potentially running (literally) into people she knew! In a flash, Harriett's feelings changed. Instead of feeling empowered, she felt exposed and vulnerable; and the irregular cadence of her feet expressed the hesitancy in her mind. *Should I turn around?*

Even as she wondered, Harriett knew to tolerate her concern long enough to conduct an emotional pros and cons. "There's only one choice," she concluded. She quickened her pace and surged forward.

My days of hiding are over!

Her stride lengthened...

I know how to accept my situation and tolerate my discomfort!

The tempo of her steps increased...

I know how to spell assume and refuse to be an ass by not suspending judgment and paying attention to the facts!

Rather than worrying over who she might see, Harriett kept herself in the present by focusing on her splits from mile to mile, intent on achieving a personal best, and employed Stop, Drop, and Roll to nod politely at acquaintances she met on the path.

Breathing heavily, she turned towards home, planning ways to complete the week's homework assignment. *I intend to condition my mind as thoroughly as I train the rest of my body!*

Harriett challenged herself to conduct an emotional pros and cons as it related to confronting Jake. She placed a three in the pros column when she realized that facing her fear would certainly be a relief because at least she'd know where she stood with Jake. Uncertain she could tolerate the pain associated with hearing that her husband no longer loved her; Harriett neutralized the positive value by placing a three in the cons column.

"Great, what happens if I do the exercise and there's no definitive outcome?"

The question made her realize that her focus was on the wrong want. "The choice isn't about confronting Jake. What I want is to break free of this morass of indecision, so the question to ask is—do the pros of moving into the future unencumbered by doubt and worry outweigh the cons of living life stuck in a state of uncertainty?"

Harriett knew Dr. Aye would endorse the choice that fueled the least discomfort.

"I'm beginning to think the pain of knowing would be more tolerable than the pain of not knowing."

Harriett experienced a wave of panic.

Paying attention to her frustration signal, she chose to discontinue her evaluation and distracted herself by focusing on her cool-down. She placed her hands on her hips and transitioned into a comfortable walk. By the time she turned right into her neighborhood, she was relaxed and breathing easily.

Keeping herself in the present, she planned the evening's activities. *After dinner, I want to make phone calls on behalf of the garden club and talk with Matt about the meeting with his advisor to discuss college visits. I can't believe his high school experience is almost over. How fast these years have flown.*

Harriett felt a pang of regret when she realized she'd hastened their passing by worrying about the future. *That's the best reason to use the Where R U Living skill. I get to savor the sweetness of the moment.*

The thought filled her with gratitude and reminded her of the plaque adorning her counselor's bookcase—*Be here, now.*

"From now on, I intend to work hard at living in the here and now. That's a significantly better choice than regretting the past or worrying about the future."

Harriett turned her attention to a regret born from her self-imposed exile. One of her favorite rites of spring was hosting a "Welcome Spring" cocktail party. She loved the way everyone arrived in their bulkiest winter gear and shed layers of clothing throughout the night. She smiled at the image of how the room looked at the end of the evening, crowded with laughing people adorned in brightly colored Hawaiian shirts and sundresses. Sadly, this year's party never occurred.

I refuse to let regret dampen my spirits!

She decided to deviate from tradition by having a "Welcome Summer" cookout on Memorial Day. Intent on making lemonade from lemons, the sound of a familiar voice caught Harriett by surprise.

"Harriett! Hello there!"

A pit formed inside her belly. *Oh, no, Phil! Just what I didn't want!*

Her mind propelled her backwards to their last meeting—the morning of the lunge. Phil embodied all that had gone wrong over the last weeks. Instead of feeling empowered, Harriett felt trapped and defenseless. She began to panic.

WARNING! WARNING! Panic is your frustration signal. PAY ATTENTION! Find a skill and find it NOW!

From somewhere deep within the recesses of her mind, Harriett recalled her newest skill. *Am I capable of using BDIO with Phil?*

Asking the self-evaluation question did little to assuage her panic. *What's the worst that could happen?*

A scenario of disasters danced in front of her eyes.

Biting her bottom lip, she assessed her options, then gritted her teeth in the same way she'd gritted them on the night she lunged. However, instead of ignoring her feelings, Harriett wisely acknowledged her panic, tolerated her fear, and changed her behavior. She forged onward...

"Hi, Phil." The wariness in her voice was reminiscent of how she'd greeted Phil on that fateful day—thin, small, and helpless.

Time to bulk up, she instructed, refusing to remain a ninety-eight-pound weakling.

Determined to persevere, a steely resilience underscored her next words. "Long time no see. How are you and Mildred?"

"Oh, we're getting by. Mildred was just saying she missed you at the last book club. We've been worried about you..." Phil's voice faded in volume, implying he expected Harriett to provide evidence that his worry was valid.

She shrugged and set a limit. "No need to worry." Intent on maintaining the offensive, Harriett followed-up with a question, "What's new with you?"

"I've been trying to organize a group to spruce up the entrance into the neighborhood."

No, Phil, Harriett silently corrected. *Do or do not...there is no try.*

"There was an implied covenant among the original homeowners to maintain the common areas, but that agreement's been voided." A dour, lawyerly expression accompanied Phil's comment. He stared down his nose and fixed a judgmental gaze upon Harriett.

She grabbed the opportunity to change her behavior. Rather than cringe in shame, her eyes twinkled in anticipation. "Phil, you're such a dear—always looking out for the neighborhood's best interest. I appreciate your concern. What can I do to help?"

Phil backed down, nonplussed by the offer. "Nothing, I suppose.

I'm just glad you understand about property values."

"I do," reassured Harriett, somewhat tongue-in-cheek. "Our homes represent a significant investment in our retirement." Setting a limit on Phil's fretting without alienating his friendship felt empowering.

Unfortunately, Phil misinterpreted her kindliness as an invitation to intrude. "I never got around to asking what actually went on at your house last month. Is everything back to normal?"

Normal? Harriett asked herself. *I might be uncertain of what I want, but I definitely don't want normal!*

"What makes you ask?" The question rolled off her tongue and she silently acknowledged how Dr. Aye's role-play had prepared her to seize the offensive.

Consternation clouded Phil's face. "I just thought there might be something you needed us to do."

The unobtrusiveness of his response confirmed Harriett's assumption. *The poor man might be a bit nosy, but he isn't an ogre.*

She smiled benevolently. "Thank you, Phil. I can always count on you and Mildred. Everything is fine." However, she caved to the pressure she felt to elaborate. "Jake and I just had a misunderstanding. All is well." She politely extricated herself from the conversation and waved as Phil turned and walked up his driveway.

Harriett released an exasperated breath. "Gosh darn it! Why did I have to add that sentence about Jake and I having a misunderstanding? I always get it wrong!"

"Always?" Dr. Aye's voice challenged.

Harriett revised the statement. "I may not have handled myself perfectly, *BUT* I definitely handled that encounter better than the last time *AND* I like the feeling!"

The affirmation made her realize how far she'd traveled, and confirmed that she was no longer on a journey to nowhere.

Feeling successful and empowered, she crooned, "I think I'm ready to confront Jake!"

Sadly, the celebratory mood fizzled the moment Harriett stepped inside the house and found Katie waiting to pounce. *Guess I'm going for another ride on the emotional roller coaster.*

Confused, she asked, "What's going on?"

"Oh, Mom! You've got to talk to Dad!"

Harriett struggled to comprehend the source of Katie's distress. *What's she talking about? Is Jake home? I didn't expect him for at least another hour. Maybe she wants me to call him at the office.*

Puzzled, she repeated, "Why? What's going on?"

"He came home in a horrible mood, saying he's too busy to drive me and my friends to the concert tomorrow night. But he promised!" Katie's wailing continued. "And now it's too late to make other plans!"

Harriett's reaction was immediate and instinctive. *Busy doing what with whom?* Her stomach churned with anger. "Damn it, Katie! For once I'd like to walk into this house and be treated in a civil manner rather than as a referee!"

Katie reared back, shocked by the vehemence in her mother's response.

Harriett paid attention long enough to pause and think more reasonably. *Hold on, I'm not as mad at Katie as I am with Jake. So stop acting emotionally and start behaving wisely.*

Obeying her edict, Harriett used Stop, Drop, and Roll to control her anger, and invoked a silent chant. *The situation's not going to adapt to you, so figure out how to adapt to the situation.*

Rubbing her hand across her forehead, she closed her eyes and took a deep breath, hoping to clear away some of the confusion. Then, Harriett enacted a do-over.

"Katie, I'm sorry for snapping. Of course you're disappointed that Dad reneged on his promise." Validating her daughter's feelings planted Harriett firmly in wise mind. "What have you done to fix the situation?"

The question implied that Katie was responsible for fixing her problems rather than running to her mother in helpless frustration.

"What do you mean? How can I fix what he broke?"

Harriett flinched, recalling how she'd used the exact words in her recent past. "Just because you're disappointed doesn't mean your world is coming to an end."

Katie's eyes filled with tears of frustration, helplessness, and despair. "Yes, it is."

Harriett found herself at another crossroads. *The old version of Harriett would rush to fix Katie's problem, but I think I'm ready for an upgrade!*

Tolerating the urge to rectify the situation, she devised another self-evaluation question. "Even if your world is coming to an end, what are you going to do?"

"Huh?" Katie asked in confusion. "Why can't you just go make Dad honor his promise? That's what you would do if I broke a promise!"

"No," Harriett corrected. "I would help you to see the importance of honoring your promise."

"So go make Dad see that!"

"Sweetheart, that's your job. Not mine."

Katie protested with typical adolescent petulance, "But, I tried!"

"How? By wailing, yelling, and crying?"

"It didn't work," she muttered.

"What else can you do?"

"Nothing."

"I disagree and can even think of a few options. Have you asked what's stopping Dad from honoring his promise?"

"He's just mean."

"That might be," agreed Harriett. "But until you check it out, you're working on an assumption. If you're going to be upset, at least be upset for the right reason. How about we go find your father and see what he has to say?"

Confused, Katie followed Harriett into the study where they found Jake hunched over his laptop. He looked up and began shouting, "Don't start with me, Harriett. I'm sick and tired of being everyone's lackey. The only reason Katie's upset is because I refuse to be her goddamned chauffer!"

His yelling escalated Katie's frustration, which increased the intensity of the conflict.

Harriett stood silently as her husband and daughter went nose to nose. At a loggerhead, they both turned, each expecting her to take their side. Exasperated, she succumbed to the urge to act as referee. "Look, you two," she began. A small voice advised her to close her mouth. She obeyed and chose to tolerate both her desire to find a perfect solution and the urge to be responsible for her family's feelings. "I suggest you stop focusing on how mad you are at each other and start working out a compromise. I have faith in the two of you. I know you'll work things out."

She left the room, gave Matt money to order a pizza for dinner, and told him she was going upstairs and didn't want to be disturbed.

Alone in the bedroom, she worked hard to resist the urge to peek downstairs and assess the damage. She remained resolute, showered, and distracted by watching Dr. Phil ask people, "How's that working for you?"

Vacillating between affirming her success at not becoming a referee and worrying over leaving her family to fend for itself, she answered, "I don't know."

Needless to say, she was relieved and somewhat amazed when Katie flounced into the bedroom, announcing she and Jake had devised a plan. "No thanks to you," her daughter added.

Harriett tolerated the sullenness of Katie's tone long enough to respond with a cheery, "Good job!" and smiled as Katie stomped out the room.

Harriett affirmed the outcome with a congratulatory thought. *Now that's progress!*

Once again, her victory was short-lived. Jake entered the room and the angry look on his face made her feelings plummet.

"Hey, what was that all about?" he growled, accusing her of ignoring the problem and dumping it on him. "How would you like if I chucked everything away and made you take care of the problem?"

Jake's choice of words made Harriett nervous. *Is he threatening to chuck away his life and go running to Julie?*

Wisely, she stayed focused in the moment. "No, Jake," she quietly corrected. "I didn't ignore the problem. I just didn't make a problem you created, my problem."

"How's that any different from ignoring?"

The insolence in Jake's voice was agitating and Harriett suspected he was provoking a fight. Again, she behaved wisely and offered a calm reply. "The difference is that I'm learning to use my energy more productively. Instead of trying to fix everyone's problems, I'm working to give everyone in this family the space required to fix their own problems."

"Did you learn that psychobabble from your shrink?"

Her husband's derisive tone tested her resolve; but once more, she chose wisely. "What I said isn't psychobabble. It's how I intend to manage my life from now on. I want to use my energy in ways that contribute quality to this family. I'm tired of wasting my time trying to do everything perfectly, only to find that I've achieved nothing but frustration."

Jake stared at her in stony silence, his arms folded. Harriett misconstrued his silence and assumed he was listening.

"Look, Jake," she began. "Every time I try to fix a situation by finding the perfect solution, I rob everyone around me of the confidence they need to fix the problem themselves and that's not fair. All that does is make you and everyone else dependent on me for the answers and it's silly for me to think my way is the only right way. That's why I've been so stressed these past months. Trying to make everything perfect is too draining. Besides, it's unrealistic. You said so the other night. I need to take care of myself. The only problems I can fix are my own."

"Your problems! What problems do you have? You have the perfect life! I work my butt off providing for you and making sure the kids have everything they need. Now you want me to be responsible for fixing this family's problems? Talk about stress! I'm the one with all the stress. Talk about needs? I'm the one whose needs aren't being met!" Jake's flushed face and labored breathing emphasized his stinging words.

Besieged with panic, Harriet's first instinct was to retreat, but somehow she tolerated her panic long enough to ask herself a self-evaluation question—*Do I have the gumption to confront him about Julie?*

Even as her mouth opened, Harriett knew she'd made the wrong choice. "Please, Jake. Can we just agree to end this conversation before we both say something we'll regret?"

Jake lobed his last volley as he turned and walked out the door. "Or what, you'll come at me with another knife?"

Jake's outburst left her feeling shaken and angry, both with Jake and with herself.

Harriett's feelings epitomized the concept of transience. One minute she'd been riding a wave of success and now she felt caught in the riptide. Her energy sapped, she sought the safety of her bed, slipped under the sheets, and lay there dwelling.

"Stupid...stupid...stupid," she repeated over and over. "How could I be so stupid to think Dr. Aye and her infamous skills would make everything better?"

Feeling tired and listless, she flopped from one side of the bed to the other, unable to find comfort. Her stomach clutched at the sound of Jake's footsteps reentering the room.

"Harriett?" Jake whispered.

She buried her face in the pillow and willed herself to be still.

"Please, honey. We can't keep sniping at each other. We need to talk."

Her body quivered. *Oh no, I've driven him to the breaking point! He's leaving me!*

Resigned, she turned to hear the word's she'd been dreading.

Jake held out a tray, his face contrite. "I brought you a cup of tea and a slice of pizza. You didn't eat any dinner. I thought you might be hungry."

She hesitated, unsure of her next move. "Thank you. Put them on the night table."

After doing as she requested, Jake gingerly positioned himself on the edge of the bed. "Look, Harriett, I'm sorry."

Her husband's tone was brusque and Harriett steeled herself for the bad news.

"I found out today that I have to go out of town for a deposition and I'll be gone most of the week. I knew I'd have to fix things with Katie and her friends, but I guess I'm tired and overwhelmed by work and just started yelling. You walking out on the situation didn't help. That's not how we've worked in the past and, if you want to change the rules, at least have the courtesy to give me a heads up."

Jake's words added guilt to her conundrum of emotions.

"I'm sorry, too," she murmured. "I've been on a roller coaster of emotion ever since..." Her words fell off, uncertain how to complete the sentence. *Should I seize the offensive and talk about the affair before he brings it up?* "...I started seeing Dr. Aye," she finished.

"I know I pushed you into seeing her and maybe that was a mistake," said Jake.

"Yes, and I was mad when you did. In retrospect, I think I was on the verge of realizing that I needed to change what I was doing. Only, maybe I changed too much too fast. It wasn't fair to leave you alone with Katie. We both know she's like a dog with a bone when she thinks we've been unfair."

Jake searched for her hand and gave a gentle squeeze. "You don't have to keep seeing Dr. Aye if you don't want to."

Her reaction surprised them both. "No, what I'm learning is important, not just for now, but for the future." A silent, *whatever that means,* completed the sentence.

Jake cleared his throat.

Harriett held her breath.

"I mean it," he reiterated. "I'm sorry for getting so upset." He gave her hand another squeeze and remained quiet.

Surprised by the reprieve, she wondered, *Is that all?* Despite her relief, she remained ambivalent. *Should I risk inserting Julie into the conversation?*

Knowing she didn't have the energy to sustain another firestorm, Harriett chose to accept her husband's apology without question or comment. She moved over and invited him into the bed. They lay beside each other, not quite touching, each lost in their own thoughts.

Sooner or later, one of us is going to have to come clean. There's definitely something going on with Jake; and if it's not Julie, then I want to know what's got him so riled up. One thing's certain—the longer I wait for him to confess, the longer I'll stay mired in worry, hoping for the answers I want to hear.

Allowing Jake to control her feelings was becoming intolerable. *I'm not sure when, but I'm getting close to taking matters into my own hands!*

Jake's absence throughout the week gave Harriett the space she needed to collect her thoughts. She offered a silent mea culpa to her counselor and renewed her commitment to condition her mind. She spent the time practicing skills and making wise choices. Each night, she reviewed the day and affirmed her successes.

She fell asleep mouthing the lyrics originally sung by Bing Crosby. *"If you're worried and you can't sleep, just count your blessings instead of sheep, and you'll fall asleep counting your blessings."*

Harriett chose to think of affirmations as blessings—both resulted in good consequences.

Acknowledging what I do right is more invigorating than beating myself up for what I do wrong. Besides, paying attention to my successes provides data I can use to correct my "faux pas." The word sounded less threatening compared to "failure" and helped her keep her mistakes in perspective.

Alone in the kitchen, washing dishes, and waiting for Jake's return, Harriett realized the time for reckoning was fast approaching. "Am I ready?" she asked out loud.

"Ready for what?"

The unexpectedness of her son's voice made her jump. "Pardon?"

"Ready for what?" Matt repeated, opening the fridge and pulling out a container of leftovers.

Harriett smiled. "Didn't you just finish dinner?"

Matt flashed an impish grin, "Yeah, but I was upstairs and the baked macaroni kept calling."

He looks so much like his father, she thought and her heart ached. She turned away before her son could see her tears, but she was too late.

Concerned, he asked, "What's up?"

"Oh, nothing," she lied, wiping her eyes with the back of her hand. "I was just thinking how much like your father you look and that soon you'll be a man with your own wife and family."

"Geez, Mom! At least let me graduate high school!" He threw the empty container into the sink, gave his mother a quick kiss on the cheek and disappeared up the stairs.

Despite everything, Jake and I have raised two pretty special kids. I'll be damned if I'm going to let anyone, including Julie, deprive them of their happiness! I need to channel as much energy as possible so that I can protect them.

Harriett devised a new strategy for harnessing her energy. *I think I'll associate energy with a savings account. Whenever I behave wisely, I'll bank the energy and watch the balance grow. I'll adopt Granddad's puritan ethics by being stingy over withdrawals made by acting emotionally. Hopefully, I'll accrue enough savings to splurge on a major purchase, like buying some piece of mind!*

She gulped, uncertain of the cost associated with her purchase.

"Why," she wondered aloud, "can I generalize the skills to more and more areas of my life, but still cannot use them to confront Jake?"

Her response felt seamless. "That's the wrong question. What stops me from confronting Jake?"

Rephrasing the question really didn't matter because the answer was always the same, "Fear."

Aware that her fear had become annoyingly irrational didn't mitigate her paralysis. *Maybe Dr. Aye's last two skills will help dispel my fear...*

18

Skill #8
Flip It!

Harriett began the week's session by asking the same question she'd asked while at the kitchen sink, "What stops me from confronting Jake when I'm able to generalize the skills to more and more areas of my life?"

"You know the answer," replied Dr. Aye.

Agitated and in no mood for question and answer ping-pong, she rebutted, "I know the answer is fear. It's always fear! I want to know what I'm afraid of!"

"The source of fear typically involves the worry of incurring an injury."

"But, we've had this discussion. I'm not afraid of Jake hurting me!"

"Maybe not physically, but what about emotionally?"

Harriett recalled how Jake ridiculed the importance of her problems. "Are you talking about verbal abuse?"

"No, although verbal abuse is as serious an injury as physical abuse because both are forms of aggressive behavior." The seriousness of Dr. Aye's tone emphasized the importance of her words.

"The type of injury I'm referring to is the damage done to your self-esteem whenever someone does something that hurts your feelings. As emotional beings, we're always vulnerable to our feelings being hurt and that's what makes us fearful. Unfortunately, there's a risk of injury associated with playing any game, including the game of life."

"Are you saying I'm afraid of confronting Jake because I'm afraid of being hurt?" Even as she asked, Harriett knew the answer.

"How much risk are you willing to incur by confronting Jake?"

"I'm not sure."

"That's because you're worried about protecting your self-esteem."

"*That's* stating the obvious."

"Well, *that's* good, because you know me well enough to anticipate the next question."

Harriett's brow furrowed in concentration but a moment later, her face brightened. "Where am I living?"

Dr. Aye nodded. "What's the point?"

"If I'm worrying about protecting my self-esteem, I'm living in the future when the only place I have control is in the present."

"In any sport, worrying about an injury inhibits the ability to play a quality game. A distinguishing characteristic among world-class athletes is their mental toughness—having an unshakable belief in their ability to win and the capacity to block out what's not important, including the worry of an injury."

"Think of yourself as a world-class athlete," counseled Dr. Aye. "Keep yourself mentally tough by blocking out the worry that your feelings might be hurt. Instead, accept that being human makes you vulnerable to injury."

"It sounds like being mentally tough contains an element of the Accept Doesn't Mean Agree skill," said Harriett.

"Mentally tough athletes accept that injuries are part of playing the game and focus on being conditioned enough to recover, should an injury occur. When my son tore his ACL, the strength of the surrounding muscles facilitated his recovery. The injury was a risk of playing the game, but my son's constant attention to conditioning was a vital factor in the speed of his recovery. Don't waste your energy worrying about an injury," suggested Dr. Aye. "Focus on keeping your mind in tiptop condition so that you're strong enough to recover quickly."

Harriett recalled her pledge to condition her mind as hard as she conditioned her body. *When I use the skills, I'm conditioning my mind and increasing its ability to cope with an unexpected injury.*

She devised her own analogy. "Mental toughness is like riding a bike."

"Meaning?"

"When the kids were little and fell off their bikes, I assessed the injury and encouraged them to get back on the bike. My feelings might be injured, but resuming the skills as quickly as possible is the equivalent of getting back on the bike."

"How might you substitute the concepts of failure identity and success identity to paraphrase this conversation?"

"Focusing on the injury fosters a failure identity and focusing on the recovery promotes a success identity," replied Harriett, surprised at how quickly she comprehended the answer.

"Which is a more productive use of energy?" asked Dr. Aye.

"But focusing on the recovery is hard. I'm sure your son would agree."

"Do I care?"

"No," she grumbled, reminded of the image of Dr. Aye dressed in workout garb. "You only care that I change my behavior."

"To what?"

"To one that stands a higher likelihood of getting me what I want."

Harriett paused, thinking about her reaction to Phil's reference to normal. "I know I have a clearer picture of how to control my perfectionism long enough to be comfortable with excellence. I also know I don't want the life I had prior to learning about self-evaluation and the skills. But, as it pertains to Jake, I still don't know what I want."

Familiar feelings of frustration and dejection surfaced, and her body slumped against the back of the loveseat.

"So flip it," said Dr. Aye. Watching the look on her client's face turn from dejection to consternation, she asked, "Are you ready for another workout?"

Caught between uncertainty and fear of the unknown, Harriett wondered if she'd hit the same wall athletes face when they run out of steam. "Do I have a choice?" she asked.

"Of course," replied her counselor. "You always have choices."

"And if I say no?"

"Then I'd ask if you were acting emotionally or behaving wisely."

Harriett made a face at the predictable comeback. *At least she's consistent.*

The thought reminded her of what Matt's coach preached about discipline and consistency being two additional aspects of mental toughness. Then, she remembered a third—perseverance.

Harriett sat back up, challenging her counselor to "Bring it on!"

"The Flip It skill is based on a concept discussed in several psychological theories—intentionality. I've adapted Milton Erickson's perspective. He's considered the father of self-hypnosis and believed in the power of neurolinguistic programming—how we talk to ourselves programs the pathways in our brain. Erickson believed that, while the mind is capable of problem-solving ways to overcome obstacles, it's incapable of devising creative ways to fix a problem unless given an object to focus on. In other words, the brain needs to hear your intention. Intention is analogous to the pictures inside your head. Dana Rayne's song, 'Object of My Desire' is a perfect example of an intention."

Without warning, Dr. Aye sang, *"Tension's fire burns on and on. My body screams, Please make love to me! 'Cause you're the object of my desire ..."*

Harriett put her hands over her ears. "Enough," she pleaded.

Dr. Aye stopped singing, her eyes dancing with unconcealed glee. "No one ever likes when I sing, but singing sure captures their attention!" She paused.

"...and exemplifies the meaning of intentionality. The object of my desire was to capture your attention. Knowing my intention, my brain devised the creative option of singing to achieve what I wanted. If intention is analogous to the pictures inside your head, then intentionality is strategizing ways to get what you want. Intentionality also means making *the choice* to enact the option that has the highest likelihood of achieving what you want. My intention was to capture your attention, but to achieve what I wanted required intentionality. I had to perform."

"Intentionality is similar to dieting," said Harriett, thinking of her snug waistband. "My intention might be to lose weight, but unless I initiate the behavior, I'll never fit into a skirt I want to wear this summer."

"There used to be a Nike ad that epitomized intentionality. The ad showed different running scenes and then flashed the tagline—'*Just do it.*' You might know what you want, and even know how to get what you want, but unless you exert the energy to go after what you want; fitting into that skirt will remain a picture inside your head."

"That's what you mean when you tell me all behavior is a choice— the choice to go after what I want or to waste energy wishing for what I want."

Dr. Aye nodded. "Since intentionality is predicated on knowing what you want, I crafted the Flip It skill to help clarify the object of your desire. Often, you tell me what you don't want. *Don't* wastes energy because the brain hears instructions to focus energy *away from* the objects you *don't desire.* Instead, flip it and tell the brain what you *do* want. This is more productive because the brain focuses energy on ways to achieve the object of your desire."

"I think I understand, but can you give me an example?"

"In third grade, I talked a lot in class." Dr. Aye wagged her finger. "Now don't you be giving me that 'so what's changed' look. Pay attention! My teacher, Sister Agnes, thought she'd correct the problem by having me write a hundred times, 'I will not talk in class.' Unfortunately for Sister Agnes, 'not' focused my energy away from 'talk,' but didn't provide my brain with the object Sister Agnes desired—silence! Making me write, 'I will be silent in class,' would have instructed my brain to devise creative options for remaining quiet. Options like raising my hand before asking a question or turning my head to avoid talking to the friend sitting beside me."

Harriett struggled to keep from laughing. "You sound as if you're using Sister Agnes as an excuse for talking as much as you do!"

"Then I suggest you find a way to make lemonade out of lemons," observed her counselor. "May I continue now that you've made your not-so-witty comment?" Not waiting for a response, Dr. Aye proceeded. "The reason you're having trouble figuring out how to confront Jake is because you're wasting your energy focusing on what you don't want."

Harriett opened her mouth in protest, but Dr. Aye held up her hand. "I understand you don't know what you want. In a minute, I'm going to ask you what you want and when I do, I want you to flip it. I want you to flip the negative to a positive by substituting the exact opposite of what you don't want. For example, if you're inclined to say, 'I don't want to be fat,' flip it to, 'I want to be skinny.'"

"How will that help?"

"Flip It allows you to approximate the object of your desire and focuses the brain's energy on achieving skinny. What are some ways to achieve skinny?"

"Go on a diet, exercise, make healthier choices." Harriett's response was automatic.

"See, you've already identified some behavioral options! Now, let's refine your intention. Instead of thinking skinny, picture yourself skinny. Describe the picture."

Harriett referred back to the summer skirt.

"What must occur for you to fit into the skirt?"

"I need to lose five pounds."

"Are you saying that your definition of skinny is to be five pounds less than your current weight?"

"Yes."

"How do you have to behave to lose five pounds?"

"For me, that means running an extra ten minutes or going to the gym."

"That would get you skinny?"

Harriett shrugged, anxious to interject. "Yes, but..."

"Then you've just used the Flip It skill to identify how you can change your behavior to get you what you want," interrupted Dr. Aye. "By providing a clear picture of what you want, you've enabled your brain to focus creative energy on devising ways to achieve skinny. You still have to

236

behave with intentionality, but now you have a strategy for getting what you want."

"But what I want is so much more than to lose five pounds!"

"I understand and we'll work to develop those pictures. However, as with all my skills, practicing Flip It is what makes you capable of applying the skill to harder issues."

"Does Flip It have anything to do with keeping my mind cognitively flexible?" asked Harriett.

"Cognitively flexible?" repeated Dr. Aye.

Her counselor's bewildered look made Harriett smile in smug satisfaction. *Finally! The tables have turned!*

Savoring her success, Harriett explained. "I'm tired of being a throwback to the past and I've been using my energy to paint a clearer picture of how to make myself more current. While I've been surfing the web looking at colleges for Matt, I've also been assessing how going back to school might satisfy *my* needs. I've also been thinking that getting a degree might make me more competitive in the job market and allow me to contribute to the family's finances." Harriett flashed a self-deprecating smile. "You know how much I *want* to outshine my sister's reputation for philanthropy, so I've been thinking about pursuing a master's degree in public health as a way to help less fortunate people achieve a healthier lifestyle. The curriculum requires knowledge of psychology, and I've been researching cognitive therapy. The Flip It skill reminds me of something I read about cognitive flexibility."

"How so?"

"Flipping it focuses my wise mind on what I want, and that makes my brain creative enough to consider various ways to achieve the pictures inside my head. That sounds awfully like cognitive flexibility and makes sense within the context of emotional mind. The more emotional I become, the more I shut off the creative part of my brain and become cognitively rigid. Like the night I lost it—I was so emotionally overwhelmed that my brain could only think of one way to get Jake's attention—lunge at him with the knife."

It took a moment to realize that Dr. Aye was quietly assessing her performance. The sparkle of admiration in her counselor's eyes made Harriett giddy. *Perhaps the student's become the master!*

Dr. Aye's next question shattered the illusion. "Then what's the purpose of practicing the skills?"

Smiling at Harriett's inability to respond, the master retained her status. "Practicing the skills conditions the brain to become increasingly flexible."

Refusing to surrender, Harriett replied, "Just like exercise! The more I workout, the more conditioned and flexible I become. That's what prepares me for the harder exercises."

Dr. Aye sighed with contentment. "Oh, Harriett, I love it..."

"I know, I know," she laughed, remembering a line from the 1980's television series, *The A- Team*. "...when a plan comes together!"

"So, in regard to Jake, what do you want?"

She automatically thought, *I don't know*. However, she suspended judgment long enough to reconsider her response. "I know I don't want to continue living with the worry that Jake's hiding something..."

Then Harriett flipped it. "...I want to know the truth."

"If you know the truth, what will you have?"

"Freedom," she replied with dawning insight. "And freedom is a need! I'll be in control of finding options that work for me as well as for my family. I might have to accept things I'd rather not, but knowing the truth gives me the choice to do what I want."

Harriett's growing invigoration waned. "I'm still awfully afraid of what the truth might reveal."

Dr. Aye offered an option. "Go away and practice the Flip It skill. Then, picture ways you can behave with intentionality to gain the truth about Jake. I don't want you to act upon your intentions. Next week I'll teach you how the last skill makes the object you desire more achievable."

"My desire to know the truth?"

"I can't guarantee you'll like what you hear, but I do know the last skill will help you learn more about your relationship with Jake."

"That sounds awfully cryptic."

"No, it's a caution. I'll show you a way to check out your assumptions, but I can't predict what you'll learn. Remember, risk is always associated with any choice we make."

Harriett remained quiet, lost in thought.

"What's on your mind?"

"Something Jake said the other night." Harriett recounted how Jake had ridiculed her problems. "He pretty much said I had no right to be stressed and unhappy because I have an easy life. When I think about the challenges other people face, I think he's right and that makes me feel stupid."

"Stupid?"

"I should just be able to snap myself out of it."

"It?"

"These feelings of confusion, anger, hopelessness...all the things I've talked about over the weeks."

"No, Harriett," Dr. Aye corrected. "You've been doing a great deal more than talking. You've refused to remain helpless to your situation and chosen to find a better way."

"Even hearing that makes me feel guilty, when so many others have so many more reasons to feel helpless!"

Harriett sat forward, intent on proving her point. "You say your goal is to help people add quality to their lives, but aren't some situations more stressful than others? What would you say to someone whose child died or victims of domestic violence and other adversities?"

She thought about her sister's comment regarding the stress of the current economy. "What about chronic stress due to things like single parenthood, or underemployment, or bankruptcy?"

"Terms like quality, stress, and severity are subjective and defy quantification," replied Dr. Aye. "No matter how stressful the situation, there's always someone whose quality of life is worse. Who determines which situation is more severe, or the quality of someone's stress? What standard do we assign to use as a basis of comparison?"

The questions made Harriett recall how Jake compared his stress to hers and arbitrarily deemed hers as nonexistent. *Even if Jake's reasons for feeling stressed are valid, that doesn't invalidate my stress. But, is one more valid than the other?*

"Minimizing anyone's stress is a waste of energy." Dr. Aye pointed to a starfish sitting in the bookcase. "The starfish parable reminds me that it's more productive to focus on helping each person cope with the unique stressors associated with their life."

> One morning an elderly man was walking on a nearly deserted beach. He came upon a boy surrounded by thousands and thousands of starfish. As eagerly as he could, the youngster was picking them up and throwing them back into the ocean.
>
> Puzzled, the older man looked at the young boy and asked, "Little boy, what are you doing?"
>
> The youth responded without looking up, "I'm trying to save these starfish, sir."
>
> The old man chuckled aloud, and queried, "Son, there are thousands of starfish and only one of you. What difference can you make?"
>
> Holding a starfish in his hand, the boy turned to the man and, gently tossing the starfish into the water, said, "It will make a difference to that one!"
>
> *Source Unknown*

"Stay mentally tough," suggested Dr. Aye. "The quality of life you achieve will facilitate quality in others."

"If I work hard to make a difference in the quality of my own life, the energy I conserve becomes available to make a difference in the lives of others and that's something I desperately want."

Harriett leaned into the loveseat, expelled a deep breath, and whispered a quiet, "Thank you."

"*De Nada.*"

19

Behaving with Intention

Harriett left the office, her thoughts focused on recovery. *I went into Dr. Aye's feeling hurt by what Jake said, and now I'm more interested in recovering from the injury caused by his hurtful comments.*

She rummaged in her purse, looking for the car keys and mulled over the difference in her feelings. *Instead of feeling hurt, I feel motivated.*

Pulling the keys from her bag, she amended, "I feel less hurt and more motivated."

The car ride home produced other realizations—*When I focus on the injury, I feel entitled to be mad.*

The thought reminded her of something Jake often said about his clients. "They're the injured party and entitled to be made whole."

"I might be injured, but I am not a victim. I don't have to depend on someone else to make me whole. Becoming whole is my responsibility!" Even though she liked the sound of her words, they provoked a sigh. "Depending on someone else would sure be nice."

Harriett was a bit surprised when she realized that the person she depended on most was her counselor. *I wonder why, since Dr. Aye never allows me to wallow in bad feelings.*

"First of all, Harriett, ask the right question."

Harriett rephrased the question. "What makes me depend on Dr. Aye, when she never allows me to wallow in bad feelings?"

Eventually the answer emerged… "There's a difference between depending on someone to understand my needs and validate my pain, and wishing for someone to take away my pain. The only person responsible for changing my feelings is me."

Harriett moved through the week, using her skills and feeling her momentum grow. She affirmed her success with the Flip It skill as she went upstairs to sort the dirty laundry. *I used Flip It when I was worried I'd be late for the flower show. After telling myself I didn't want to be late, I flipped it to "I want to be early" and arrived with time to spare!*

A similar outcome occurred after flipping "I don't want to spend money on a new dress" to "I want to wear something in my closet." This time, the result was an ensemble of previously worn garments accessorized with a stylish panache she'd stolen from one of Katie's fashion magazines.

Her mind's growing suppleness was impressive. However, unbeknownst to Harriett, a significant success was about to unfold…

Carrying an armful of laundry down the stairs, she looked out the window and saw the mail truck stop in front of the house. *Oh good, I sent away for some information on public health; maybe the catalogs came.*

She walked into the laundry room, dumped the clothes into the washer, and turned on the machine. Slipping into a pair of clogs by the garage door, she made her way to the bottom of the driveway. The tight buds on the ornamental maple had blossomed into a willowy cascade of red that caught her attention and made her stop to survey the property.

"Things are coming together nicely. But I still haven't planted…." She held up her imaginary stop sign. "Stop! Don't start overlooking what is by emphasizing what isn't." She continued towards the mailbox, granting herself permission to ignore the empty planters outside the front door.

Strolling back to the garage, she casually flipped through the newest edition of *Rhode Island Monthly*. The magazine's first page boasted about bringing its readers the very best of what Rhode Island had to offer—from people to politics, food to finance.

Directly under the headline was a picture that eradicated her positive thoughts. The mayor of Providence stood in front of a newly renovated Georgian mansion, flanked on either side by her sister and Randy. In front of the trio was an enormous red ribbon announcing the opening of another restaurant. The caption read, "The city of Providence continues profiting from local couple's beneficence."

Standing in the middle of the driveway, she quickly turned the pages and read the accolades heaped upon her sister. The upgraded version of Harriett worked hard to be loyal and proud, but the old version reared its ugly head. *Dam, Faye's one-upped me again!*

Disgusted, she shut the magazine and returned to the laundry room. *Just when I'm feeling good about myself, Faye comes along to remind me of how little I matter.*

Harriett's thoughts vanquished the good will garnered from Faye's understanding of her problems and made setting limits on her sister's capacity to intrude upon her feelings impossible.

Even if I do get that degree in public health, I still won't be on the cover of a magazine! I don't want to be some anonymous administrator working for the government!

"What do you want?"

The self-evaluation question, the New York accent, Harriett's own voice, weeks of practice and hard work—all integrated into a seamless transition.

"Stop!" she commanded for a second time. "Keep focused on what you want, and what you want is to use your essence in ways that improve the situation of others."

Knowing what she wanted helped clarify the object of her desire. "As long as a degree in public health helps me achieve what I want, does it really matter if there's a picture in the *Rhode Island Monthly*?"

"Well...maybe just a little," she admitted.

Instead of wasting energy comparing herself to Faye, Harriett used her energy to conduct a more thorough evaluation.

Growing up, Mother stressed to Faye and me the value of helping others to lead better lives. She taught us to be nurturing and caring, as well as the importance of being the best we can be. Mother might be a bit of a pill, but she's all those things and so is Faye. It's silly of me to waste my energy comparing myself to them when there's no benchmark for comparison—Mother cares in her way, Faye in hers, and me in mine. That doesn't entitle any of us to improve the situation of others, but caring does make us all want to improve the situation of others. We just behave differently on our wants.

The new insight helped mitigate some of her negative feelings. *However, I can't deny being jealous of my sister.*

She lifted the washer's lid and transferred the clothes to the dryer. *After all, I am human and, as Dr. Aye constantly reminds me, I'm an emotional being.*

Harriett validated her emotions, allowed herself to accept her negative feelings even though she didn't agree, and used her energy to consider her options. *Maybe I could become a member of the school committee or even run for a seat on the town council! After all, most people in Bayview know me for a lot of different reasons...* A rueful chuckle accompanied the completion of her thought... *Some good and others not so good!*

Her reflections continued as she moved through the house, putting plates in the dishwasher, making the beds, and tidying up after her family. *I still think I'm responsible for the everyday tasks associated with this family's well-being.* She realized the thought made her feel good (*sorry for the insipid adjective*).

"How can that be," she wondered aloud. "When I've been working hard to set limits on their ability to make me responsible for their well-being?"

The answer seemed obvious. "Managing the day-to-day welfare of my husband and children is the role I want to play in this family. However, I refuse to be responsible for their happiness. Their job is to make themselves happy and mine is to help them achieve what they want."

A gremlin wormed its way into her mind, whispering the question, "What about Julie?"

The whisper drowned out the buzzing of the dryer and rekindled her fear.

Harriett reiterated what she'd said to Dr. Aye. "I want to know the truth." Yet, the words did little to assuage either her ambivalence or her mounting panic. *I want Jake in my life and I'd probably forgive him even if he did admit to an affair. He's a kind man, a good partner, a loving father, and an excellent provider. But is that enough to outweigh his betrayal?*

Harriett tolerated her panic long enough to conduct a pros and cons and concluded, "Yes."

Surprised, she wondered what her family and friends would think. "Does it matter?" she asked.

Again, she answered, "Yes," knowing she'd always be vulnerable to the judgment of others. "However, I can't let that trap me into acting emotionally. I have to do what's best for me and the kids."

Wisely said, but an impossibly hard choice.

"I don't want a perfect life," she reminded herself, as she walked back into the laundry room. "I want a partnership with a man who values the things I value and appreciates me for who I am. Jake used to be that man. Am I capable of trusting that he's still that man?"

I'm not sure. The admission created a lump in her throat.

She leaned into the dryer and pulled out a pair of her husband's jeans, contemplating his erratic behavior over the past weeks. *He's been increasingly preoccupied and distant, abrupt with the children and sniping at me.* She shook the wrinkles out of his pants. *Even if he's been feeling unappreciated, does that give him the right to cheat on me?*

The question made her angry and the sound of denim whipping through the air seemed to punctuate her anger.

Why should I accept his choice to have an affair? THWACK!

Why would I want to tolerate looking like a fool? SMACK!

I don't want to be the cuckold spouse! I want some respect! SLAP!

Working hard, Harriett resisted the urge to succumb to her anger. She grabbed the rest of the clothes from the dryer and took the bundle into the living room, dropping the warm clothes onto the sofa. Picking up the remote, she tuned into a rerun of the *Brady Bunch*, vaguely remembering that Mrs. Brady once thought Mr. Brady was having an affair with a neighbor.

"Enough of living in the past! Find a more present-day distraction!"

A political debate among panel members on *The View* helped keep her engrossed until Matt and Katie came home, filled with news about the day's events at school.

"My guidance counselor's waiting for my list of college options," Matt confessed. "If I don't have something by Monday, I guess you should expect another phone call." The tone of his voice contained a mixture of annoyance and resistance, tinged with fear.

Harriett recognized his vulnerability and yearned to protect him from life's disappointments. *I don't want him hurt.* Then, with seemingly little effort, she flipped it. *I want him to feel confident enough to manage life's disappointments.*

Tolerating her desire to put her arms around Matt and soothe away his fear, Harriett replied, "Maybe we should spend a few minutes discussing your options."

"Oh man, not again! I told you. I plan to go to whatever school recruits me for soccer."

"And you should."

"Then why are we talking about it? All I can do is wait until the coaches contact me."

Before opening her mouth to argue that Matt's excuses were becoming tiresome, Harriett asked herself a self-evaluation question— *Whose behavior can you change?*

Reminding herself that the object of her desire was to help her son find ways to manage his fear of rejection, Harriett behaved with intent. Adopting a non-judgmental, but decidedly firm tone, she said, "That's where we differ, sweetheart. I think there's a lot more you can be doing."

Ill-tempered and sulky, Matt asked, "Like what?"

"Do you really want to know?"

"I guess," he muttered.

Harriett set a limit. "No, Matt. I will not risk upsetting either of us if you don't really want to know. Which is it, yes or no?"

"Is this going to turn into another lecture about me not living up to my potential?"

The defensiveness in Matt's voice was irritatingly familiar and typically succeeded in curtailing further dialogue. This time, Harriett changed her behavior. "No, Matt, I promise, no lectures. Just some thoughts I'd like to share with you."

Matt's "okay" was filled with obvious suspicion.

"You know I've been seeing someone to help me understand why I got so upset with your father a few weeks ago."

"Yeah," he interrupted. "But how's that gonna help me get into college? Do you want me to start seeing a shrink? Because the answer is a big N-O."

Despite her irritation, Harriett dropped the urge to argue. "No, honey, I want to share with you something I think might make your college search a bit easier."

"By using psychobabble?"

Harriett chose to overlook the derisiveness of her son's question. "No, by treating you as a maturing young man, capable of making your own choices."

"Oh, yeah! As long as those choices are the ones you and Dad think are right!"

"There are lots of right choices and, as your parents; our job is to help you find options that best fit the needs of this family."

"Why do *my* choices have to suite *your* needs? It's my life!"

"Because, like it or not, we're your parents and part of being a parent is to help you succeed. You're going to make lots of wrong choices as you get older—we all do. Doesn't considering our input make sense if it helps you avoid some of those wrong choices?" The challenge to self-evaluate came easily.

Clearly baffled, Matt crossed his arms in silent resistance.

Thinking she'd failed to make her point, Harriett panicked.

Recognizing her panic as a frustration signal, she opted for a do-over. "Perhaps I'm not explaining myself as well as I could. What I'm saying is that my counselor's helped me to understand how emotions can sometimes cause us to make bad choices."

"Like when you went after Dad with that knife?"

"Exactly, and I am sorry that my choice was so upsetting to this family."

Matt shrugged. "No big deal."

"Yes, Matt. Lunging after your father with that knife was a big deal and one you shouldn't minimize. I take responsibility for what I did. I've learned the importance of acknowledging the impact our behavior has on others. Yes, I was upset. I had a right to be upset, but I should have chosen a different way to show how upset I was."

"Why? Dad sure got the message."

"Yeah, he sure did. But the cost to deliver the message was too high. That's the consequence of making wrong choices. If you learn nothing else from me, please learn the value of considering the consequences that come with any choice you make. And in the case of college, that includes the choice of doing nothing."

"Wow, Mom, that's a little heavy."

"I don't mean to sound melodramatic, but taking responsibility is pretty heavy."

"So how does this conversation help get me into college?"

"I'd like to help you evaluate if what you're currently doing is getting you what you want. If you decide it's not, then I'd like to help you find ways to change your behavior. Together, we can strategize ways to increase your odds of getting into the college that you want."

"But how can I do that if I don't know which colleges want me?"

"I guess our first step is to identify the colleges that might want you and then convince them they'd be foolish not to recruit you." A flash of inspiration swept over her. "You know what, Matt? Let's flip it."

"Flip it?"

"Yeah, it's pretty neat. Instead of saying, 'I don't want to go to a college where I can't play soccer,' flip it and say, 'I want to go to a college where I can play soccer.'"

"What's the difference?"

"You tell me. Which way makes you feel more optimistic?"

Relieved, Harriett watched her son seriously consider the question. His face brightened. "The second way...how come?"

"The second way is a more productive way to think. Rather than worrying that no college wants you, you can focus your energy on identifying the colleges that *might* want you. Then we'll figure out ways to sell you to those coaches. The plan might not be perfect, but it will increase your odds of getting into the college you want. How does that sound?"

Harriett's heart broke as she heard her son's small voice admit, "I'm still worried that no one's gonna want me."

Paying attention to Matt's concerns, but behaving differently on the way they made her feel, Harriett validated his fear without rushing to find a perfect solution. "I know, sweetheart. Applying to college is a big risk because no one likes rejection. But does flipping it help you feel less worried?"

"Only a little."

"Then let's capitalize on that little bit and make a plan that might make you even less worried." Determined to push her son's self-evaluation to the limit, she asked, "What can you do?"

"Some of the guys have been using websites to look at different schools in different soccer divisions. They've been comparing their stats to what the colleges say they're looking for. I guess I could do that."

"Oh, Matty, that sounds like a good start. Why don't you spend some time this weekend surfing the net and bring the information to your father and me. Then we'll discuss the next step. Is that an acceptable plan?"

"I guess."

"What makes you hesitate?"

"Dad will probably disagree with whatever I come up with."

Working to keep her son focused in the present, Harriett offered, "You gather the information and I'll handle Dad."

Remembering the importance of specificity, she asked, "When would be a good time to review the list?"

"I'll try to do it by Sunday night."

"Sorry, but I can't accept the word, *try*. Either you're going to have it done by Sunday or you're not."

"I said I'd get the list done! Are you going to nag me until Sunday?"

"No, and your plan sounds good with one exception."

Matt's hesitancy escalated to opposition. "Here we go. I knew there was a catch!"

"Yes, sweetheart, there's always a consequence to our choice. In this case, if I don't hear back from you by Sunday night, I will nag you."

"You mean you won't nag me until Sunday?" Matt's doubt was evident.

"Well, tolerating the urge will be hard, but I'll do my best."

Matt conceded. "Okay. We have a deal. Should we seal it with a handshake?"

His tongue-in-cheek response contained an element of sarcasm, but Harriett allowed herself a sigh of relief. "What I really want is a hug."

After dinner, she apprised Jake of the conversation. She'd expected an agitated reaction and was caught off guard by his response.

Barely looking up from his laptop, he replied, "Whatever."

"Pardon?"

Still disinterested, he closed his eyes and shook his head. "Harriett, I'm too tired to care."

"But, Jake, you have to care!"

"Why?"

"Because caring is what you do!" Her husband's erratic behavior had taken an alarming turn.

Jake sighed. "I know. Caring is all I do."

"Jake, please! You're scaring me."

The fear in her voice captured his attention. "I'm sorry, sweetheart. Of course we'll look at Matt's list. I just need a quiet weekend to recharge my batteries."

Harriett walked away, feeling helpless and vulnerable. She used her skills to navigate through the weekend, relying on her next session with Dr. Aye to shed light on her options. However, a significant injury occurred on Monday night when Jake called to say he'd be late...

"I have a client dinner."

"Jake! You can't keep doing this! We need to talk."

"There's nothing to talk about. I'm the sole provider for this family and this is what I have to do to keep you and Katie in designer clothes and make sure there's enough money for Matt's college."

Her husband's words made Harriett gasp. "Jake, that's not fair! You know I don't wear designer clothes and neither does Katie. I'm just wondering what's changed. The number of client dinners has grown dramatically. Until recently, you conducted most of your business in the office or on the phone at home." Hoping she could get her husband to self-evaluate, Harriett repeated, "What's changed?"

"Maybe I'm not nearly as worried about one of my clients coming after me with a knife because I decide I don't want beef for dinner."

Harriett was at another crossroads. The old Harriett would respond helplessly to the feelings of guilt and shame provoked by Jake's retort. However, the new Harriett found his remarks hackneyed and wearisome. She still felt pangs of guilt and shame, but this time she chose to behave differently. The time had come and, despite her counselor's cautionary warning, Harriett behaved with intentionality.

"Jake, until we talk about what's going on between us, I can't guarantee anything that happens."

"That sounds like a threat."

"No. It's a fact."

Jake's response was a distinct click that ended the conversation.

A tsunami of anger crashed over her. "He hung up on me! He actually hung up on me!"

Mentally, she pushed the replay button on the conversation, feeling her anger build. Then she realized the folly of her actions.

"Stay mentally tough," she advised. "I have a choice. I can continue pushing the replay button or I can find a more productive way to cope."

With effort, Harriett began the recovery process...

Remembering her mantra—the situation's not going to adapt to you, so figure out how to adapt to the situation—she began to chant, "Stop thinking, start doing."

She searched her list of distracting behaviors until she found what she wanted. Picking up the phone, she placed a call.

"Hello?"

She took a deep breath. "Beth? It's Harriett. I really want to talk about what's going on between Jake and me. Are you free for dinner?"

Hanging up the phone, Harriett knew she'd made the right choice. *If I can't talk to Jake, at least I can depend on my friends to validate my pain and understand my needs.*

Like storm troopers, Beth, Lissa, and Brenda converged on their favorite Thai restaurant, ready to defend their friend, even though she'd yet to reveal the reason behind the call to arms.

Harriett was amazed. A short time ago, she'd resisted sharing herself with her friends and now, she was prepared to divulge her worst nightmare. Tears of gratitude filled her eyes as she affirmed how, on some level her friends satisfied all her needs. She also affirmed how the associated sense of fulfillment was the product of her hard work.

"Ladies, the time has come! What would you do if...."

Beth and Lissa were proponents of direct and immediate confrontation. Lissa opted for a straightforward show down with Jake, while Beth thought Harriett's phone call should have been to Julie rather than to her.

True to form, Brenda pronounced, "I knew it! The moment I saw Jake and that woman at the Crowne Plaza, I knew something sinister was going on!"

Harriett realized she had to behave assertively and set a limit on her friend's behavior. "Look, Brenda," she began and watched Brenda's head snap up, somewhat shocked by the firmness in Harriett's voice. "I got myself in trouble for acting emotionally the last time you implied Jake was having an affair. You might be right, but your assumption might also be wrong. *My* assumption might be wrong and I want help finding ways to check out my assumption. I don't need anyone making me more worried. I'm worried enough."

Stunned, her friends were at a loss for words. They sat in strained silence as each woman contemplated how news of an affair would affect her life. Finally, Beth leaned across the table and touched Harriett's hand. "Just remember, we're here for you."

The words echoed in the faces of her friends, and once again, Harriett's eyes filled with tears. "Thanks."

Shaking the pall that covered the table, she changed topics and asked Lissa about gardening. "This is the longest I've ever delayed in filling the planters by my front door. I guess I got tired of lugging those heavy pots in and out of the garage. Now I think I might wait until the summer annuals arrive."

Lissa studied her friend. "You know, Harriett. There's something different about you. I've never known you to blow off getting the house ready for spring. I always thought you were in some kind of race, but I could never figure out why. I can't explain what's changed, but somehow you seem more relaxed. What's been going on in your counseling sessions?"

Harriett smiled as she pictured Dr. Aye sitting in her brown leather swivel. "I've been learning a lot," she replied. "Dr. Aye helps demystify my life. This way the answers to my problems are easier to find."

"What answers?" demanded Brenda. "Doesn't she just tell you how to fix your problems?"

Harriett laughed at the absurdity of Dr. Aye telling her what to do. She shook her head. "Just the opposite. She asks me tons of questions that force me to self-evaluate and figure out my own answers."

"What questions does she ask that you can't ask yourself?"

"Actually, that's what I've learned. The right questions to ask and how to problem-solve the answers."

"That sounds way too cut and dry," objected Beth.

"Yes," agreed Brenda. "There must more than that. I help people figure out their problems all the time. She must do something more complicated or why can't we all be counselors?"

Harriett gave her answer serious consideration, wondering how to explain the rationale behind self-evaluation and using skills to control emotions long enough to behave wisely.

"Are you feeling better?" asked Lissa.

The question reminded Harriett of the importance of being specific, and she shared her wisdom with her friends. "Dr. Aye's taught me that *better* is a subjective word. Am I feeling better, meaning back to the way I was? No, then I'm not feeling better because I don't want to be back to the way I was."

She nodded her head at Lissa. "You're right. I'm feeling relieved."

"Isn't that the same as better?"

Harriett recalled how only a few weeks earlier she too didn't comprehend the subtle difference. Paraphrasing her counselor, she explained how relieved was more specific and less insipid. "I'm relieved that I don't have to continue acting the way I've been acting for all these years. Relieved that I get to choose how to think, feel, and behave."

Again, her response took them aback. "Does that mean you're thinking of divorcing Jake?" Beth gasped.

"That's not the point," corrected Harriett. "The point is that I have a choice."

"But," Brenda protested. "What would you do if you left Jake?"

"Wait a minute." Harriett knew she must set another limit. She couldn't allow her friends to drag her into the future. "I didn't say I was divorcing Jake. What I said was that I'm relieved to realize I have a choice. Dr. Aye's taught me how to prepare for my future by focusing on the present and that's what I intend to do. Now, can we please order some dessert and discuss what I heard on *The View*?"

20

Skill #9
Communicate

Harriett wandered around the room, eager for Dr. Aye to make an appearance. She tapped her foot impatiently as she searched through the magazines lying on the rattan table in front of the couch. On the far wall, an article tacked into a cork bulletin board caught her attention.

Walking across the room, she perused an expose about life being too short to waste time. She glanced at the author's name, wondering if he was a client because there really isn't much difference between wasting time and wasting energy.

The squeak of the waiting room door made her turn. "I've decided what I want and now I want you to teach me how to get it."

"Hello to you, too," responded Dr. Aye. "Would you care to step inside and elaborate?"

Following her counselor into the office, Harriett plopped onto the loveseat. "I'm sick of wasting energy worrying over what Jake might say if I confront him about the affair! I've decided whatever he says can't be any worse than living in this limbo."

"Limbo?"

"Vacillating from day to day about what I should do and making assumptions based on his every move. I get so angry when I think how much energy I've wasted trying to be perfect. I know that's not Jake's fault, but the uncertainty of not knowing what's happening between us has become intolerable and I refuse to waste another ounce of energy worrying."

"What have you been doing?"

"Most nights I distract by going out with friends or staying in my room reading and watching television. I'm beginning to think I'm a prisoner in my own home and I'm ready to make a different choice."

Harriett paused, reflecting on some of her more productive choices. "I've also been spending time with the kids. Instead of focusing on why I'm not the perfect mom, I've been giving them the chance to take responsibility for their thoughts, feelings and behaviors. It's hard," she flashed a wry smile, "but not nearly as hard as trying to make their lives perfect."

"Is what you're doing getting you what you want?"

"Yes, because what I want is to raise my children to be responsible for their choices. The best way to achieve what I want is by modeling the skills."

"Meaning?"

"When I use the skills to control my emotions long enough to change my behavior, I'm showing my children that feelings aren't what get us into trouble. Behaving unwisely on our feelings is what often leads to trouble. My willingness to acknowledge how my behavior impacts a situation and my ability to risk changing my behavior to make the situation better, helps them understand the difference between making excuses for a mistake and taking responsibility for making a mistake. Failing isn't the issue. Knowing how to problem-solve ways to minimize risk and how to recover from an injury is what fosters a success identity. Besides, every time I show Matt and Katie how to behave wisely, I reinforce the lesson in myself."

Harriett concluded her soliloquy with a question. "Would you like to know the secret to living a quality life?"

Dr. Aye raised her eyebrows in silent invitation.

"The secret is to remember that feelings come and go. One minute you can be ecstatic that you've found the perfect dress..."

"Or sweater," interrupted Dr. Aye.

Harriett smiled. "And the next minute that positive feeling can be overshadowed by an equally negative feeling because someone on the road cuts you off on the way home from the mall."

"So feelings are transient?"

"Yes! Feelings change, but how we behave on the feelings can produce lasting results."

Harriett settled comfortably into the loveseat, considering her next words. "I've been helping Matt and Katie to accept their feelings and use their energy more productively by changing their behavior. I tell them what you told me—changing our behavior is what changes the negative feelings."

She saw Dr. Aye open her mouth in response and rushed to complete her thought. "I know some feelings are less transient than others and rooted in the extent of the injury. That's why I have to stay mentally tough and pay attention to the signals warning me of potential danger."

"Does this mean I no longer have to be your keeper of hope?"

Harriett studied her counselor. "You've taught me how to hope for myself, but I think I'll always carry you on my shoulder as a reminder not to get sidetracked by my vulnerabilities."

"There's another option." Responding to Harriett's puzzled look, Dr. Aye inquired about messages.

"Are you telling me to stop listening to old messages?" Harriett asked.

"You can choose to listen to whatever message you want. However, I'd encourage you to challenge the message before behaving."

Harriett nodded. "Instead of thinking I have to blindly accept the messages I've heard."

"Blindly?"

"Without evaluating how they apply to my life. For instance, my mother sent my sister and me a message about doing our best. The message was appropriate, only we each interpreted my mother's words differently. I understand how my uniqueness caused me to distort the message, but I made the choice to adhere to the distortion. That's when my efforts to honor the message transformed into my obsessive want to be perfect. A wiser choice would have been to evaluate how the message contributed to the quality of my life."

Harriett paused, apprehensive about Dr. Aye's response. Unable to endure the silence, she asked, "Are you proud of me?"

"Is that important?"

Little girl Harriett would always be part of her essence. "I'd like if you were."

"I'm pleased that your hard work resulted is such a nice outcome." Adding a caveat, Dr. Aye noted, "I never expected anything less."

Harriett savored the affirmation. "That's what makes confronting Jake imperative. I've worked hard to learn wiser ways to cope with my life and avoiding a confrontation with my husband is no longer a wise choice."

Harriett tempered her exuberance. "I know I'll always be vulnerable to injuries. Nevertheless, I feel more confident about coping with most aspects of my life and I want to feel confident in all aspects of my life. The only way to achieve what I want is to resolve the event that precipitated finding you."

"What was the event?"

"Through lack of conditioning, I wasn't mentally tough enough to recover from the injury I caused by assuming Jake was having an affair. I was too drained to behave wisely and acted emotionally on that assumption by not controlling my emotions long enough to use wise mind to check out my assumptions."

"If you know what happened, what's left to resolve?"

"I need to rectify my mistake by checking out the original assumption. While that will never justify lunging after Jake with the knife, at least I'll get the information I need to choose my next behaviors."

"Meaning?"

"What to do about the affair. Do I divorce Jake? Do I acknowledge my role in his choice to have an affair? Do I forgive him and ask him to forgive me? Do I accept that staying married is important enough to warrant tolerating his behavior even if I disagree? The only way to answer the questions is to validate my assumption. You've helped me understand that being afraid of information is a waste of energy. You once said that information is empowering. I think that's what resonates the most from our time together. Information gives me the power to evaluate my options and choose the one that's best for me. The choices I make are what make me a survivor."

"I'm curious. Have you ever considered your assumptions might be wrong?"

Harriett rebuffed the question with a dismissive wave of her hand. "Maybe, but I don't think so."

"Life has a way of surprising us and that's why I stress the importance of preparedness. Jake may be having an affair, but there may be other reasons why he's become disengaged. I'd be remiss if I didn't caution you to consider other explanations."

"I know you're telling me to suspend judgment on my assumptions, but I'm ready to close this chapter of my life."

Recalling another life lesson posted on the bulletin board—"If you don't ask, you don't get," Harriett asked, "Please teach me the last skill."

"How do you define communication?"

There was an abrupt shift in her counselor's demeanor that Harriett found unsettling. "I hate when you do that," she complained.

"Do what?"

"When you switch from a discussion that makes me think we're colleagues to one that reminds me of being a school girl, I think I'll never fully understand all that you have to teach. Instead of feeling empowered, I feel vulnerable."

Dr. Aye remained speechless.

Well, that's a first, thought Harriett.

"Sorry," apologized Dr. Aye. "What you said surprised me because the way you phrased your complaint was a perfect example of the Communicate skill...and I do mean perfect!"

Harriett smiled, enjoying the victory even though she didn't fully comprehend the source of her counselor's surprise.

Responding to Harriett's complaint, Dr. Aye explained. "Like all relationships, our relationship is a system comprised of individual components that mesh together to perform a specific function. Each component of the system has a discrete purpose and the more efficient the components, the more productive the system."

Harriett recalled how Dr. Aye described people as systems comprised of three components—thoughts, feelings, and behaviors... "And a change in one component forces a change in the other components."

"Ours is a system containing two components, you and me. My purpose is to demystify the difference between acting emotionally and behaving wisely. Your purpose is to use what you learn to cope with the stressors in your life. Our relationship is like a dance in that the lead-follow interaction contributes to the overall quality of your life. You rely on me to choreograph the skills, but your creative interpretation is what makes the dance uniquely satisfying."

"Are you saying I feel empowered when my interpretation of the dance is affirmed?"

"Yes. What makes that important?"

"Affirming my interpretation motivates me to expand on what I've learned. As long as I take my toolbox into every situation I encounter, I don't have to be dependent on you to choreograph my next steps."

"Your observation to your friends the other evening was correct. I've taught you how to ask yourself the questions required to problem-solve your life. Your answers are what determine the quality of your life."

Suddenly worried, Harriett asked, "Are you discharging me from counseling?"

"How am I going to respond?"

Harriett lowered her head and evaluated her thoughts. *Initially, I was resistant, now I'm reluctant to have this relationship end. What changed?*

Me!

Meeting her counselor's gaze, she replied, "The choice is mine."

Once again, Dr. Aye took the lead by repeating her initial question. "How do you define communication?"

"I suppose communication is the same as talking."

"Actually, the goal of communication is to obtain a mutual understanding and that requires more than talking. Communication requires an exchange of information and the Communicate skill facilitates a productive exchange of information. Using the skill allows you to share your thoughts and feelings regarding the impact someone's behavior has on you. Only, instead of acting emotionally, you share your thoughts and feelings wisely."

Harriett grinned. "Is acting emotionally a euphemism for yelling?"

"Possibly, or...," Dr. Aye tilted her head and looked at Harriett through the corner of her eye, expecting her to finish the statement.

Sobering, she realized her counselor's intent. "...Or lunging after someone with a knife."

"The Communicate skill helps you check out the intention behind the other person's behavior. You might assume you know the meaning, but like all assumptions, check it out before you behave. Using the Communicate skill promotes a back and forth exchange of information that enables both parties to derive a mutual understanding of the situation."

Leaning forward, Dr. Aye picked up her yellow pad. Sitting back in her seat, she began teaching the skill.

"I adapted the Communicate skill from a negotiation concept called Fair Fighting. The rules are easily accessible on multiple websites. Fair Fighting offers a framework for people involved in a dispute. Fair Fighting helps them negotiate their differences and come to a mutual understanding of the issue."

"Rules for fighting?" Harriett thought the idea sounded absurd.

"I've developed a script that I encourage clients to use as a way to practice the Communicate skill," said Dr. Aye. "The logic behind the script is similar to the reason I suggested you make a list of distracting behaviors."

"So that I have something to refer to when I'm too emotional to behave wisely?"

"Scripted words provide a higher likelihood of success because they offer a roadmap to follow when you want to transition from emotional mind into wise mind. With practice, you'll begin to modify the script into words that work for you. In your case, that would be called, 'Harriett-ifying' the script."

"I'm sure I'll be in emotional mind when I use the skill with Jake," she replied, eager to reach the final chapter of her story.

"Harriett," cautioned Dr. Aye. "I urge you to practice in situations less stressful than the one with Jake. Negotiations always begin with good intentions because we begin them in wise mind, but fail because of our inability to stay wise. Effective use of the Communicate skill requires the combination of all the skills in your toolbox."

"I understand and promise to choose wisely."

Dr. Aye took a pen off the credenza and wrote:

HOW TO GIVE AND RECEIVE INFORMATION

Giving information:
> *When you* (state the behavior you wish to discuss),
> *I think* (state what you think).
> *When I think* (restate what you think),
> *I feel* (state what you feel).

Asking for information:
> *Is that what you want me to think?*
> *Is that what you want me to feel?*

Clarifying a "NO" response:
> *Help me to understand—if you didn't intend*
> *for your behavior to impact me that way,*
> *what did you intend?*

Ripping the page from the pad, Dr. Aye handed Harriett the script. She watched as her client studied the paper and mouthed the words.

Satisfied that she'd committed the lines to memory and fortified by the knowledge that she'd unwittingly enacted the Communicate skill earlier in the session, Harriett felt confident in her ability to use the script to achieve the closure she sought. "This sounds pretty straightforward."

Dr. Aye flashed a knowing smile. "Remember, we learn the skills in wise mind, but initiate them in emotional mind."

The reminder made Harriett gulp as she imagined the emotion she'd feel when she confronted Jake and invoked Julie's name. "The purpose of the script is to alleviate some of the emotion because I won't have to worry about what to say."

"Preparation is another aspect of mental toughness," replied Dr. Aye. "In some ways, a prepared script is like a role-play because it gives you a chance to anticipate and prepare for the various outcomes that might occur during the negotiation. A prepared script also gives you more confidence to behave wisely on the inevitable emotions arising from the negotiation."

"I see how rehearsing the questions and anticipating the questions prepares me to seize the offensive when I'm feeling defensive. I also understand how the script gives me a way to behave after I've accepted the situation and tolerated my feelings."

Harriett paused, speculating about other benefits of having a script. "Rather than worrying about what to say next, I can stay focused long enough to pay attention to what Jake says. I still have to suspend judgment on what I hear, but using the script is a way to get the information I need to choose my next behavior."

Comprehending the value of the script, Harriett concluded, "That's why you say the Communicate skill depends on using the other skills in my toolbox."

"You left out three skills."

Once again, Harriett pictured the confrontation with Jake and imagined how she could easily slip into emotional mind.

"If we start fighting over who's right and who's wrong, I can remember that I don't want to fight, and use Flip It to remind myself that I want to know the truth. Then I can call a do-over and use Stop, Drop, and Roll. The script can be the new behavior that I roll out."

"And how does Communicate help you check out your assumptions?"

Harriett thought the answer intuitively obvious. "Isn't that the whole purpose of the Communicate skill? I might assume I know the meaning behind Jake's erratic behavior; but unless I check it out, I won't really be sure." She suddenly realized why the skill might not work. "What if I tell Jake how his behavior's been impacting me and he dismisses me?" Her mind recreated the knife scene, and her body trembled.

"That is a risk. What would you do?"

"I don't know!"

Dr. Aye provided a hint. "You could use something you learned by doing your first homework assignment."

Harriett struggled to recall the assignment. "You asked me to differentiate between thoughts and feelings." Confused, she wondered how to apply what she'd learned.

"If Jake dismisses your feelings, you reply, 'I understand that's what you think, but that's how I feel.' Remember, no matter what Jake thinks, your feelings are valid. Then ask for more information."

Harriett looked down and recited, "Was that what you wanted me to feel?"

"The question is a self-evaluation question that encourages Jake to consider how his behavior impacted you, and his answer provides you with information that recalibrates your thoughts and feelings."

"This sounds like a recipe for a good fight!"

"But the fight will be fair. One that stays focused in the present and has the greatest likelihood of obtaining what you want—a mutual understanding of the situation."

Not convinced, Harriett found another flaw in the skill. "But what happens when I know his answers are lies?"

"Sounds like you need lots more practice," observed Dr. Aye.

"Why?"

"If you know the answer is a lie, what else do you know?"

That I'm being an ASS.

"That I didn't suspend judgment long enough to check out my assumption," she replied.

"Even if you suspect the other person is lying, your best choice is to continue asking self-evaluation questions designed to confirm your suspicions. Only then can you determine your options."

Thinking ahead to her confrontation with Jake, Harriett projected a different result. "What if Jake blames me for his behavior, like when he says he's distant because I went after him with the knife? Or what if he refuses to engage, like when he hung up on me?"

"Then what have you learned?"

"That he doesn't care." No longer exuberant, Harriett now felt dejected.

"That's another assumption and your assumption may be wrong. What you've learned is that something's stopping him. Maybe he's scared, maybe he's not ready, or maybe he just doesn't know how to tell you without hurting your feelings."

Dejection turned to gloom. "What do I do then?"

"Rely on your options. They're what empower you to behave wisely."

Worrying about the future inflamed Harriett's despair. "But what choices do I have if he refuses to engage?"

"There are numerous options. Your inability to identify them is a frustration signal warning you to transition back into wise mind. One option may be to set a limit and explain to Jake the consequences of his refusal. A second option might be to table the discussion until you gauge that Jake is ready to tolerate the discussion. Or, you might use a clarifying question like the one I scripted."

Harriett looked down at the paper and read, "Help me to understand. If you didn't intend for your behavior to impact me that way, what did you intend?" She looked up, comprehension written across her face. "The power of 'what.'"

"Meaning?"

"If Jakes says, 'I don't know'—I ask, 'What might have been your intention?'"

"Good, very good," affirmed Dr. Aye. "Tell me what resonates."

"I think the purpose of the Communicate skill is to suspend judgment long enough to behave in a way that gets me the information I need to plan my next behavior." Harriett giggled. "I have this image of myself as Mata Hari, relying on my good looks and steaming sexuality to seduce Jake into revealing what I want to know."

"I like that! Whenever you're about to act emotionally, ask yourself, 'What would Mata Hari do?'"

"Because Mata Hari would behave wisely," finished Harriett.

"Remember, the inane pictures we create inside our heads are useful ways to stay focused on our intentions."

"Like the picture of yourself as a swan?"

"How do you know about my picture of a swan?" Dr. Aye asked, her voice demanding an answer.

Harriett tittered in triumph as she pointed to the picture of two swans in her counselor's bookcase. "I suspected that picture was significant and I've been waiting for the right time to check out my assumption. I think the picture reminds you to behave in ways that get you what you want."

"Very clever, Mata Hari, very clever," muttered Dr. Aye.

"How does the picture help you to get what you want?"

"I'm tempted to tell you to go away and figure that out for yourself! However, since you've worked hard, I think you deserve a reward."

Settling into her brown swivel, Dr. Aye revealed. "A swan sits atop the water looking peaceful and graceful, giving the appearance of being in control of her surroundings and effortlessly gliding wherever she wants. Underneath the water, she has to paddle furiously to keep her body from succumbing to the water's current. Whenever a client presents me with a situation that feels discombobulating, I remind myself to be a swan. Outwardly, I try to present as calm and in control, while underneath I'm paddling furiously to keep up."

"Try?"

"Pardon?"

Harriett smiled, secretly amused by her counselor's choice of word. "You said, *try*." Invoking Yoda, Harriett intoned, "Do or do not—there is no try."

"You're starting to annoy me. Stop analyzing your counselor and go behave in ways that get you what you want! Just remember, practice makes proficient."

Snickering, Harriett replied, "You almost said, *perfect*."

Working hard to disguise her laughter, Dr. Aye pointed to the office door. "Leave!"

21

What Would You Do?

Harriett walked out of the office, feeling pleased with the session's outcome, and decided to reward her hard work by getting a manicure. She headed across the bridge towards her favorite nail salon, unconcerned about who she might meet or how to explain an event that seemed a lifetime ago.

In a way, it was a lifetime ago. I'm certainly not the same person. She amended the thought. *My essence is the same...I'm just choosing to behave differently.*

Harriett reveled in her contentment, aware that her happiness was largely due to the satisfaction of her freedom need. She also comprehended how acknowledging her hard work contributed to her happiness. *Affirming my behavior makes me think I've achieved something and that satisfies my need for power.*

She focused on one of her more recent achievements. *I can't believe I was able to tolerate my embarrassment long enough to fulfill my obligation as president of the garden club. Even though I wasn't a perfect president, I feel proud that I completed the term. I consider that an awesome achievement!*

Taking gratitude in the moment, she applied her energy to the situation with her husband. *Until I confront Jake, I'll be nothing more than a truck stuck in the mud and I'm tired of spinning my wheels.*

Talking to Jake is the only way to get on solid ground.

The Hummer's engine was revving and she considered driving into Boston to put an immediate end to her torment.

"Stop," she instructed, knowing she must keep a tight reign on her emotions. "Behave wisely. Tolerate the urge long enough to practice the Communicate skill."

While prudent, Harriett wondered if she'd be able to follow her own advice. "Be patient. Tolerate your feelings for just a few more days."

She decided to utilize her energy more productively by staying focused in the moment and using the time to prepare for the confrontation.

I'm going to practice the Communicate skill until Friday. This way I'll be more prepared to choose my words carefully when Jake admits to the affair. I'll have to tolerate all the hurt and anger I'll feel when he confirms my assumption. I wonder if I'm strong enough to withstand the pain.

Harriett dismissed Dr. Aye's warning to consider other explanations for Jake's erratic behavior. However, her thoughts instigated a second worry. *What if Jake denies the affair? I might be prepared to have my assumption confirmed, but I don't know how I'd cope with a lie.*

Aware she'd drifted into the future, Harriett yanked herself back to the present. "Stop worrying and keep planning!"

She chewed the inside of her lip until a strategy emerged. "I know! I'll pull a Jake!"

Recalling a tactic that worked when she suspected the kids of lying, Harriett hatched a plan that adopted the same dispassionate persona that Jake used to cross-examine a witness. Her mind conjured a vivid picture of herself as an English barrister, donned in a powdered wig and pointing a finger at her husband as he stood in the witness box.

In some ways, pulling a Jake is similar to the Communicate skill. If I suspect that Jake is lying, I'll check out my assumption by presenting him with the evidence and then ask him to explain the meaning. If we start arguing, I'll stop, and drop the urge to prove I'm right. But, what new behavior should I roll out? I'd be smart to have something prepared, especially since the odds of maintaining my composure are low.

Thinking about the odds made her anxious, so she chose to apply her energy towards making her plan more specific.

When Jake gets home tonight, I'll tell him we really have to talk. Then I'll suggest we go out to dinner on Friday. I'll use a public place as an ally so things can't get too out of control—a place that's quiet enough to talk, but not so quiet that we become the center of attention if things turn ugly.

Harriett mulled over her options and settled on the Outback Steakhouse because the booths would provide privacy and the crowd of people on a Friday night would be large enough to cover the sound of raised voices.

Remembering the outcome of their previous talk in a restaurant, wise mind asked a question, "How will you get there?"

Harriett's response was to use what she'd learned from the past to plan in the present for the future she wanted.

Last time I had my car available, but I don't think that's an option because we'll be coming from the house and driving two cars would seem odd. Yet I need a crisis plan in case there's an emergency. I'm not exactly sure what constitutes a crisis, but I want to prepare for the worst.

Her face crinkled in concentration as she considered her options. Tricia's face appeared before her eyes. *I'll ask Tricia to be my wingman! Jake and I will drive together and if the conversation does turn ugly, I'll have Tricia waiting across the street at Target. She'll get a kick out of helping me play Mata Hari and I know I can depend on her to come to my rescue.*

Harriett smiled at the thought of her friend leaping out of an ambulance, dressed in blue, stethoscope dangling from her ears. *Tricia's version of rescue will be to take me to the nearest bar and ply me with Cosmos!*

She approached the salon and scanned the busy street, looking for an available parking spot. She parked, set a limit on her thoughts about Jake, and walked towards the shop's entrance. The rhythm of her steps kept time with her chant—*Be here now*.

Settling into the salon's familiar coziness, Harriett acknowledged how life's simple pleasures could satisfy a need. *I used to think of manicures as frivolous and simply a part of the daily minutia associated with my life. Now I realize how little things, like being among people I know, are what satisfy my need for belonging.*

Harriett affirmed her hard work. *The situation's the same, but my perspective of the situation's changed.*

Sighing with contentment, she enjoyed the nectar of a success that tasted so much sweeter than a Cosmo!

Looking around the salon, Harriett watched the owners, Janine and her husband Drew, work hard to adapt to their situation. While Drew kept a careful eye on his wife, Janine struggled with a patron's complaint.

"We rotate the polish regularly," assured Janine, disagreeing with the woman's premise that the salon used old nail polish.

Despite Janine's assurance, the woman remained skeptical. "I don't know," she replied. "I've heard about salons using thinner to dilute thick, overused polish. I think I want a new bottle."

Accepting the woman's skepticism, Janine responded, "I'm sorry if that's happened in other salons." Then Janine seized the offensive by asking a self-evaluation question, "What made you decide to try our salon?"

"You come highly recommended as a reputable shop."

Armed with the new information, Janine offered the woman a compromise. "Perhaps you might like to finish the pedicure and see what you think after we've painted your toes."

Harriett soaked her cuticles and watched Janine quietly tolerate the woman's suspicions long enough to complete the pedicure. Afterwards, the woman bent over her toes, carefully inspecting each dab of polish. Sitting upright, she grudgingly acknowledged the salon's reputation, made another appointment, paid, and left the shop.

Janine's ability to keep her emotions under control long enough to behave wisely was impressive and made Harriett appreciate how running the salon necessitated carrying a toolbox filled with tools similar to the skills taught by Dr. Aye.

Watching Janine simultaneously cope with the wants of her clientele and employees also caused Harriett to have a completely different interpretation of Jake's favorite phrase, "Success comes to those who can multitask." *Multitasking means using the skills to juggle multiple emotions at the same time. That's the most productive way to stay in control and avoid being overwhelmed and exhausted!*

The insight shed light on her grandmother's ability to manage life with grace and elegance. *Perhaps Granny knew that controlling her emotions gave her the energy to juggle Granddad, Mother, and Faye.*

Harriett searched for a word to encapsulate how she wanted to conduct her life. *From now on, I want to manage situations with...quality!*

An incisive nod of her head affirmed the thought.

Janine slipped into the chair across from Harriett and reached over, plucking Harriett's right hand from the water. "Miss Harriett, why do some people have to be annoying just for the sake of being annoying?"

"I don't know," Harriett replied. "But I'm very impressed by how you tolerated your annoyance long enough to behave wisely."

Janine stopped her inspection of Harriett's hand and looked up. "What do you mean?"

Harriett smiled. "Oh, it's just something I've learned over these past few weeks."

Janine returned the smile. "We're glad to have you back. You've been away for a while." She shook her head in mock horror. "Just look at these hands!"

Harriett chose to practice the Communicate skill. "You know, Janine, when you say that, I think you've missed me; and when I think I've been missed, I feel glad to be back."

The smile on Janine's face broadened.

The Communicate skill might achieve a mutual understanding in favorable situations. I wonder how it works in negotiations that aren't as amicable.

Little did Harriett know, her hypothesis would soon be tested...

Pulling the Jeep into the garage, Harriett entered the house, hailed a quick greeting to Matt and Katie, and walked towards the kitchen. Her stomach tightened when she heard the phone ring. Assuming the call was from Jake, she chose to let the machine record a message. *I'm not in the mood to hear another excuse about working late.*

Refusing to ruminate, she hung up her coat and retrieved the yellow paper she'd pocketed on her way out of Dr. Aye's office. Smoothing out the wrinkles, she hung the script on the fridge and distracted herself with a reminder to "Practice! Practice! Practice!"

Walking over to the phone, she pushed the play button and steeled herself for the anticipated message.

"Mr. Bartlett here," announced the vice-principal. "While I'm pleased at Matt's attention to tardiness, he left school before last period and we've no record of his being excused. Please call me."

Exasperated by the perfunctory message, she called up the stairs, "Matt, we need to talk."

"Sure, Mom! Be right down."

The sound of his footsteps bounding down the stairs filled Harriett with ambivalence and she conducted a quick emotional pros and cons.

He's really been working hard to take responsibility for school and the college search. Maybe I shouldn't come down on him too hard. But, can I tolerate Matt's repeated disregard of the rules? No! Not only do today's antics make me feel annoyed and disappointed, I'm also worried that he's slipping back into bad habits.

Matt entered the kitchen, the wariness in his eyes indicating he already sensed trouble.

"Matt, the school called to tell me you skipped last period..."

"Oh, Mom," Matt interrupted. "It was just study hall and..."

Harriett put up her hand, signaling him to stop making excuses. Glancing at the fridge, she began again. "Matt, when you skip class, I think you're slipping back into bad habits; and when I think you don't care about school, I feel disappointed and annoyed. Is that what you want me to think? Is that what you want me to feel?"

"No, Mom, I just..."

"Matt, did you hear what I said?"

"Yeah, you want to know why I skipped school."

"That's not what I said." Tolerating her annoyance at Matt's inattentiveness, she used a carefully modulated tone to repeat what she'd said.

"Look, Mom. I can understand how what I did makes you worry that I'm screwing up. Believe me, I don't want you or Dad to start coming down on me like you were a couple of months ago. But, the day was great and some of the guys wanted to take the Saab over to the beach. We didn't do anything wrong. We just played the radio, listened to music, and chilled."

Aggravated by Matt's confidence in his ability to sway her, Harriett worked hard to suspend judgment on her son long enough to gather more data. "If you don't want me to think you're slipping back into bad habits, what should I think?"

"That I'm just your typical male adolescent screw-up!"

Biting back an angry response, she relied on the yellow paper to behave wisely. "Matt, help me to understand. You tell me the colleges you've selected as your top picks, all require a 3.2 minimum grade point average. Right now, you're barely at a three zero. All your teachers say the 3.2 is within your grasp as long as you do really well on your finals. They also offered to help you achieve what you want."

Harriett held Matt's gaze in hers and asked, "How does leaving school early make your teachers inclined to help?"

Matt broke her gaze, casting his eyes to the floor. "It doesn't."

Harriett's no-nonsense tone demanded his full attention. "So how are you going to fix this situation?"

"I guess I better apologize for screwing up. Maybe they'll have pity on me, especially if I ask them for some extra credit work."

Harriett nodded in satisfaction. "That's a good plan and one that I hope, for your sake, works."

Her nod made Matt gush with relief. "Thanks, Mom. You're the best." He leaned over to give her a hug.

"Just a minute, mister, not so fast. I said the plan was good, not good enough. Driving the Saab to school is a privilege that you just lost for a week. You better reconcile yourself to the bus because I certainly don't intend to drive you."

"MOM," came an injured moan.

"Don't 'mom' me. You know the rules."

Matt continued his cajoling, but Harriett remained firm. Finally, she set a limit and instructed him to leave. He stomped off in wounded outrage.

I don't care what he thinks or feels. I only care that he learns!

During dinner, Jake commented on Matt's long face.

"Mom took the car away from me for a week!" Responding to his father's questioning look, Matt continued. "I skipped last period and got caught."

"Damn it, Matt!" Jake's angry outburst surprised everyone. He looked at Harriett. "Just a week? This is your idea of raising a perfect family? You can't even make the punishment suit the crime!" He threw down his napkin, pushed back his chair, and retreated into his study, slamming the door for added emphasis.

Harriett, Matt, and Katie looked on in stunned silence.

Matt was first to recover. "Gee, Mom, good thing he didn't have a knife."

Harriett elicited a small smile, despite being shocked. "Listen, kids. Would you please clean up? Your father and I need to talk."

She got up from the table and quietly followed Jake into the study where she found him sitting in his recliner, channel surfing, and breathing heavily. Casting an irritated look in her direction, his eyes returned to the television. "Don't you dare start in on me!"

"I'm not," she replied, struggling to tolerate her hodgepodge of emotions. "But we have to talk."

"About what? How I didn't back you up in there? How I don't validate you? How I don't satisfy your needs?"

"No, Jake," Harriett responded softly. "We have to talk about what's going on between us so we can do what's best for our children."

"What about what's best for me?" Jake stared at the television, refusing to make eye contact.

"That, too," she continued, swallowing the lump in her throat. "Because doing what's best for you will be what's best for the kids."

Jake shrugged. "So let's talk."

"No, not tonight." Both her tone and limit were firm. "Tonight we must remain calm and work as a team. You and I both want the same thing. The children are our first priority and making them feel safe is essential. We have to control our emotions long enough to let Matt know what we expect from him without causing him or Katie to worry about a violent outcome."

Despite his obvious distress, Jake acquiesced and allowed Harriet to explain the afternoon's interaction with Matt, including the planned apology to his teachers. "Do you really think losing the car for a week is too light a punishment?"

"No, not really."

"Then why don't we go tell him?"

To his credit, Jake's "sterling" character enabled him to regroup in a way that rectified the situation. However, his largess didn't extend to Harriett. After talking with Matt and Katie, he returned to his study and stayed there for the rest of the evening.

Remembering how Jake's pleas did little to coax her out of the bedroom a few weeks earlier, Harriett chose to leave him alone and opted for a behavior that had a higher likelihood of achieving what she wanted— she made a phone call to Tricia.

Behaving with intentionality, Harriett asked, "Can you meet me tomorrow at Panera? I want to talk without interruption and the deli's too distracting."

The next day, Harriett confessed her fears and solicited her friend's help. Tricia quickly agreed, "Don't worry, kiddo. I make a great wingman!"

They decided Tricia would wait at a nearby shopping plaza and have her cell phone available should Harriett require assistance.

Harriett breathed a sigh of relief. "I'm glad I can stop pretending that my life's perfect."

"Harriett, the only one who thought your life was perfect was you."

"Pardon?"

"Most of us think Jake's a bit aloof. He gives the impression of knowing a secret that makes him superior to everyone around him."

Tricia's comment left Harriett flabbergasted. "Jake? He's usually so affable!"

"Don't get me wrong. Jake's always friendly, but sometimes I feel like I bore him."

No, Tricia, that's what you think and I wonder how that makes you feel?

Knowing her thoughts were irrelevant to the discussion, Harriett asked her friend to elaborate.

Tricia shrugged. "Look, no one's perfect. What I think doesn't really matter as long as your relationship with Jake works for you. No marriage is perfect and the best we can do is the best we can do."

"Dr. Aye says there are pros and cons to any choice we make and the best choice is one that maximizes the pros while minimizing the cons."

"Are you sure you really want to confront Jake?"

"No, I'm not sure. But I do think confronting Jake is the only logical choice."

Harriett picked at her lunch while she and Tricia finalized their plan. After dumping a half-eaten sandwich into the trash, Harriett turned and gave her friend a tight squeeze. "Thanks for being there for me."

Tricia returned the hug. "Always. All you have to do is call."

By Friday evening, Harriett felt ready to burst with nervous energy. Her heart raced as she descended the stairs and found Jake waiting in the kitchen, looking equally tense. *Oh great, tonight's going to be really hard.*

"Use your skills," reminded wise mind.

The couple strained to maintain a civil conversation as they drove towards the restaurant. Rummaging through an assortment of CDs,

Harriett managed to distract herself from the "*what ifs*" playing in her mind. Relieved she'd taken advantage of the Outback's phone-ahead priority seating policy, they avoided the added stress of waiting for a table. Settling into a booth, each requested a hefty drink.

"I might need several," Jake commented, handing her the car keys.

Harriett placed her order before delivering a well-rehearsed opening line. "Jake, we both know our marriage is unraveling. What I don't know is why."

Jake replied with an expected refrain, "Because you came after me with a knife."

"No, Jake, I came after you with a knife because I could feel you slipping further and further away and I was scared."

"Scared of what?"

"That what I thought was a perfect life was coming undone and I didn't know what to do to make things right."

Studying Harriett's face intently, Jake leaned across the table and took her hand in his. "Things were never perfect," he began.

"I know that now," she interrupted. "That's what I've learned in counseling. Perfection is an illusion. I was trying so hard to maintain the illusion that I was incapable of enjoying what I had. I'm so sorry." She withdrew her hand and dabbed her eyes with the napkin. "What I don't understand is why you're still so distant."

"Trying to live up to your standards is just too damn hard." Jake's voice was taut with emotion.

"When you say that, I think you want out of this marriage and when I think you want out, I feel petrified."

Intent on delivering her lines, Harriett failed to pay attention to Jake's mounting distress.

"Don't you dare lay a guilt trip on me!"

"I don't mean to. But, what should I think when you say that?"

"That you should lower your standards!"

"Stop, drop, and roll," she chanted under her breath. Biting back an angry retort and curbing her overwhelming urge to prove that Jake's words made him sound foolish, Harriett summoned the energy to roll out a different response. "Jake, are you having an affair with Julie Butler?"

Surprise forced the beer he'd just sipped to spurt from his nose. Grabbing the other napkin, Jake wiped his face and looked at Harriett in wonder. "An affair with Julie! Where'd you get such a wild idea? No wonder you've been acting crazy. An affair with Julie? That's the least of my problems!"

Harriett studied the face she'd come to know so well. For some inexplicable reason, she believed her husband. "Then help me to understand. If you're not having an affair, how do you explain being seen with Julie at the Crowne Plaza and all the clandestine client dinners?"

"First of all, Harriett, stop paying whatever detective you hired to spy on me because he's obviously a rip off. Yes, I go to the Crowne Plaza and so does Julie. We're involved in that class action suit I told you about months ago. For God sakes! You've been around lawyers your whole life! You know that sometimes dinner's the only available time to discuss a case. If you'd asked, I'd have told you that Julie's one of about six lawyers present at these *clandestine* dinners!"

Speechless, Harriett slumped into the booth, watching Jake take another deep gulp of beer.

"Then what's making you so distant? You're always so grouchy and irritable. Is the case that exhausting? Do you want to change your job and worried what Granddad will say? Are you having a midlife crisis? It can't be just because my standards are high. They've always been high. That's the reason you married me."

"Not the only reason," muttered Jake.

This time, Harriett paid attention. *What's he alluding to?*

Holding her breath, she asked, "What do you mean?"

"Harriett, I know what I'm about to tell you is going to come as a shock and I wish to God I could go on pretending, but I can't. I just can't do it anymore."

"Do what?" she exclaimed, sure she didn't want to know.

Horrified, she cried, "Jake, are you sick?"

"No, Harriett. I'm gay."

Harriett recoiled in dumbfounded disbelief. "Pardon?"

"You heard correctly. I'm gay."

The arrival of their salads added to the absurdity of the moment. She remained mute as the waiter fussed, asking if they wanted freshly ground pepper. Harriett shook her head—outwardly indicating no, while her mind worked to shake away a fog of confusion that prevented even a single, coherent thought.

Gay? The word reverberated in her ears. *Jake's gay?*

From somewhere far, far away, Harriett heard Jake's pleading voice. "Harriett? Harriett! Please say something!"

She managed to croak, "Gay?"

"Yes, sweetheart, and I know telling you destroys everything we've built over the years."

Harriett fumbled for her drink in the vain hope that alcohol would numb the pain emanating within her. Again, she studied her husband's face, this time in dazed bewilderment. "Please explain." The two words sounded stilted and devoid of expression.

"I think I've always known," Jake began. "I've tried to ignore it, maybe the better word is, deny. I couldn't risk disgracing my parents and you know your grandfather's reaction to a gay lawyer practicing in his firm. Keeping up pretenses has always been easier. I told you I didn't date much in college and let you believe focusing on the law was more important. In reality, I was neither comfortable trying to be a heterosexual, nor was I ready to accept the alternative. After college, I continued the charade by having the occasional date, followed by the occasional one-night stand. Flirting was easy and provided a good cover. Then I met you..."

The look on Harriett's face made him quickly recant. "No! Please don't think you were a convenient cover. You were never a cover! I truly loved you and still do love you."

Jake's words did nothing to abate her pain. "But why would you marry me?"

"Because you legitimized me."

"Legitimized you? What does that mean?"

"I thought being married to a bright, creative, lovely woman would eliminate suspicion in anyone's mind. I also thought having your grandfather sanction our marriage would prevent anyone from questioning my status as a heterosexual man. Most of all, Harriett, and please, please hear me. I believed we could build a good marriage. I love you deeply and I wanted to, or at least thought I could, make a happy, successful life with you."

Trying to right a world tilted on its axis, Harriett struggled to absorb what she'd heard. "But the sex?" Angry, she castigated the years she'd wasted blaming herself for their lackluster sex life.

Jake shrugged, his look guilty. "A natural conclusion to some wonderful and intimate moments. Please don't let what you've heard tonight rob you of the joy we've shared over the years."

"Then what's changed?" she asked.

Jake stared at her in wretched silence.

"What's changed?" she repeated, her anger rising. "Why tell me now? Why not go on pretending? Why make me miserable all these months thinking I was the reason you were so unhappy?"

Her stomach turned as another horrific question formed on her lips, "Have you met someone?" The look on her face demanded an answer.

Jake's eyes slid left, unable to withstand her scrutiny. "Not exactly."

"What does that mean?"

"Ignoring my needs is becoming more and more difficult."

His choice of words made her swoon. *Which of Dr. Aye's needs applies to this situation?*

Suddenly, her hands flew to her mouth. "The kids! What's going to happen to our children? Their lives? Our lives!"

"Oh, Harriett, I wish I knew! The only thing I know is that, while I can't undo the past, I can't go on living this lie."

"Jake, I've got to get out of here! I think I'm going to be sick!" Throwing the car keys at him, she scrambled from the booth. "Don't worry. I have a ride home."

She fled the restaurant in desperate search for the bathroom. Stumbling into a stall, she became violently ill. As she heaved up the meager contents of her stomach, Harriett realized her body was also expelling the last remnants of perfection.

22

The Choice is Yours

Dr. Aye was waiting at the office door when Harriett arrived. "Come on in. I'm glad you called."

"I didn't know what else to do." Her blotchy face and red eyes told the story.

Dr. Aye assessed her client with quiet concern. "How can I help?"

"I wish I knew." Harriett reached blindly for the box of tissues as another onslaught of tears ran down her face. Bit by bit, she related Jake's horrid admission.

"Of all the horrid parts, which part is most horrid?"

"I feel so betrayed...and stupid!"

"Stupid?"

"How could I not know my husband's GAAAAAY?"

She leaned forward, wrapped her head in her hands and began wailing. "I hurt so much," she keened, rocking back and forth in a futile attempt to soothe her pain. "Where have I been all these years? How can you be with someone you think you know and suddenly find out everything's a sham? All those years of living a lie!"

"Harriett."

The firmness in Dr. Aye's voice demanded Harriett's attention.

"You can waste your energy searching the past for clues you missed. Yes, you'll see your life through a different filter but, in the end, you'll be left with the same outcome."

"That my husband's gay," she moaned.

"Yes, you're husband's gay."

A shudder ran through her body. Hearing the words made the nightmare real. She huddled into the loveseat, attempting to shield herself from the horror, but Dr. Aye continued, "I understand you feel deceived and think you've been living a pretense. Both your feelings and thoughts are valid, and you have every right to grieve. However, if you waste your energy living in the past, your present will contain nothing but shattered memories that rob you of the happiness you had with Jake. You know you can't change the past, but you can focus on surviving the present."

"It's too hard," she wept, pulling tissue after tissue from Dr. Aye's ample supply.

"Hard, yes—impossible, no."

"Please don't tell me I have to work hard and use my skills. There's no energy to feel better."

"Harriett," persisted Dr. Aye. "You've had a devastating injury. The skills will help you recover, but first you have to grieve."

"Grieve? Jake's not dead; he's GAY!" New sobs wracked her body.

"Grief accompanies any loss. You've lost a perspective of your husband and your marriage that you've held for almost two decades. You're entitled to grieve."

"I feel so guilty! I was so busy pursuing perfection that I completely missed that Jake and I had stopped communicating. Last night I started wondering when we last talked about things that really mattered. Like sex, for instance. Maybe if I had kept pushing him to talk, I would have seen the signs earlier."

A sense of panic overwhelmed her. "How will I explain to the children? What can I possibly say to my friends? I think I'd rather die than tell my family."

She quickly pacified Dr. Aye's look of alarm. "No, I'm not suicidal. I just can't face the questions, condemnation, or jokes that are sure to come in the following weeks."

"Where are you living?"

"In the future, but the present's just as bad!" A mound of tissues collected in her lap.

"The present may feel as bad as the future, but there is a difference."

Wiping her eyes, she blew her nose and looked at her counselor, silently imploring her to say something that would magically take away the pain. "What?"

"In the present you have the ability to take control and the capacity to survive. Through self-evaluation and practice, you've become mentally tough and now's the time to use that toughness to redefine your meaning of quality. You still have choices."

"What choice do I have? I can't change the fact that Jake's gay!"

"No, you can't," agreed Dr. Aye. "However, you do have a choice regarding what to do about Jake being gay."

"What to do! What do you mean I have a choice? No matter what I do, Jake will always be gay. Have can I redefine something so absolute?"

"I didn't say redefine Jake's sexual orientation. I said redefine your quality of life within the context of Jake's sexual orientation."

"I don't want to! I want my marriage back! I want my husband back! I want what I've always had!"

"Which is?" Dr. Aye asked the self-evaluation question in a soft voice.

"A normal life and a normal marriage to a man who thinks of me as more than a way to legitimize his homosexuality!" Anger co-mingled with guilt and pain.

"Define normal," challenged her counselor.

"What do you mean 'define' normal? All these weeks you've been counseling me to self-evaluate my life and control my emotions long enough to behave wisely. While I've been working hard to fix what I broke, I completely misjudged the magnitude of the disaster looming on the horizon. How is that being wise? Now you're asking me to define normal? You know what normal means!" Instead of sobbing, she gasped with outrage.

"Normal is subjective. Normal according to whom?"

"To society!" Harriett screeched, the extent of her loss crashing down on top of her.

Dr. Aye waited, allowing Harriett time to accept the situation long enough to consider ways to cope her new reality.

Eventually, Harriett asked, "What do you mean about normal being subjective?"

"We've had this conversation. There's no benchmark to compare one person's definition of normal to someone else's definition. Your definition depends on the quality of life you want to live, not whether Jake's gay."

"But my quality of life includes Jake!"

"And still can. Just not the Jake you thought you had."

"But how can I be partners with a man who might not want to be partners with me?" Utterly confused, she sorted through her options, her efforts fruitless.

"You're right," agreed Dr. Aye. "Jake might not want you as a sexual partner, but I wonder if he still wants you as a partner in other ways."

"Isn't that obvious? If he still wanted to be partners, he would have continued living the lie."

"That's an assumption," observed Dr. Aye.

Harriett wanted to scream. "You can't possibly want me to check it out!"

"What would stop you?"

The self-evaluation question reigned in Harriett's emotions. Pushing through a haze of confusion, her lips formed a familiar answer, "Fear."

"Fear of what?"

Fear of rejection by a man who I've depended on for my entire adult life. The thought made her feel powerless.

"The fear of being alone and helpless," she replied.

"Would you be able to tolerate that fear long enough to ask Jake the questions and gather the information you need to inform your choices? That might help you regain some of your power."

"I only see two choices and both are revolting."

"What are the choices?"

"The first is to accept Jake for who he is, even though I don't agree."

"What are the pros and cons?" prodded Dr. Aye.

A film of memories glazed Harriett's eyes. "I keep remembering our wedding...when we vowed to stay together for better or worse. I was naïve in so many ways. Everything was shiny, new, and perfect." She grimaced at the word. "Even as the shine faded, Jake and I still managed to create a life that felt good, warm and safe. A life based on mutual caring and intimacy. Not sexual intimacy," she qualified. "But just as close because we were intertwined by love and commitment. The addition of Matt and Katie rewove the fabric of our marriage and strengthened our relationship. The perspective changed, but the partnership was still good." She turned to Dr. Aye. "I don't think I can cut Jake out of my life without the fabric completely unraveling."

"And your other choice?"

"How can I possibly turn a blind eye to the reality of what is? The vows we made were made under false pretenses. From an attorney's perspective, that makes the contract null and void. In a sense, Jake's admission absolves me of any responsibility should I decide to abandon the marriage. I don't have to feel guilty." Unable to tolerate either option, she pleaded, "Oh, Dr. Aye, what should I do?"

Her counselor quietly responded, "You know the answer."

Harriett bowed her head, knowing that the only choice that mattered was the one she was willing to make. She thought about all the things she'd learned over the past weeks—needs, wants, self-evaluation, and the difference between acting emotionally and behaving wisely. She thought about the skills and their ability to help her get the better life she wanted. Mostly, she thought about the choices she'd made over the course of her life, and wondered if she was capable of using what she'd learned to make the wisest choice regarding her relationship with Jake.

As the silence between client and counselor lengthened, a picture developed that seemed to fill the void. A picture similar to the one she'd painted all those weeks ago—a picture of a glorious summer day, laughing with family and friends. Harriett wasn't sure how or if she wanted to include Jake in the picture.

Looking up at the woman who'd been her guide over these past weeks, Harriett replied, "I know the choice is mine, and the wisest choice I can make is to continue walking my walk."

LESSONS FROM *HARRIETT*

I wrote *Harriett's Walk* because I wanted to demystify the difference between acting emotionally and behaving wisely. Using a fictional character to illustrate how to apply self-evaluation and the skills enabled me to achieve my goal in a way that is accessible to a broad audience. While the concepts contained in *Harriett's Walk* are appropriate for professionals and students involved in counseling relationships, the fictional story format makes them available to anyone interested in learning ways to cope with life's challenges, and useful to people seeking to improve their quality of life.

The lack of a resolution to Harriett's dilemma is purposeful in that the story's ending encapsulates the meaning of making wiser choices for a better life. Living any kind of a life requires risk—the risk of the unknown. Living a quality life isn't about eliminating the risk—living a quality life is about acknowledging the risk, and managing the subsequent emotions in ways that work for you. Whether you use the book to help others or you use it to help yourself, make Harriett's walk your walk, and utilize the strategies to make choices that are uniquely satisfying for you.

Like Harriett's, your story is unfolding choice by choice. I challenge you to ask questions, pay attention to the answers, evaluate your responses, and choose wisely. Life may be a roller coaster, but learning the skills and adopting the strategies will empower you to enjoy the ride!

Clients often bring me quotations that epitomize the underlying concepts presented in this book. I share them with you as a final summary of the lessons contained in *Harriett's Walk*.

Self-Evaluation
Can it be, Ischomachus, that asking questions is teaching? I am just beginning to see what is behind all your questions. You lead me on by means of things I know, point to things that resemble them, and persuade me that I know things that I thought I had no knowledge of.
Socrates (Quoted in Xenophon's "Economics")

Differentiating Thoughts from Feelings
A little kingdom I possess, where thoughts and feelings dwell; and very hard the task I find of governing it well.
Louisa May Alcott

Tolerate
A man who cannot tolerate small ills cannot achieve great things.
Chinese Proverb

Stop Thinking! Start Doing!
Hutchinson's Law: Any occurrence requiring undivided attention will be accompanied by a compelling distraction.
Robert Block

Where R U Living?
If we fill our hearts with regrets over the failures of yesterday, and worry over the problems of tomorrow, we have no today in which to be grateful.
Fulton Oursler

How Do You Spell ASSuME?
We simply assume that the way we see things is the way they really are or the way they should be. And our attitudes and behaviors grow out of these assumptions.

Stephen R. Covey

Stop, Drop, and Roll
When you do the wrong thing, knowing it is wrong, you do so because you haven't developed the habit of controlling or neutralizing strong inner urges that tempt you, or because you have established the wrong habit and don't know how to eliminate them effectively.

W. Clement Stone

Accept Doesn't Mean Agree
Acceptance is the observation of life and suspension of judgment about whether what is happening is good or bad, right or wrong.

Ron Smotherman

The Best Defense is a Good Offense
I have heard there are troubles of more than one kind.
Some come from ahead and some come from behind.
But I've bought a big bat. I'm all ready you see.
Now my troubles are going to have troubles with me!

Dr. Seuss

Flip It!
It is not good enough for things to be planned—they still have to be done; for the intention to become a reality, energy has to be launched into operation.

Walt Kelly

Communicate

Communication leads to community, that is, to understanding,
intimacy and mutual valuing.

Rollo May

Perseverance

Two frogs fell in a deep bowl.
One was an optimistic soul,
But the other took the gloomy view.
"We shall drown," and he cried adieu.
So with a last despairing cry,
he flung up his legs and said goodbye.
The other frog quoted with a merry grin,
"I can't get out, but I won't give in!"
I just swim around till my strength is spent,
then will I die the more content.
Bravely he swam till it would seem,
his struggles began to churn the cream.
On top of the butter at last he stopped,
and out of the bowl he gaily hopped.
What is the moral? 'Tis easily found—
if you can't hop out, keep swimming around.

Author Unknown

RESOURCE LIST

BOOKS

Choice Theory: A New Psychology of Personal Freedom, William Glasser, MD (Harper Paperbooks, 1999)

Counseling with Choice Theory: The New Reality Therapy, William Glasser, MD (HarperCollins, 2001)

Dialectical Behavior Therapy Skills Workbook: Practical DBT Exercises for Learning Mindfulness, Interpersonal Effectiveness, Emotion Regulation, & Distress Tolerance (New Harbinger Self-Help Workbook), Matthew McKay, PhD, Jeffrey C. Wood, PsyD, and Jeffrey Brantley, MD (New Harbinger Publications, 2007)

Getting Together and Staying Together: Solving the Mystery of Marriage, William Glasser, MD and Carleen Glasser (HarperCollins, 2000)

Leadership, Rudolph W. Giuliani (Hyperion, 2002)

Patterns of the Hypnotic Techniques of Milton H. Erickson MD, Vol. 1, Richard Bandler and John Grinder (Metamorphous Press, Inc., 1997)

Take Charge of Your Life: How to Get What You Need with Choice Theory Psychology, William Glasser, MD (iUniverse Publishing, 2011)

The Feeling Good Handbook, David D. Burns, MD (Penguin Books, 1999)

WEBSITES

Dialectical Behavior Therapy: Behavioral Tech, LLC
www.behavioraltech.org

Choice Theory/Reality Therapy: The William Glasser Institute
www.wglasser.com

LOCATING A QUALIFIED CT/RT, DBT, or CBT PRACTITIONER

Referral from a primary care practitioner, insurance provider referral list, local outpatient mental health facilities, or:

Mental Health & Psychology Resources Online: www.psychcentral.com

National Alliance on Mental Illness (NAMI): www.nami.org

Substance Abuse and Mental Health Services Administration (SAMHSA): www.samhsa.gov

ACKNOWLEDGMENTS

Making *Harriett's Walk* a reality depended upon the love, support, and efforts of many people. I am indebted to them all. I especially thank:

Paul—my champion and knight in shining armor. He is the quintessential husband and I love him.

Luke—my son epitomizes how great achievements require a blending of intelligence, curiosity, and perseverance.

Peter and Joan Notaro—my parents are an endless source of encouragement who contribute their time and wisdom to nurture me in every way. Thank you, Daddy, for being my "rock." Mom, your inspiration and insights are responsible for the creation of Harriett. Thanks for being her advocate.

My early readers—their critiques were extremely helpful, and never hurtful: Aunt Anita, Beverly Ash, Dana Bliss, Patsy Bove, Janet Calvitti, Sue Clough, Pat Derobertis, Linda Dickey, Joie Hand, Ann Hays, Cathy Lavin, Maria Nicolas, Karen A. Pelczarski, Eileen Schwartz, Pat Spencer, and Carolyn Strain.

Gina Woelfel—my "everything."

Marly Cornell—an extraordinary editor whose efforts make me

feel blessed.

William Glasser and Marsha Linehan—the founders of Choice Theory/Reality Therapy and Dialectical Behavior Therapy gave *Harriett* her foundation.

Larry Litwack—my teacher, mentor, and friend, whose ability to infuse quality into the lives of others is sorely missed.

ABOUT THE AUTHOR

From New York City, to Atlanta, to Detroit and London, Lucia Matthews now lives in Rhode Island with her husband, son, and two dogs. She is a licensed psychologist who capitalizes on a wide and diverse set of experiences to help people get what they want. She is a graduate of the Georgia Institute of Technology, studied in London, England, and received her PhD from Northeastern University in Boston, Massachusetts.

Prior to establishing a private practice as a psychotherapist, Dr. Matthews was a manager for companies, including IBM and General Motors, and a therapist in a Massachusetts state hospital. As the director of Adolescent Services, she developed programs designed to reunite families by teaching family members how to tolerate their emotions long enough to behave wisely. She is a certified Reality Therapist and former faculty member of the William Glasser Institute of Reality Therapy. She has published several articles on cognitive behavioral psychology, and her insights into the effects of transracial adoption on family dynamics are included in the book, *Understanding Diverse Families: What Practitioners Need to Know*. She and her husband travel extensively and enjoy visiting different cultures throughout the United States and abroad.

With more than fifteen years of clinical experience, Dr. Matthews teaches individuals, couples, and adolescents how to cope with significant lifestyle adjustments.

Reader feedback is welcome.

Please visit Drluciamatthews.com